A Field Guide to Demons, Fairies, Fallen Angels, and Other Subversive Spirits

A Field Guide to Demons, Fairies, Fallen Angels, and Other Subversive Spirits

Carol K. Mack
and Dinah Mack

An Owl Book

Henry Holt and Company   New York

Henry Holt and Company, LLC
Publishers since 1866
115 West 18th Street
New York, New York 10011

Henry Holt® is a registered trademark
of Henry Holt and Company, LLC

Published in Canada by Fitzhenry & Whiteside Ltd.,
195 Allstate Parkway, Markham, Ontario L3R 4T8.

Library of Congress Cataloging-in-Publication Data
Mack, Carol K.
A field guide to demons, fairies, fallen angels,
and other subversive spirits / Carol K. Mack
and Dinah Mack—1st Owl books ed.
p. cm.
"An Owl book."
Includes bibliographical references and index.
ISBN 0-8050-6270-X (pbk.: alk. paper)
1. Demonology. 2. Fairies. I. Mack, Dinah. II. Title.
BF1531. M26 1999 99-20481
133.4'2—dc21 CIP

Henry Holt books are available for special promotions and
premiums. For details contact: Director, Special Markets.

First published in hardcover in 1998 by
Arcade Publishing, Inc., New York

First Owl Books Edition 1999

Designed by Sean McDonald

Printed in the United States of America
All first editions are printed on acid-free paper.∞

3   5   7   9   10   8   6   4   2

This book is dedicated to Eliza,

may she always be surrounded by love,

joy and compassion, the demon vanquishers.

Willingly I too say, Hail! to the unknown awful powers which transcend the ken of the understanding. And the attraction which this topic has had for me and which induces me to unfold its parts before you is precisely because I think the numberless forms in which this superstition has reappeared in every time and in every people indicates the inextinguishableness of wonder in man; betrays his conviction that behind all your explanations is a vast and potent and living Nature, inexhaustible and sublime, which you cannot explain. He is sure no book, no man has told him all. He is sure the great Instinct, the circumambient soul which flows into him as into all, and is his life, has not been searched. He is sure the intimate relations subsist between his character and his fortunes, between him and the world: and until he can adequately tell them he will tell them wildly and fabulously. Demonology is the shadow of Theology.

RALPH WALDO EMERSON,
"ESSAY ON DEMONOLOGY," 1875

CONTENTS

Although far more commonly sighted than angels, demons are still the most misunderstood of the ancient spirits. Many demons were once ancient deities or nature spirits who were degraded or demoted over the millennia by later cultures that settled in their areas. Together they form the most archaic spirit strata on earth and they've never lost their power to enchant us. Often described as unpredictable, magical, and riveting, demons have always lived close by — much closer than angels — too close to ignore and yet too "Other" to get to know. Humankind has always regarded demons with ambivalence: as supernatural adversaries who must be combated, yet also as a source of superhuman secrets, which can be wrested from them.

Universally demons have been considered agents of both good and evil, and have been looked upon as vital or negative forces, but share key characteristics: all demon species are supernatural spirits of semi-divine status with limitless energy, excessively passionate natures, shape-shifting talents, and preference for concealment, "indwelling," and darkness.

Demons are everywhere, in every part of the world and in every moment of recorded history. They are as invisible as microbes. They inhabit every grain of sand and drop of water. They lurk at crossroads, crouch at the door, hide in trees, slip into bed, wait in caves, slide down chimneys, hover at weddings and childbirth, follow caravans, pretend to be friends, mates, or grandmothers. They slip into your mind and become your self.

Demons include the genii loci who imbue and protect their natural habitats at any cost and fairies who've retreated farther and farther into the remaining pockets of wilderness. These underground operatives await the trespassing human traveler, expecting their usual tithes, and when ignored they can be vengeful. Other demons are personifications of our own passions, impulses, and desires, lurking about in the dark, hidden terrain of our unconscious, and their habits hold profound insights into the nature of our minds. Still others serve as explanations of misfortunes or aberrant events, or are seen as portents bearing chilling prophecies of death or doom. The wide array of demon functions and roles are as fascinating as their intense personalities.

Some demons serve as portals to sacred ground. Because demons can be protective (at times overprotective), they were often employed as guardian spirits to watch over the sanctuary entrance. They stood at the portal, baring their fangs, and ferociously repelled malevolent spirits who would fly head-on into their terrific images and take off in horror. They had a riveting effect on any human who entered in the wrong spirit. This useful, evil-averting demon function is still displayed in many cultures at places of worship, and it continues in a more concealed form just as the mythic traveler approaches a forest, or attempts the ascent of a mountain, a passage through the desert, or stands at the banks of rivers, at the well, at the doorstep.

This demonic protector/portal function is regarded by the Guide as one of its most relevant. In all cultures, the very presence of a demon — or of his reputation for lurking about a specific spot — alerts the traveler to some taboo that in itself indicates the presence of divine powers. The sacred nature of Forest, Desert, Water, and Mountain is to be assumed if demon warnings are in effect. These indwelling spirits are reminders to avoid a certain action or to perform it in a prescribed way — or risk incurring divine wrath. "Although it's commonly known that modern humankind has been destroying the environment on which its existence depends; that it is ever faster exhausting nonrenewable sources of energy and other riches of this planet ... that although contemporary humanity has been aware of these dangers, it does almost nothing to confront or avert them," said Václav Havel. "It is my deep conviction that the only option is a change in the sphere of the spirit, in the sphere of human conscience, in the actual attitude of man toward the world."

Demons, like blazing stop signs, demanded attention and defined limits in earlier times. Their lore in the Guide expresses an animistic worldview in which wilderness held "forbidden" places and earth was believed to be imbued with sacred spirits, some beneficent, some harmful, some capricious. The geography of demon encounters and quellings is marked by many peoples on sacred maps, and throughout the world these places are still sites of ceremonies. Many peoples today believe in the literal existence of the figures and tales in the Guide, while others see them as metaphor. In either case they serve to remind us with their retaliatory gestures of avalanches, floods, sandstorms, and acts of mayhem that there are consequences to acts of greed, despoiling, and deforestation, and that an attitude of humility is more appropriate than hubris in the face of nature's awesome power.

Demons are also the essence of human storytelling. People everywhere tell similar tales, which serve to transmit values and contain clear messages about what traits are considered desirable or undesirable. The demons are brilliant performers who entertain us marvelously as the mischievous trickster, the town menace, the sultry temptress, in what have become our classic plots. As you'll see in the Lore sections of the Guide, all these plots provide us, as Mircea Eliade said, with "models for human behavior and, by that very fact, give meaning and value to life."

Without the choice between the demonic and, for lack of a better word, the angelic, there can be no moral to the story. There cannot even be a plot. There can be no story without internal or external struggle; no hero without antagonist; no pain, no gain; no quelling, no quest. The demon is always a challenge.

Demonic lore was pre-media campfire entertainment. Many grisly scenarios seem concocted as thrillers. The spirits outdo each other: What's worse than a buffalo-headed giant? A skinless centaur. What's worse than meeting it on a secluded mountain path? How about in your bed when you were least expecting it? Worse? How about if you always thought he was your husband? Many of the bogey features of the demonic creatures were probably intended to scare young children into staying nearby, and the humor in the Guide's retelling of these stories is not intended with disrespect but seems implicit in the over-the-top nature of certain folk tales.

Note that most demons, fairies, and fallen angels are encountered, trailing their gory reputations behind them, just when they are about to be defeated or outwitted, so we see them in their final burst of glory, roaring and brilliant like fireworks' finales before "The End," when the light of reality or day comes back on.

The demon is the quintessential performance artist with an infinite repertoire of roles. His motive is to deceive, to "lie" so as to utterly enchant his victim — sometimes with a fatal denouement, but sometimes for only a bit of entertainment (they never know when to stop). When a human actor sacrifices his very being to the character he plays, lending his body, gesture, voice, and energy to create a "real" fictional being, he enchants the audience and transports it to his make-believe world. The demon, like a brilliant actor, is a virtuoso who will go to *any* extreme to create the illusions that so convince his audience that they suspend their disbelief and forget themselves entirely. Human audiences can learn from such demonic performance to appreciate the power of the art of fiction.

The demon, in addition to his function as protector at the portal of sanctuary, performer, and plot enhancer, also holds up a magnifying mirror to our passions — each so eloquently expressed by the species. When they crave they are relentless and almost unstoppable and the harm they do is rarely gratuitous, unless you get in their way. They're unconscionable, but only when blinded by passion. Obsessive workaholics (they "work like a demon"), outrageous in wrath — do they begin to sound familiar? We can gain valuable insights into the nature of our passions from these distilled incarnations of our most havoc-wreaking emotions. What is human love without desire? Yet to see where Desire can lead, follow the furry fanged-creature heading toward Lust with his usual fiendish verve (see the *Seven Deadly Sins* in Psyche). Demons have no word for moderation.

Much of the demon lore's humor exists in the repugnant habits of the irrational, uncivilizable demonic species who act out in outrageous ways: the incredibly uncouth Japanese *Oni* ingests several vineyards of wine and all his dogs in one sitting and spits out rivers when he laughs (see Forest); and the *kappa* always reaches greedily for a cow's liver through the anus, only to have his arm broken off every time as the animal bolts, yet he never learns (see Water); the eccentric *Wood-Wife* can't stand caraway seeds and goes screaming off indignantly, "They put caraway seeds in my loaf!" and curses the farm family forever. All this over-the-top behavior provokes laughter in part because it is recognizable: all those unconscious desires, unbridled lust, and gluttony normally repressed is what the unthinkable, insatiable creatures are made of.

Demons would be virtually unstoppable were it not for the few important attributes they universally lack: they have no capacity for reason, love, or compassion. The human hero has the light of day as well as reason on his side because most demons are doomed to vanish at dawn. Many of the most powerful demons can be as easily tricked as little children because, although supernatural, they lack the intelligence of angels or the human's potential ability to think logically or gain wisdom. They also lack the human ability to rationalize or justify action. They simply are. They are also quite literally heartless and love is so alien it can melt them.

Like human beings who can't act reasonably when in the throes of rage, or reflect on past history when determined to get what they want, demons are driven entirely by instinct. In fact many are only hypostatizations of desire (see *Id* in Psyche). When human heroes use consciousness, reason, love, and compassion as their "weapons," the demon is rendered helpless. The towering *Djinn* is tricked into returning to his bottle and then sealed within; the *Dodo* who's eaten the entire wedding party continues bingeing, this time on a proffered sword, and he dies, releasing all the guests; *Lilith,* when dragged to a mirror and revealed for who she really is, instantly vanishes.

Finally, it is the demon who guards the treasure (whether it be gold or an immaterial reward) and must be conquered before any hero or heroine can claim it. Frequently, in the Guide's Lore, the hero who encounters the demon is transported to the Other World by abduction, or sometimes by his own choice. In either case, when the explorer returns he is radically transformed by the journey. The spirits who pilot the journeys are always double-sided — holding knowledge and danger — and are capable of bestowing gifts of supernatural powers of healing and of art (like the *Ponaturi* water fairies who are the source of all Maori carvings).

The mythic traveler who successfully harvests the benefits of his demonic encounter needs special qualities to succeed. Motivation counts, and somehow all the diverse demonic spirits — the Jewish *Shedim,* the Arabic *Djinn,* the Russian *Leshii* — discern what is in the heart of the hero. To the guileless goes the prize; to the innocent third son the victory; to the humble passerby, the gold ring. All mean, miserly, envious, vain human travelers end badly.

Throughout much of demon history, the genus has been associated with malign forces (or life-eating powers), such as storms and disease, in part because they had long served as explanations for aberrant natural phenomena. Demons have been held responsible for such events as eclipses, comets, volcanic eruptions, and illness both mental and physical of various kinds (a "stroke" is left over from the "fairy stroke," which was understood to be the cause of sudden paralysis), and some were considered agents of both fortune and misfortune, portents of death when sighted, and choreographers of Fate.

Throughout all traditions the demonic spirits have avoided the light of sun, love, truth, or reason. However, by circling Goodness darkly, or ignoring it altogether like swarms of fairies, or attacking it head-on like fallen angels, all these subversive spirits throw our universal ideas of Good into illuminated relief. They are the grace notes that accentuate the human chorus of Joy. They (inadvertently) contribute to humankind's idea of Goodness.

This Guide is an introduction to humankind's most ancient spirits, the demons, and is planned to aid the beginner approaching the field. Patterns and habits of a diverse spectrum of demonic spirits, including many fairies and fallen angels, are described, as well as where to find them, and what equipment and amulets are necessary to disarm and dispel them.

The Field Guide points to the commonality of features and motifs as it observes the creatures side by side, fang by talon, in their natural habitats of Water, Mountain, Forest, Desert, Domicile, and Psyche. In this way, they cross the artificial boundaries that seem to separate them by era, culture, or spiritual tradition. Whether these spirits were spawned from a collective unconscious or by diffusion of stories from culture to culture is unknown. It is clear, however, despite their variations, plot twists, and details, that they illuminate the universality of humankind's most profound concerns.

When in the realm of subversive spirits — and we always are — you must carry a map. You don't ever want to be stuck relying on one of them for directions. You want always to travel in goodhearted company and be sure you know your companions well before you set out. You don't ever want to ask the time, for a supernatural hour may equal a year or century back home. You will also want to know what you can and cannot eat if you intend ever to go home again. In case of emergency, you'll want to know how to find the exit. This information can be found in the Lore sections of the Guide. Dispelling & Disarming Techniques are supplied for most entries.

As with bees, don't bother them and they won't bother you is a good rule to follow. Especially with fairies. However, as you'll see from the Guide's Lore sections, sometimes they expect a sacrifice, or at the very least a porridge offering. After all, most were once seen as deities. And when you picnic in a forest or on a mountain, remember, *they* believe you're trespassing. Keep a respectful distance. Since some spirits travel the universe in one step and fly faster than the speed of light, the recommended distance is, unfortunately, undefinable. Lest you think all this too lighthearted, know that human laughter is one of three sure sounds to instantly drive off demonic spirits (the other two are church bells and firecrackers).

Only those demonic species who seem of particular interest because they manifest spectacularly, or inspire good tales, or are important in their traditions, or have idiosyncratic twists, are seen here. The Guide's bibliography is extensive, with the hope the reader will use it to continue exploring.

The demon is universally regarded as an incorporeal spirit who can actualize in many ways, yet is usually depicted as a grotesque hybrid: part *Homo sapiens*, part wild beast, it always walks upright. It has other recognizably human features, but often quite unnatural or uncommon ones, such as way too many fingers or none at all, no bones, no skin, or perhaps several heads. There is something about its mouth and teeth that is always alarming.

The entire species is composed of supernatural, composite feral creatures with telltale tails (often hidden from view), hooves or talons, batlike wings, and intense heliophobia. In its basic shape, scales or fur covers at least half its body (the hidden half), and its "real face" is one that inspires terror. Even when at a village dance, dressed to kill and looking irresistibly attractive, it can always be recognized by its feet: whether they are those of a rooster, goat, goose, or pig, webbed, or fish/snake bottom, a discreet glance down will confirm its true nature.

In tales of enchantment the human kisses the bear, frog, or ugly crone only to find in its place a handsome prince or beautiful maiden. With the demonic spirit, an inverse transformation occurs: the human is lured out in the night by a beauty or handsome stranger for a tryst, only to discover a hideous serial killer with a fanged overbite. In some traditions the person is enlightened by this encounter as to the nature of reality and illusion, and with that insight, vanquishes the spirit; and in others the creature must be destroyed by wit or sword, but it is always a learning experience.

The "Basic Demon," as depicted, obviously cannot be the being that attracts a traveler; all these creatures enchant by "shape-shifting" into someone or something highly desirable to that special traveler. Some say the noncorporeal spirits hide within natural shapes (some even inhabit corpses). Others claim they never actualize by shape-shifting but simply project illusory images like film stars, designed to ensnare and seduce. Like love, they do manage to alter reality for a while.

Shape-shifting is the supernatural art of creating illusory appearances and transformations out of thin air. Demons, using only their energy, can appear as smoke, as temptresses, animals, grains of sand, flickering lights, blades of grass, or neighbors. These magical antics are kept up tirelessly, heartlessly, and innovatively all night long. The Basic Demon shown here can only be seen by the viewer who sees through its seductively packaged masks. It is when one finally sees through the Basic Demon itself that it is utterly disempowered and vanishes without a trace.

HOW TO IDENTIFY A COMMON FAIRY

Fairies cast a "glamour" over their prey like moonlight, an illusory attractiveness so utterly bewitching that one is too enchanted to ask who they really are until it's too late. Fairies are usually depicted in a positive light: they are usually of feminine gender and seen as dainty, winsome, small or even tiny humans with wings that are often gossamer, sometimes like those of a butterfly, and sometimes angelic. But a glance down will reveal talons instead of feet. Fairies tend to vanish rather than shape-shift. They can shape-shift if they want to, however, and are often sighted in human guise at village dances and markets. There is no certainty about their essential form, but the consensus is they are transparent.

Fairies live in a subterranean parallel universe of their own that is often entered via holes in the ground, a mountainside, or a hill, and also in subaqueous castles entered via a lake or river. Fairyland is not one of everyday experience; it is Other, and only visible from time to time to special adults and children, not because the viewers will it, but because they somehow fall upon it by chance.

Fairies, like demons, may be the residue of ancient deities, diminutive nature spirits, and have also been considered the souls of the dead (especially unbaptized babies), or fallen angels (those angels who weren't so evil as to be thrust into hell, but instead landed in the subterranean realms of earth). Fairy lore is often interchangeable with demonic lore, although demons have a worse reputation because they've been confused with "devils." The Devil is of quite a different family that originates later from *Diabolos,* Greek for "slanderer" or "adversary" and referring to Satan or the Devil. Most "devils" are in hell and not in the Guide. In the opinion of the Guide, both fairies and demons are in a Class of Supernatural Subversive Spirits that share most of the same traits and habits and lore. Fairies, like demons, are considered to be supernatural helpers from time to time, but their attitudes vary considerably, and they are always dangerous.

Except when they kidnap human babies or borrow human males to propagate their species, fairies prefer to have nothing to do with the human community. They are very private, and when disturbed by gawkers or intruders they react violently. Some fairies were categorized by W. B. Yeats as "sociable" and some as "solitary." The latter are always malevolent, but all of them, despite their small size and adorable guises, can be surprisingly sinister. Fairies generally are more aloof and laid back than their energetically engaging demonic cousins, and provoke fewer involuntary encounters, but they are equally vengeful when stepped on or rejected. (See the *Abatwa* in Mountain who sends a lethal invisible arrow into the foot of any human who steps upon him, and the *Sea Fairy* in Water who will rise to the occasion when rebuffed and kiss her ex-lover to death in his own home.)

It will be shown that if a human visits Fairyland and eats fairy food, he or she will usually not return to the land of the living. Joining a dancing fairy ring — Celtic fairies are always dancing in rings — is as dangerous as ingesting fairy food. Once enchanted by this species, it is almost always too painful to return to everyday life, and returned people have been known to waste away pining for lost bliss.

The Guide identifies all these creatures, demon, fairy, and fallen angel, as "subversive spirits" because they overthrow all civilized order, reason, rules, and expectations. Where they live, deep within our Psyche, or the waters or woods of our planet, all is chaos, darkness, and turbulent creative energy that can erupt, break through, and overturn routine daytime existence. Nowhere to travel without a Guide.

When and where can the various species be found? Location is a more ambiguous issue, since the Other World surrounds us like undetectable ether, but the surest way to encounter a demon manifesting itself in our world is to venture alone, at night, outside town boundaries. Your presence will probably invite an abundant display of demon plumage. According to every source on the demonic spirits, from canonical texts to occult books, epics, myth, folklore, and superstitions of all peoples, the dark spirits rise at sunset.

The Guide is arranged by habitat. The nature of the habitat seems to shape the nature of the spirits who reside within, or perhaps the specific nature of each habitat as seen by humankind at its most terrifying and unmanageable is expressed by its particular indwelling spirits. They seem to represent the very nature of nature as experienced by humankind, and arise from the Psyche, a terrain of unfathomable depth that represents the nature of human nature.

The Guide begins with WATER, the element of formless potential from which creation and consciousness emerge. Its distinctive characteristics are seen in its teeming population of aquatic femmes fatales who cause mists, drownings, and shipwrecks. It is the most chaotic and profoundly mysterious of all habitats, and all its creatures are unpredictable. Its amphibians lurk about the land at night fishing for humans and return to their unknown depths by morning. In each lagoon, well, lake, and river, beautiful bait waits to hook a voyager. The encounters produce oceans of stories.

The MOUNTAIN, considered the sacred abode of the divine spirits, holds in crevices and caves a huge hidden population of fairies, who often hover like flickering lights over precipices. They serve to guard treasure and warn any encroaching humans that they are trespassers by creating hazardous conditions, falling rocks, and mud slides.

The FOREST houses a wild kingdom of (mostly) predatory male demons, often camouflaged as beasts or trees, who spring suddenly from shadows to catch and devour hunters and domestic animals. Entering a forest, usually the nearest habitat to a village, is crossing over into a dangerous, dark world beyond and wholly unlike the safe community at its edge.

The species of the DESERT frequently display as whirling powerful sandstorms but also appear in friend guise and soon shape-shift to alien form, or instantly vanish along with their tented villages, all expressing the powerful state of flux and shifting reality of this terrain. It is in this vast, hostile wilderness that three Western world religions have placed their most powerfully radical species to wage battle with spiritual journeymen who seek them out.

For armchair travelers, the DOMICILE houses the most variegated species of demons: they lurk in the doorway (pouncing if the home is approached incautiously); in the bedroom, where seductive succubi or incubi often appear to any solitary spouse whose mate is away; and in the kitchen or basement is the genius loci puttering about all night (fed or propitiated by the humans who share its abode). Dangerous disease spirits attempt to fly in through windows, and fairies enter the nursery and take babies in exchange for their own. Each portion of the home defines its demon specialties by its fears and has shelves of preventative measures.

Lastly, closer than home, is the terrain of the PSYCHE. One doesn't have to leave one's mind to witness the lively *Dybbuk, Werewolf,* or *Kitsune-Tsuki,* who leave their prey looking quite normal but for that telltale vocal change and a new je ne sais quoi behind the eyes. The Psyche, once home to the medieval *Seven Deadly Sins,* in this century has the *Id* and *Shadow,* who often require an exorcist or rather, psychoanalyst, to address them directly. Most important, the Psyche is the place to recognize all of our personal demons and to discover transformation techniques.

The Field Guide will not discuss philosophical issues

associated with demons, like Evil or how it arose (a vast, fascinating mystery inextricably linked to the question of theodicy — how there can be suffering and evil if God is good). It will avoid Halloween and bhuttas and witch hunts entirely and the only mention of "ghost" will be the *gui* or *shen* origin of certain Chinese spirits. The "devils" and infernal demons who have not come up for air or interacted with living people will not be identified in these pages. With 20,000 demons in a sole epic battle of the *Ramayana*, a modest medieval professional estimate of 7,405,926 demons in the world, and a Talmudic guess of one demon per person, the Guide must be highly selective and has included only those personalities who, by their nature, appearance, or stories, offer the reader an insight to the genus — or genius — of them all.

In the beginning, invisible hordes wing through the universe faster than the speed of light. In this world each tree, lake, rock, wall, and hearth pulse with indwelling power, and any abnormal change of weather, fortune, or health is attributed to unseen agencies of shadowy, anonymous collectives. This is the origin of many Western species who slowly spin into focus. The daemonic remains unnamed and highly charged as quantum energy, beyond human understanding, always present, causal forces of good or misfortune.

In ancient Greece, Hesiod refers to innumerable invisible *daimons* of two general types: the daimons of the hero cult (which the heroes of the Golden Age became after death) that act as guardian spirits, and the other daimons, evil spirits of disease that can cause harm. There is an ambivalence concerning the nature of the species: they can act for better or worse, but either way their effect is powerful. In Homer's *Odyssey*, the daimon is seen as that supernatural force (but not one of the gods, like Zeus or Athena) which intervenes in uncanny, preternatural moments, the kind that produce sudden insight, wild inspiration, peculiar behavior, or incomprehensible events. These fateful moments (for they are always that important!) loosely connect the daimon to Fate itself. This notion evolves into the concept that each person houses a daimon of his/her own. In Horace, the daimon becomes the "companion who rules the star of birth, the god of human nature, mortal in each man," and is inextricably linked with Fate.

It is Plato who definitively classifies and establishes the function of the daemonic species for us, in his *Symposium*: the Daimon is an intermediary spirit, described as neither god nor mortal but something between them. The gods had no direct contact with mortals and it was only via the Daimon that intercourse between gods and humans became possible. It is the Daimon that carries man's prayers to the gods and the gods' will to mortals. The Daimon itself continues to express a mercurial nature. Subject to passions and impulsivity, it is known to fly off the handle and grow so enraged that it demands placating and sacrifices. But so do the gods of this time. This Daimon is a mediator; a halfway creature that lives in the gap between the Divine and mortal.

The gap widens to a gulf as a pessimistic view of this mortal world sets in like ground fog. Over the next few centuries we see a radical shift in demon status. Starting in the fourth century B.C.E., after Alexander had changed the geography of Greece by adding vast conquered territory, borders widened and villages became urban and people no longer knew their neighbors. For many, a sense of alienation set in. All seemed left to Chance. Diviners and magic practices sprang up all over to soothe the increasingly anxious public.

We begin then to see a major downgrading of belief in the sacrality of earthly life as the ancient world became seen as "sublunar." The ancient gods fled for "higher places" and without them, it was darker here. The idea took root that perhaps an inferior demiurge (a dark daemon who was either an angel in revolt or a totally evil impulse) was the actual creator of this material world, so entirely cut off, it now seemed, from the heavens.

This divide of spiritual versus material realms became increasingly severe over the next century. A radically dualistic chasm opened wide. New religious systems of the East and some mystery cults entered the thinking of Greece and Rome, along with migration of peoples. By the first century C.E. an age of syncretism began. It affected the Daimon adversely. As Christianity spread, all pagan spirits were demonized and shoved down under to new dwelling places, and now the "angel" inherited the function of the Daimon and began blithely circling around the old daemonic realm. The angel was becoming the new intermediary spirit, so it had to grow less aloof, more approachable, and it smiled benignly as the ancient daemon/demon sunk to new lows and fell, stunned and soot-winged, into a subterranean abyss.

John Milton wrote about this time (calamitous for demonic spirits in the Western world) his famous poem, "On the Morning of Christ's Nativity" in 1629. Here is a sampling of the verse that tolled the death knoll for many ancient deities:

XIX

The Oracles are dumm,
No voice or hideous humm
Runs through the arched roof in words deceiving.
Apollo from his shrine
Can no more divine,
With hollow shriek the steep of Delphos leaving . . .
The lonely mountains o're,
And the resounding shore,
A voice of weeping heard, and loud lament;
From haunted spring, and dale
Edg'd with poplar pale.
The parting Genius is with sighing sent,
With flowered-inwoven tresses torn
The Nymphs in twilight shade of tangled thickets mourn.

Judaism never officially recognized demons, but several species were very popular in Jewish folklore and called *shedim*, *seirim*, or *mazzikin*. They were much discussed, and from the *Hagigah* (a tractate of the Babylonian Talmud) comes this description:

Six things have been said about demons: They are like angels in three particulars, but resemble men in three others. Like angels they have wings, and are able to fly from one end of the world to another, and know the future. . . . Like men, the demons take nourishment, marry, beget children, and ultimately die.

Shedim were demons (borrowed from neighbors of the ancient Israelites) to whom other peoples performed sacrifices. In Deuteronomy (32:17) is an admonishment not to borrow the practice: "And they shall offer no more sacrifices unto devils after whom they go a whoring." In Leviticus (17:7), the *seirim* (hairy ones), satyr, goatlike spirits, are clearly mentioned as forbidden objects of worship. These prohibitions generally indicate that contrary customs were popular.

One Jewish source related that the demons were created on the Sixth Day of Creation when the Lord was producing many creatures, but He was interrupted by the approaching eve of Sabbath, and so there was not enough time to give all the souls He had created bodies of their own. Another Jewish source claimed that a demon race existed long before humankind and grew so arrogant that finally humans were created to replace them. They were left hanging about in resentful droves. The notion of the demon as an elder sibling/spirit who came before humankind is found in the folklore and myth of many traditions. It is said to explain their attitude and their sense of prior claim on property, thus expecting tithes or sacrifices from mortal usurpers.

Meanwhile, in India, ancient spirits were winged hovering siblings of equal power. They were all brilliant shapeshifters who shared the power to create illusion (*maya*). Their struggles were a kind of recognizable sibling rivalry for the same turf known to so many human families. Even the word *asura*, which came to mean anti-god, in early Vedic mythology meant "gods." But the *devas* (gods) and the *asuras* became locked in battle until one major incident divided the spirits forever:

Myth has it that the gods and *asuras* were working together cooperatively to churn the cosmic ocean and produce the Elixir of Immortality when Vishnu appeared as a tortoise with the World Mountain on his back wrapped round with the World Serpent. The gods grabbed the serpent's tail and the *asuras* its head. When the Elixir was ready, the serpent spit venom at the demons, temporarily blinding them while the gods gulped down the drink. In another version, it is said that

Vishnu showed up disguised as a temptress, and the *asuras*, influenced by their slightly "lower" nature, were so distracted by this sexy illusion they didn't even notice the Elixir was gone.

In any case, in Hinduism, the *asuras* lost immortal status, but kept a longevity of eons. From then on, the *asuras*, semi-divine, with a nature unsuitable for angels, have become their warring adversaries. A tad greedy, too lustful and envious, too "human" to fly eternally, the *asuras* provide the action. On earth they become the Guide species of *Rakshasas* and include the formidable *Ravana* and *Mahisha-Asura*. But none remain radically evil. They often transform from one lifetime to the next and can be reborn as saintly human beings. In the lore of India, all demons are born with the seeds of their own self-destruction set in place by their own action, and they will come to their inevitable end by their own actions.

Farther east in Asia we witness demonic power as the wrathful or terrific aspect of a deity, to be harnessed for various uses. In Buddhism, the demon was considered basically as an obstacle to Enlightenment. Various techniques and methods were practiced to vanquish it. In Tibetan Buddhism we see how the "weapon" of Compassion can utterly transform a demon. Powerless in the force field of love and compassion, they melt, truly vanish, and leave a luminous, empty landscape in their place.

In China, the yin/yang symbol shows a bit of light extending into the dark, and a bit of dark in the light, all in a whole circle of inextricable Oneness. The original characters for yin and yang were the light and shaded side of a mountain peak. This points the traveler to the inseparability of the spiritual and material terrain of this worldview.

The Chinese *gui* (deceased persons who do not become *shen*) become demons, devils, and goblins who prey upon mankind if not fed and given offerings by the living. These restless spirits cast no shadow and usually serve the gods who govern the universe and punish evildoers. They can possess humans or cause misfortune. The *gui* of suicides go about wearing a red ribbon around their throats and try to convince others to do the same (and so take their place in hell).

Chinese lore of demons springs from a mix of Confucianism, Buddhism, and Taoism. It is rich and colorful and much is found in Taoist tales. When visiting Eastern habitats, one finds oneself in a constantly transforming, dreamlike reality where there is no sure footing, and *shen, gui,* the world itself, can vanish instantly.

In many cultures we run across subversive spirits who are creative although anarchic and unconscionable. They often play important roles in creation stories and remind us of the sheer energy and innovative brilliance of these ancient powerful, shape-shifting, intermediary figures. They proliferate in the four corners of the world, practicing specialties that account for all human urges, passions, impulses, ambitions. The demon hovers near every one of life's special occasions, and it appears at every border where we may cross too dangerously near the realm of the Divine.

Demons wait to trip us up at birth, at weddings, at death,

at the building of houses, at setting out on travels, at having too good a piece of luck (the kind that incites envy), or when accounting for a piece of bad fortune. They are ever present and uninvited. Naturally, they produce oceans of advice on how to avert them, how to conjure, control, or tame them, how to exorcise them, how to rid the house or mind of them. Yet worldwide, like flying grace notes, they point clearly and universally to the good life, highlighting love and compassion and all they are not. The tales in the Guide attest to the powers of a demon-filled universe, to the unexplained, to human capacity for wonder and ambivalence, to the extraordinary richness of human Imagination, the faculty Blake calls "Divine."

WATER

WATER, CONSIDERED TO BE THE ELEMENT OF FORMLESS potential, beyond order or cultivation, covers two-thirds of the earth's surface and holds a vast supernatural population in its fathomless depths. In the lore of Japan, India, Egypt, and Babylonia, and in the Jewish tradition, it was the primal sea from which creation emerged. Ancient deities imbued the Nile, the Euphrates, the Ganges, and the fountains of ancient Rome.

As a sacred element, water is believed to hold purifying and healing powers. It can relieve thirst, renew the earth, or destroy by flood. If water is withheld there will be drought and death. It is both the elixir of life and the source of the deluge. Approaching a body of water is still an occasion for prayer in many traditions. The washing of hands and feet, the baptismal font, the sacred spring, and the holy well — all flow with myth. Human sacrifices were routinely cast into water to propitiate the spirits within, and then fortunes were told by oracles at the riverbank.

Vast seas with their still uncharted depths and their mysterious hidden creatures have prompted many sailors' tales. Watch Water for its unpredictable, creative figures, its subaqueous fairy kingdoms, sunken demonic treasures, fierce guardians, and oceans of stories.

WHO'S WHO IN WATER

TIAMAT	Mesopotamia
MERMAID	Global
MERMAN	Global
KAPPA	Japan
RUSALKA	Russia
MUNUANE	South America
WAHWEE	Australia
MADAME WHITE	China
KELPIE	Scotland
NIXIE	Teutonic
TIKOLOSHE	South Africa
NUCKELAVEE	Scotland
BUNYIP	Australia
VODYANOI	Russia
MBULU	South Africa
MERROW	Ireland
PONATURI	New Zealand

TIAMAT
Mesopotamia

Tiamat, of the Babylonian Epic of Creation (first millennium B.C.E.), is an ancient sea goddess who gave birth to all. Part glistening cosmic serpent, part winged animal, her image may superficially appear more dragon than demon. But within, she holds the essential DNA of all demonic species: the dark, creative, turbulent, protean spirit of the unconscious deep.

LORE

> *When skies above were not yet named*
> *Nor earth below pronounced by name*
> *There was water . . .*

and *Tiamat* mingled her salt seas with the fresh waters of Apsu, her consort, and bore populations of gods who lived within her darkness until finally Apsu could no longer bear the disorder and clamor of the young gods. He attempted to destroy their offspring. Naturally enraged, *Tiamat* collaborated with her son and destroyed Apsu. Generations passed until her great-great-grandson, the solar god Marduk, challenged her dominion.

Marduk was a perfect hero. He had four eyes and four ears and could breathe fire. In preparation for the battle, Marduk made a bow and arrow and a huge net. Carrying a spell on his lips, an herb in one hand that worked against *Tiamat*'s poisons, and a mace in the other, he mounted his terrifying storm chariot and marshaled the seven winds to follow him into battle.

Tiamat was infuriated. From her rage came forth monsters, demons, horned snakes, bull men, fish men, filled not with blood but venom. Her army was radiant and terrible. She appointed Kingu, a monster offspring, to be her spouse and to lead her brood into battle. But Marduk challenged her to single combat. He caught her in his net and then sent evil winds toward her. She opened her mouth like a mammoth cave to swallow them, but the winds were of such power her jaws were forced to remain open. The winds distended her belly. Marduk entered and saw within her an entire army of gods, snakes, and demons. He shot his arrow. It split her heart in two. She perished. He stood on her body and smashed her skull with his mace.

Then Marduk sliced *Tiamat* in two like a cosmic clam, and raised one half of her to become the roof of the sky. He bolted it to hold the waters in check. With her lower half, he created the earth above the subterranean waters. From her eyes he created two rivers; from her udder, mountains and foothills. From her saliva he made rain and clouds; from her poisons, fog. After Marduk named each thing and set the stars and gods in their places, he created man out of the blood of Kingu, poisonous spouse-creation of *Tiamat*.

This Epic of Creation was read annually at the Babylonian new year's festival, and since most of it featured the slaying of *Tiamat* by Marduk, the supreme god of their pantheon, the story was naturally told from his point of view. The ancient goddess is seen as demonic in the eyes of the new hegemony: male sun god defeats dark feminine life force of chaos and creates civilization.

Yet without her essence nothing could be created. *Tiamat* is primordial chaos. *Homo sapiens* can only walk about and build civilizations in an ordered universe, and so *Tiamat* must be divided and named, but within and of *Tiamat* is all life. From this inchoate broth come tides, fish, birds, flowers, weeks, night and day.

Water is, with rare exception, seen as female and quintessentially *Tiamat,* and its anarchic, untameable spirits surface globally. Despite its terrific dangers, we also arise from these fertile depths both in body and consciousness.

MERMAID
Global

The *Mermaid* is a species of human size, rapacious, salt-water femmes fatales (though they've also been sighted in lakes and as far inland as many coastal fishes). The characteristic shape of the *Mermaid* distinguishes it from afar. From ancient sailors we hear, "It is a beaste of the sea, wonderly shape as a mayde from the navel upwarde." The *Mermaid* always has shining hair streaming in wavelets over ample breasts and very fair skin — a skin so strong, however, that it could be used for making soles of boots that would last three years or more. Her seal-like lower torso that ends in one or two fish tails is conveniently hidden by surf. The species is long-necked and comely with distinctive voice and luring song.

From ancient Greece come three supernatural spirits whose images and attitudes contribute to the development of the *Mermaid:* Skylla ("Bitch"), the six-headed monster with triple rows of teeth in each canine mouth who could devour six sailors at a time when their ships sailed close enough to her cave; the Sirens, with women's heads and bird bodies, later seen with fish tails, who sang irresistibly (it was to avoid the

Sirens' lure that Odysseus had himself tied to the mast and wore earplugs); and most important, the fifty Nereids, ancient sea fairies who lived in an underwater kingdom but came up to the surface to play. Nereids, who had whole human bodies, were often seen riding naked upon sea monsters that resembled dogfish. They were considered responsible for shipwrecks and storms, and, like the Sirens, had irresistible singing voices. They were fickle. They were never what they appeared to be. They were slippery and incredibly dangerous. And they were enchanting.

There has been some debate as to whether the *Mermaid* is utterly malicious or just forgetful about human ability to breathe underwater. The available information is ambivalent at best. With oblivious impulsivity (a demonic trait), she is said to grasp her mortal lover so tightly that he is crushed to death. Call her irresponsible rather than malevolent. In some lore she shows a bit of remorse by heavy sighing at the loss. There are tales of men lured to the dazzling undersea kingdom of the sea-fairy-type *Mermaid* who do manage to live and to return to shore, but when they have stayed dry awhile, they so miss the subterranean depths that they pine to death.

Sighted singing on rocks, combing their long hair, with looking glasses in hand that wink in the sunlight, they are irresistible to sailors far from home and desperate for female company. Sailors' maps have been found with spots marked "Here be mermaydes!" written with obvious enthusiasm, but none of these seafaring cartographers has lived to tell his *Mermaid* tales.

Mermaids habitually eat their victims after drowning them. From Portugal comes a seventeenth-century sighting that claims they eat only the nose, eyes, tips of fingers, and private parts of their prey, and toss the rest on the sand, where the dismembered corpses are eventually found. On the other hand, once in a while, a human man follows a *Mermaid* to her world beneath the waves and lives underwater in splendor. (This is the sea fairy branch of the family, indistinguishable at first glance from their demonic cousins, but generally fatal in the end.)

LORE

One night a man was walking along the beach and saw a group of *Mermaids* and mermen dancing in the moonlight. Their sealskins, which enable them to live at the depths of the sea, were piled up on the sand beside them. After the dance each *Mermaid* and merman picked up its skin and dove into the water.

One of the *Mermaids* forgot her sealskin, and the man found it and took it home. The next day when he returned to the water he saw a beautiful maiden crying on a rock. She was weeping over the loss of her sealskin; without it she could not live in her home beneath the sea. The man had never seen such a beauty and he fell passionately in love with her. When she begged him to return her skin, he refused, asking her instead to live with him. He promised to love her so much that she would forget all about her watery dwelling. She realized she could not change his mind, and so agreed.

The two were married and had two children. The man was happy but his supernatural wife wanted nothing more than to return to the depths. Every day she would sit on the rocks and gaze sadly at the water. One day her son found the sealskin that his father had hidden, and he innocently brought it to his mother to ask her what it was.

She wept with joy. She kissed her son for the last time. "Farewell!" she called, as she ran across the sand. At that moment the man saw his wife running toward the water, sealskin in hand, and hurried to stop her. But he was too late and she never returned to him again.

At their best, such as in this tale from the Shetland Islands, mermaids are not reliable. In most tales of *Mermaid* capture it is usual for the kin to retaliate by causing heavy mists, storms, gales, and shipwrecks, cutting off all trade and livelihood to the coastal human community.

The famous German tale of Undine reveals the true nature of a wild sea fairy:

A fisherman and his wife lost their beloved young daughter, Bertha, who fell into the lake and presumably drowned. During a tempestuous storm the following evening, the grief-stricken couple heard a knock on their door, and in from the winds and torrential rain came a pretty laughing child who said she did not know where she had come from but she had fallen into the lake and her name was Undine. The couple raised her as their own and tried to ignore her wayward disposition and her habit of running wild through the rain and singing, although it caused them great anxiety.

One evening, when the child had grown to young womanhood, a knight named Hildebrand passed by the cottage. He was lost and seemed quite sad because of his hopeless love for a proud young woman named Bertha. A sudden storm raged outside and the knight was forced to stay for several days until it had subsided. He became enchanted by Undine, and finally proposed marriage. (The true story: When Bertha fell into the lake, the sea fairies decided to send their own Undine to be raised by a human family, marry a human man, and thus gain a soul. They delivered Undine to the bereaved couple and sent Bertha farther down the lake to a childless noble couple who raised her as their own.)

Undine worried at the wedding ceremony that "there must be something extremely awful about a soul," but out of love she went on with it and seemed to undergo a radical change. She became oddly tender, meek, and helpful and even seemed content doing domestic chores. But after a short time there was a reunion of Bertha and Hildebrand and he realized he loved Bertha still. He spoke angrily to Undine, although she warned him never to speak to her harshly — especially near water — because the result could be dreadful. In response to his cruel outburst as they were out boating, she fell into the lake, saying only "Woe" as she vanished into the water. Hildebrand made plans to remarry, but on his wedding day he saw the door of his bedroom chamber open very slowly and watched in terror as the spirit of Undine entered. "You will die," she said quietly. Then she took him in her arms and kissed him to death.

DISPELLING & DISARMING TECHNIQUES

Some say placing barrels on the side of ships discourages the species from getting too close. Once they do there's no getting away, so it is important to be well informed. There *are* aberrant, gentle mermaids who behave benevolently to sailors and even share their supernatural skills and buried treasures, but they are exceedingly rare and have received inordinate amounts of attention. This overreported variety may have originated in the Middle Ages when sightings were frequent and there was debate in the Church as to whether or not a mermaid, who was part animal, could gain a human soul and whether her status changed if she married a human being. The Hans Christian Andersen tale "The Little Mermaid," which evolved from this Undine tradition, has propagated a pasteurized, radically denatured spirit in an unlikely story with a mawkish ending in which the mermaid herself becomes the sacrificial victim. Not only did Andersen remove the spirit's ability to sing or speak and her wish to bite, he tamed her, and rather than seek revenge at her betrayal, she opted to turn into foam. And why? To gain a human "soul" at some future time. Andersen's mermaid is a Christianization of a sea spirit that is incredible to anyone acquainted with genuine accounts of this ancient, ferocious, proud, exuberant, and unremorseful species.

The Guide sets Thackeray's literary account of the species in *Vanity Fair* against Andersen's disinformation:

> They look pretty enough when they sit upon a rock, twanging their harps and combing their hair, and sing, and beckon you to come and hold the looking-glass; but when they sink into their native element, depend on it those mermaids are about no good, and we had best not examine the fiendish marine cannibals, revelling and feasting on their wretched pickled victims.

MERMAN
Global

The *Merman*, male of the species, is said to have a powerful, attractive upper torso, a fish bottom, and a hollow look in his eyes. He is reputedly always lusting after human females and carrying them off whenever possible, making it a general rule of thumb that "no woman should adventure to come near the sea, except her husband were with her."

It is said that the *Merman* keeps the souls of drowned sailors or humans under pots or in cages in his underwater palace at the very depths of the sea, lake, or river.

LORE

Once there was a *Merman* who befriended a neighboring farmer, some say a miller, and invited the human being to dine with him in his underwater palace. The neighbor accepted the invitation, and found himself fathoms deep, enchanted by the magnificent rooms all filled with golden treasures, the floors made of pearls, emeralds, rubies, and the walls of shells studded with jewels, all blazing with light from huge crystal chandeliers. After a sumptuous meal, the man was about to leave when he noticed many pots overturned on the floor in the long halls. He asked what the objects were for, and the merman replied casually that they held the captive souls of the drowned he was known to keep. The neighbor said nothing, but he was deeply disturbed by the proof of such rumors and could not forget it. Sometime later, when he was sure the *Merman* had gone out, he carefully descended and again came to the enchanting palace. He retraced his steps to the long halls and there, one by one, he overturned the pots and all the souls floated up through the water to finally be delivered.

DISARMING & DISPELLING TECHNIQUES

Nothing is said of the fate of the human neighbor after his exploit, however, since mermen and mermaids are well known for their vengeful natures, and since the weather, mists, rains, and floods are influenced by these spirits, it can only be assumed that inclement weather arose and the farmer may have found himself in the depths again as prisoner. The sign of the cross can help, as can metal objects such as knives to avert the species, and various food offerings and lit candles may placate the mermen under normal circumstances.

KAPPA
Japan

The *Kappa*, a life-sucking amphibian, usually lives in swampy pools, but watch for it while swimming in any river, lake, or stream. The *Kappa* is the size of a ten-year-old boy; it has webbed hands and feet, a tortoise shell covering its back, the face of a monkey, a long beaky nose. It is quite slimy and emits a putrid odor. Its most singular characteristic is a large bowl-like indentation on the top of its head, filled with a clear, gelatinous fluid. This mysterious substance is the secret of the *Kappa*'s power. Around this indentation it wears its black hair in a short pageboy style.

The *Kappa* pulls its human victims into the water and sucks the life out of them. Avoiding the neck, it always sucks out their entrails through the anus. It is said to enjoy the human liver most of all. Sometimes the *Kappa* will just take a bite of flesh as a snack and nibble. Often it challenges passersby to a game of pull-finger, whereupon it grabs at the victim and pulls him into its home. The *Kappa* always wins.

LORE

Long ago, in the river of a small village in Japan, there lived a *Kappa*. He had eaten a number of residents and farm animals. One day a horse went to the river to drink. Soon as the *Kappa* struck, the horse reared and ran back to his master, ripping one of the demon's arms off in the scuffle. In terrible pain, the *Kappa* ran to retrieve his arm from the farm. He promised to leave the villagers alone if he could only have his arm back. The farmer made him sign a document, which he did, with a webbed handprint. He never bothered the villagers again. Furthermore, if he knew of another *Kappa* in the water, he warned the villagers of the danger. The demon print can be viewed to this day in a small temple that contains the original document.

In another village, a *Kappa* got stuck to a cow as he reached into the animal by his usual route. The cow reared and ran home, breaking off his arm in the process. When the

Kappa went to retrieve his arm from the cow's owner, the man was reluctant to give it back to him. The *Kappa* promised that in exchange, he would teach the man how to set broken bones. From then on the man became a famed healer and passed the art down to his son.

DISPELLING & DISARMING TECHNIQUES

Although the *Kappa* usually gets its prey, there is one well-known method of escape. It is based on the fact that a *Kappa* is notoriously courteous, that bowing is a national custom, and that the creature's head indentation holds all its power in liquid form. So, when encountering a *Kappa*, travelers should keep bowing to it as a sign of respect. The *Kappa* will have no choice but to bow back. As it bows lower and lower to the ground, the vital fluid begins to drip from the *Kappa*'s indented head. When there is no fluid left, the demon will be powerless. Take this opportunity to run as far from the water as possible.

The *Kappa* is also said to love cucumbers, eggplants, and fleshy melon. Many throw a cucumber inscribed with the name of their loved ones into the water, for there's a good chance that the *Kappa* will accept this offering and leave them alone. When there is fresh produce floating atop the water, it's most probable that there's a *Kappa* just below the surface, eating.

It is evident that humans can gain healing skills from this supernatural creature, and protection as well. But to obtain anything from a *Kappa*, the challenger must have heroic qualities of strength and fearlessness.

RUSALKA
Russia

The *Rusalka* (pl. *Rusalki*), a charming, amphibious lake/river species, is best sighted on a clear night when the moonlight reflects off her long pistachio green hair. With delicate pale skin and comely features, she is as much a temptress as any of her saltwater cousins, but she can also shape-shift into toad, frog, or fish with alacrity.

The original *Rusalka* is a Russian underwater princess who lives in a palace at the utmost depths of the river or lake. She is always on the alert for a mortal playmate to share her palatial digs. She uses her amphibian prowess to roam about on land luring children with baskets of goodies and young men with her obvious charms. Unfortunately she is doomed to remain lonely; either her partners drown or she tickles them to death before they have a chance. This serial behavior keeps her in continual prowl mode. Yet she never seems to learn.

The *Rusalka* is able to live on land for long times at a stretch, years, according to some lore. This is because she keeps with her a magic comb that she uses to conjure up water, bringing some element of home to whatever habitat she visits.

Rusalki are thought to be the souls of babies who died before being baptized and also of drowned virgins. In the spring they leave their underwater worlds and head for the field and forest to dance in circles with garlands in their hair. They are especially powerful and dangerous during the

Rusal'naia week festival in mid-June. In this celebration of spring, there was an old rite among peasants in southern Russia and Ukraine of creating an effigy of the *Rusalka*, which was buried or torn apart. Offerings were made to the *Rusalki:* eggs and garlands to appease them. Songs were sung to avert their powers.

LORE

One June, a young hunter met a *Rusalka* in the woods. She was lovely, with bits of flowers clinging to her long pale hair; and she was breathless as if she'd been running or dancing in the woods. He was immediately enchanted. He asked her to marry him and she accepted. For months they were blissfully happy. The *Rusalka* seemed almost sad to part, but summer was over and she had to leave for her home in a nearby stream. Her husband pleaded with her not to leave him until she agreed to leave her address. The poor man felt so dispirited after she'd gone that he roamed the woods hollow-eyed and grew thin, for he couldn't eat. Finally he bravely approached her stream and dove straight to the bottom to find her. She was waiting for him and embraced him hungrily. It seemed an eternity, that moment between life and death, and in it he regained his senses and realized he was about to die in the arms of his "wife." He managed to make the sign of the cross, and instantly he found himself back in his own village, a wiser but sadder man.

In other tales where a mortal man is enchanted by a demonic spirit or fairy species his return to terrestrial realm only *seems* instantaneous, but in fact fifty years or more may have passed. He may return from the dead, as it were, and upon reentry to the mortal world, will instantly turn to dust. A real time difference exists between worlds and should be kept in mind by all travelers.

DISPELLING & DISARMING TECHNIQUES

The sign of the cross, so effective in this tale, can disarm many Western demonic spirits, and when it does, proves them to be of that ilk. Another method is to draw a magic circle and drag the *Rusalka* inside. This was reportedly done by a brave villager in the past century after being attacked by a group of *Rusalki*. The one he captured worked for him all year, but she had to return to the water the following spring, as these spirits always do.

MUNUANE
South America

The *Munuane* is a toothless, gray-haired guardian demon with eyes in his knees. He always travels on a simple raft. He carries a bow and only one arrow, for he never misses his target. He is very large and somewhat slow-witted but equipped with charismatic power and can psychically lure his victims to him. The *Munuane* is considered by the Sikuani to be the "Master of Fish," and will appear wherever there are many fish in the water.

LORE

Once a man went to the lagoon to fish. When he got there he climbed up into a tree and carelessly shot many arrows into the water from above. After a while, he climbed down into the water to retrieve his catch. But when he pulled at his arrow, only a stick came out. He knew this was a bad sign, but he persisted, climbing back up into the tree to shoot at fish. The *Munuane* came sidling by on his raft, pushing his way through the water with a long pole. Seeing the reflection of the tree man in the water, the *Munuane* shot an arrow into it, and was surprised when it didn't hit him. Finally, with a slow-wittedness large demonic species mercifully exhibit, he realized it was only a reflection he had shot in the water. He retrieved his arrow and aimed at the real thing.

This fisherman had certain shamanic powers, and the *Munuane's* arrow was unable to kill him. But the impact of the arrow made the fisherman fall into the water, whereupon the *Munuane* pulled him up onto his raft and paddled away determinedly, calling out to his wife: "I'm bringing something home to boil for soup!" He repeated his words over and over again as he headed for home. But as the *Munuane* pushed forward with his paddle, the fisherman crept slowly to the back of the raft and slipped silently into the water. When the *Munuane* realized what had happened, he shouted out, "My soup escaped!"

The *Munuane* began to feel around rather stupidly in the

water with his hands while far away ashore the fisherman watched his futile search. Then, suddenly, the *Munuane* spotted the man, climbed from the raft, and the chase began. The man climbed up a palm tree and, using his magic powers, made it grow taller until it bent over like a bridge to the other side of the lagoon. He jumped off, and immediately the tree shrunk back to its original size, thwarting the demon's pursuit.

The following day, the *Munuane* reached the man's village. When his family saw him approaching, they tried to shoot arrows into its body, head, and arms. But the fisherman knew the important secret: A *Munuane* must always be shot in the knees! The man shot the *Munuane* in the knees and it immediately perished.

DISPELLING & DISARMING TECHNIQUES

When fishing in Sikuani waters, it is said a person must take only what he truly needs. The *Munuane* lives to protect local residents and, as their guardian, considers all human beings edible and destructive. If, by acting greedily, the hunter should encounter the *Munuane,* its knees are its weakness.

WAHWEE
Australia

The *Wahwee* is a deep-water-hole amphibian of the Aborigine with a froglike head, a long tail, and three legs on either side of its body. It is nearly thirty feet long. It is known for its insatiable appetite and for its supernatural power to cause flooding, rains, or drought.

The *Wahwee* is best sighted after everybody has fallen fast asleep, when it slithers silently over the ground to a campsite and selects its human meals. It swallows its victims whole, and after thirty or fifty average-size humans is still hungry. It will also eat bush animals such as kangaroo, wallaby, and wombat.

LORE

Two children, a boy and a girl, used to play near the *Wahwee*'s deep water hole and dig for shellfish. They were young and innocent and never realized that the place was owned (and occupied) by a *Wahwee*. The elder members of the tribe knew of the *Wahwee*, and that it might be getting angry. They tried to warn the heedless children, but to no avail.

Meanwhile the *Wahwee*, who could see the children through its hole, watched and waited. Time is nothing to demons. It waited until they grew up. It saw how deeply the boy loved the girl. One day, as the girl (now a young woman) waited for her sweetheart, an old woman approached her, weeping. The girl asked why she wept, and the old woman said it was because she knew what destruction the girl would cause her people by stealing shellfish from the *Wahwee*'s home. Shocked, the young woman said she would rather sacrifice herself than cause any harm to her people or to her beloved childhood sweetheart.

"Then return tomorrow," the old woman said. "And I will tell you what you must do." After the girl left, the old woman turned into an eel and slithered down into the water hole. The next day the girl met the "old woman" as she had promised, and was given a choice: if the girl had courage enough to plunge into the hole, all would be forgiven; if not, the *Wahwee* would call for the rains and destroy the village. The girl immediately agreed to follow the old woman into the water hole.

When the boy came to meet his sweetheart, she had vanished. Everybody knew that the *Wahwee* had taken the girl. The boy wept and wept, crazy from loss. Every day he sat by the water hole and sang for her. One day he noticed a little green leaf unfold in the water. Each day, as he sang, another green leaf unfolded before his eyes. He called again for his friend, and this time a red lily opened in the water. The boy plunged into the water hole and found his sweetheart. She clung to him. He was changed into a water rush, and soon, the water hole was covered with lilies and rushes.

DISPELLING & DISARMING TECHNIQUES

It seems in this case that it was true love that conquered the *Wahwee* and transformed his habitat into a site of great beauty. However, one must consider that the lovers were sacrificed in the effort. It seems there is nothing other than extreme measures here, so to avoid loss, the Guide advises a healthy respect for such powerful nature spirits as the *Wahwee*.

MADAME WHITE
China

Madame White, a lethal, possessive, eerie demon of Taoist lore, appears as a fabulously beautiful human woman dressed in white. She has typical fairy features: a dainty, cherrylike mouth, a tiny waist, and petite feet. She is always accompanied by a demure maid dressed all in blue. Her appearance is utterly illusory, and she will revert, under stress, to her demonic form: a white python. Her maid is a blue fish.

LORE

In a famous legend, *Madame White* was sighted by a young man named Xuxuan who was on his way by ferry to a temple on the bank of West Lake in central China. It was early spring, during the Qing Ming Festival (a time of remembrance of the dead during which many supernatural sightings take place). He was charmed by her, paid her fare, and, as it had begun to rain, loaned her his umbrella.

Madame White invited him to visit her at home, and soon after his arrival, she gave him many silver pieces, declared her love for him, and even proposed marriage. Unfortunately, when Xuxuan arrived in his own hometown with the silver, the pieces were discovered to bear treasury marks and he found himself under arrest. He protested his innocence and told the authorities where and how he had acquired the silver. They all went to visit *Madame White*, but found her "mansion" to be an abandoned ruin. Just as the inspectors entered, the demoness made a flittingly brief but astonishing appearance, then vanished, leaving in her stead the rest of the silver.

Xuxuan was exonerated but, perhaps because of his contact with unnatural spirits, was forced to leave his native province to work in a far-off place. There, he again ran into *Madame White*. She persuaded him that the silver incident had been a simple misunderstanding. They married and lived happily for a while. When spring came, Xuxuan went again to the temple for the Qing Ming Festival, and there met a Taoist priest. As they stood outside the temple talking, *Madame White* approached on a boat with her maid in blue to bring Xuxuan home. Seeing her, the priest called out: "Demon!" She vanished. So did the boat and maid. Xuxuan was very upset. The priest told him to go back to his hometown. He did, only to find "Madame White" lying in wait for him as his "wife." By now he was very frightened that at any moment what he now knew to be his supernatural wife would do him harm. He asked the local village priest for help.

The priest gave him a bowl and told him to press it on Madame White's head as hard as he could. Xuxuan did and watched as she became smaller and smaller under pressure. When she had shrunk to almost nothing, the priest commanded her to name herself. She confessed that she was a white python who had fallen in love with Xuxuan from a distance, and thus changed into human form to gain his affection. The priest chanted incantations that kept her in the bowl in the form of a small white snake accompanied by a blue fish. They still live under a pagoda near a lake.

In an eerier sighting, again on Qing Ming, another vulnerable young man, Xuanzan, was out by himself passing by the Broken Bridge when he saw a little girl crying. He stopped to help. She said her name was White and she lived by the lake. She had been walking with her grandmother and was now lost. He took the child in. Soon the grandmother showed up, and in gratitude she invited him home for dinner.

Home turned out to be an exquisitely furnished grand palace near the temple that he had never noticed before. A beautiful woman dressed all in white came to greet him, saying she was the little girl's mother. They all drank a bit and then it was suggested that Xuanzan should become her new bridegroom. "Yes," she said, "and have the other prepared for an appetizer." So the servants dragged her old lover from a chamber where he had been resting, tore him apart, cut open his belly, and removed his heart and liver. They offered some of this appetizer along with hot wine to Xuanzan.

Xuanzan wanted desperately to flee. However, he managed to spend the night with the woman in white and before he noticed a month had passed. At this point a new groom arrived. Xuanzan knew he was slated for vivisection, but he was saved by the little granddaughter. She flew him home, for she had certain magical powers. Unfortunately this was not the end of it. Next Qing Ming Festival, it happened again. It was not that Xuanzan was gullible, or that he did not learn from experience, it was a case of holiday possession. He was again saved by the skin of his teeth. But this time the demon woman in white was furious. She turned up at his home and claimed he owed her his heart and liver. Fortunately, Xuanzan's uncle was a Taoist priest and realized his nephew was under attack. He recited incantations, burned incense, and successfully exorcised the demonic creatures.

DISPELLING & DISARMING TECHNIQUES

Watch for this species on holidays like Qing Ming, the Festival of the Dead, when the boundary between the spirit and terrestrial world is fragile and the air is filled with spirits. There are no ordinary measures known and these matters must be left to professionals.

KELPIE
Scotland

The *Kelpie*, also known as *Each-uisg*, is a male amphibian species that can be found in and near all moving water and notably in Loch Ness. The Scotland west coast *Kelpie* is described as a young, sleek, handsome horse, black or brown in color, who can shape-shift into human form. The east coast variety has been sighted only as a golden yellow "horse." The *Kelpie* has skin like glue. After enticing humans onto his back, he gallops away with his victims stuck on for the final ride into the depths of the river. When plunging into the water, the *Kelpie* slaps his tail hard against the surface, making a tremendous banging sound, and disappears under the water to devour his prey.

There are, unfortunately, many stories of children who are out playing much too close to the water's edge when a handsome horse suddenly appears. He draws the children onto his back, and can actually lengthen his body to make room for as many as twenty of them.

LORE

One west coast *Kelpie* shape-shifted into a handsome young man and had great success with consecutive mortal maidens. One night he fell asleep by the side of his latest, when she happened to notice a bit of sea grass in his hair and something equine about his appearance. She fled. He followed her home, vowing to get her back. After a while the poor maiden managed to forget the brief encounter and met her true sweetheart. But on her wedding day, just as the bride was on her way out the church door, she was seized by a huge black horse and was last seen heading to the water. Some say her face bobs up from time to time, looking quite pale in the light of the moon.

A *Kelpie* can be caught only by trapping it with a bridle that is engraved or adorned with a cross. A captured *Kelpie* can be used for hard labor. It is tireless, works like a demon, and has such stamina it can carry its rider endlessly. Unfortunately, at the end of each day it must claim one human victim.

One day, some people working in a field heard a strange voice crying: "The hour is come but not the man!" Just then, they sighted a *Kelpie* rising from the water and then sink down again. Suddenly they saw a rider appear on a horse who was speeding toward the water. The workers jumped up from their labors, and tried to catch hold of the rider. They warned him about the nearby *Kelpie* and the dangerous water, but he paid no heed. Determined to save the strange rider despite himself, they carried him, struggling, to a nearby church, and locked him within. They told him they would free him soon as the prophesied hour had safely passed. But when they returned to unlock him after the dangerous time, they found the poor man drowned in a trough of water near the door.

DISPELLING & DISARMING TECHNIQUES

When approaching loch country, remember: *Kelpies* are an unflaggingly persistent species and fatal encounters cannot be averted by usual methods. Even entrapment with a cross-engraved saddle or working the creature overtime ploughing hard land will not stop its eating habits. There is only one thing that can stop a *Kelpie*. Though they live in moving water, *Kelpies* cannot be exposed to still water of any kind: puddle water, rain or tap water, or non-fizzy bottled water. Travelers usually pack a small bottle of puddle water. And beware of barbecuing near the loch. There's a story of one man who did and unwittingly attracted the *Kelpie* with a roast. The fellow unfortunately lost his daughter, who was sitting nearby and was devoured whole. It is commonly said that the *Kelpie* species tends to come out mostly in November.

NIXIE
Teutonic

The *Nixie* is a freshwater femme fatale amphibian. Like the mermaid, she has a characteristic profile of breasts and fish tail. But watch for some odd features here. She has been said to be completely green: skin, hair, and teeth. She has even been sighted from time to time as a gray horse (these may be misreported Kelpie sightings). She is often found in the mill pond. Unlike the traditional mermaid, the *Nixie* always dwells very close to and mingles with human communities.

LORE

The *Nixie* can usually be distinguished from a mermaid because she is a shopper. Because of this habit, she is often found in town, where a mermaid would never travel. She is sometimes seen in the marketplace in the guise of an old woman. How can one tell if it's a *Nixie* and not a new neighbor? The discovery is usually made when somebody, a child or clever villager, raises the hem of her long skirt slightly, exposing her fish tail. She also drips fresh water behind her, leaving a telltale trail of wetness in the marketplace for some observant human witness.

Aside from shopping, the *Nixie* loves to dance. As a frequent visitor to village dances, she always appears in the guise of an attractive young woman. There she entices many a victim and lures them home to the nearby millstream. In pagan times, she was given at least one sacrifice a year, so now she takes her own as her due. In fact, rescuing a drowning person can often cause a reprisal by the *Nixie* (who feels understandably unhappy about the food loss and disrespect). She expects to be propitiated, not scorned.

The *Nixie* can live on land for extended periods; she has been known to marry a mortal man, and even to raise an entire family. However, these long absences present problems among her original water demon kin, who sometimes come to claim her. Whenever a young wife vanishes, it is certain she was a *Nixie* if she is last seen sinking into a body of water, and the water turns the color of blood. These occurrences are not infrequent as the *Nixie* often chooses human mates to propagate her species, and her frequent intermingling has caused much talk of changelings. (See Changeling in Domicile.)

The male of the species is the *Nokk*. He lives in lakes, ponds, rivers, and waterfalls. He resembles an old man with green eyes, huge ears, and a long wet beard. The *Nokk* drags people down, especially small children if they play too close to the edge of the water or attempt to pick water lilies. He is most dangerous after sunset, and to see or hear the *Nokk* means someone will drown. He is often heard shrieking during shipwrecks. The *Nokk* often takes the shape of a bird that perches on the surface of the water. He has also been seen as a horse or half a horse, also as half a ship, or a gleaming silver coin or ring. The *Nokk* plays music on a golden harp to lure his victim closer if his precious-object disguise doesn't work.

DISPELLING & DISARMING TECHNIQUES

Travelers who may need to drink water inhabited by a *Nokk*, spit in it first to avert harm. In Sweden, when planning to go swimming, first throw a steel knife or scissors into the water and say: "Nokk, Nokk, needle thief, thou art on the land but I am in the water." Conversely, when emerging say: "Nokk, Nokk, needle thief, I am on land, and thou art in the water."

Like many demons, the *Nokk* loses his power when called by name. The best prevention against the *Nokk* is to say his name three times: Nokk, Nokk, Nokk. It may sound oddly familiar, but it is not followed by "Who's there?" and it works.

TIKOLOSHE
South Africa

A *Tikoloshe* is a river amphibian demon of the Xhosa people. Short and hirsute, he walks on land swinging his arms like a baboon. The *Tikoloshe* is known for his voracious sexual appetite, and preys upon local village women. But the *Tikoloshe* can also be seen in urban areas as far away as Natal and Johannesburg, where he often travels to copulate.

A *Tikoloshe* wheedles his way into a woman's heart by offering to carry her heavy bundles or her water jar in return for sexual favors. Like most amphibian river species, *Tikoloshe* mingle with the human community in many forms. They can appear at dances in the village, dressed quite convincingly like attractive neighbors. They are extraordinarily charming and seductive, and it is well known that many women find them irresistible and fall under their spell. However, if a woman does not succumb to his charms, a *Tikoloshe* will become vicious and take her by force.

LORE

One morning a man entered his hut and was horrified to see what looked like a *Tikoloshe* on his way out. That night the husband pretended to leave the hut again, but this time he hid just outside and waited to see if the *Tikoloshe* would return. When he did, the man silently entered his hut and, much to his dismay, witnessed his wife copulating with the short hirsute demon. He killed the *Tikoloshe*, but resisted killing his adulterous wife. He demanded that she tie up her slaughtered lover, and when she had done so, they marched together into the village carrying the corpse to show the others what had happened. The man no longer wanted the woman as a wife and the other villagers understood that. They returned the cattle he had paid for his wife's dowry, and with the cattle but without a wife, he sadly returned to his hut. The other husbands knew it was only a matter of time before the *Tikoloshe* struck again.

DISPELLING & DISARMING TECHNIQUES

One common custom is to raise one's bed on bricks: this prevents the very short *Tikoloshe* from snatching a sleeping female away in the night. There is a twin Chinese species called the White Monkey (see Mountain). He is very tall and no defensive measures are known.

NUCKELAVEE
Scotland

The *Nuckelavee* is a lethal amphibian centaur. He has a head the size of a small human, and his mouth, which rests on a snoutlike piggish projection, is several feet in width. His human-shaped upper body rises from his horselike torso. He has only one eye, which is huge and bloodshot. However, what makes the *Nuckelavee* uniquely unsightly in appearance is that he has no skin at all!

The *Nuckelavee* is from the Fuath (Foo-a) family. Many of the male Fuaths have tails, manes, webbed feet, and are noseless. The females sometimes marry mortal men.

It is said that if a *Nuckelavee* breathes on a vegetable it withers, and if he breathes on an animal it could die on the spot. He is blamed for crops that are blighted by sea winds, and for the death of cattle that fall from the rocks near the edge of the sea. He is also blamed for epidemics and for droughts. He seems driven by a vengeful desire to do as much harm as possible by land, sea, and air.

LORE

It was on a moonless night near the sea that Tammie first saw the *Nuckelavee* approach him on a deserted road. He had first thought the creature was only a horse galloping toward him, but identified the demon by the fins flapping loudly on his legs and the hideous wide mouth snorting steam in his direction. What caused Tammie utter terror was the skinless body. He saw it all: the muscles and sinews all raw and dark and pulsing as the thing moved closer and closer. Riveted, he couldn't turn his eyes away from the *Nuckelavee*. He knew it was futile to try to run. It was just then, as the horrid maw of the demon opened for its dinner, that Tammie remembered the antidote.

It was well known that the species was repelled by fresh water. For one thing, it never appeared in the rain. Hoping desperately that this was true, Tammie headed straight for the loch. When he neared it, just ahead of the *Nuckelavee*, he accidentally splashed the demon's horse legs with some loch water. The *Nuckelavee* reared and backed off instantly. So it was true! Tammie leaped into the freshwater loch. He crossed it, to fall exhausted on the bank, but lived to tell this story.

DISPELLING & DISARMING TECHNIQUES

Travelers in the Scottish Isles carry a bottle of spring water with them. As a rule of thumb sweet water and not salt-water dispels demons. All Fuaths can be harmed by steel or sunlight.

BUNYIP
Australia

The *Bunyip* is an important lagoon species of the Aborigine, at least four times the size of a seal or about the size of a small bull. It is covered with gray hair (or sometimes feathers). It has hoofed feet like those of a horse, a flat, wide tail, and a very wide mouth filled with large sharp teeth and two walruslike fangs. It is said to have an equine mane down the middle of its neck like the Kelpie, a head like an emu, and big flippers. The *Bunyip* can be heard long before it is seen. It has a distinctive loud and repetitive roar.

The *Bunyip* stays primarily in the lagoon and seizes any-one who comes too close to its habitat. Instead of devouring its victims, it holds them prisoner, makes them work, and eats them later. The *Bunyip* also is said to have a long-lasting supernatural claim over its human victims; even if they escape, it will cause them death or misfortune. The *Bunyip* also has power to control or cause floods or drought.

LORE

Once many young men of a tribe disappeared after going out to hunt. Their footprints all led to the lagoon and ended abruptly at the water's edge. Thinking that crocodiles might have killed the men, people began to avoid the lagoon, but it had been an important source of food and soon the people became hungry. One old visionary did not believe that croco-diles were responsible for vanishing hunters, so he went home and looked into his magic glass. There he saw all the young men imprisoned in a cave on the other side of the lagoon. He bravely set out for the cave, and it was then he first noticed the strange, hooflike footprints on the shore. He followed the tracks, then suddenly, out of the water rose two large animals, four times the size of a large dog, covered with gray hair, with fangs like a walrus, and short tails. *Bunyips!* He ran for his life. The *Bunyips* followed, until finally the old man was forced into a cave, the very one he'd foreseen, and there were all the missing men.

Bravely clutching his magic stick, he told the hunters not to worry because before he'd left the village he had arranged for his friend to follow his tracks, and to listen to the ground for certain tapping sounds that he could make with his magic stick from deep below the earth. There, he'd instructed his friend to dig a hole large enough for a man to climb through, and prepare a tree ladder. The old man began tapping and soon they saw a hole opening up above them. A ladder came down, and despite near capture by *Bunyip* guards, all prisoners climbed out and safely returned to the village.

After much celebration, the people grew afraid of the wrath of the *Bunyip*. They sang drought songs to dry up the water in the lagoon and destroy the crocodiles and *Bunyips*. Then they sang rain songs and the lagoon filled up again and was soon teeming with fish. Later the villagers found the bones of the crocodiles, but the remains of the *Bunyips* were never found.

These villagers were fortunate, for the wrath of the *Bunyip* can be overwhelming. In another village some young men were out fishing late one afternoon and one of them strung some meat on his hook. Soon something pulled hard on his line. Very hard. Frightened, he called his friends to help pull up the heavy catch, but when they pulled the creature up they all began to tremble. None had ever seen a *Bunyip* before, but they knew at once that what lay before them on the bank was a child of the legendary species.

Despite an ominous, distinctive roar from the lagoon, the fisherman defiantly announced he planned to take the *Bunyip* home and give it to his betrothed as a present. They warned him as he hoisted it on his shoulders, and then suddenly all saw the head of the *Bunyip*'s mother rise up from the lagoon, and at her roar they ran for their lives. But no human can run from the wrath of a *Bunyip* and, after glaring with horrid flaming eyes at the fleeing fishermen, the mother vanished. Instantly the water rose, and began to spread beneath the feet of the men. The waters continued to rise as the men ran just ahead of the mounting flood that roared into their village home. As they reached their families, all was swept away: hills, trees, houses, were all swallowed by the violent waters. The young man dropped the *Bunyip,* reached his sweetheart, and embraced her. Trying to climb the tallest tree to save her, he felt his feet grow cold, and when he looked down they were talons, then his arms turned to wings. He looked at his sweetheart still held in his embrace and she had become a black swan. No trace of earth was left and all had become water. He floated there with his friends, for now they were all black swans, and they never became human again. After the *Bunyip* was safely carried home by his mother, the waters slowly receded. Much later, when new people came to live near the lagoon, they knew never to disturb the *Bunyip.*

DISPELLING & DISARMING TECHNIQUES

There is nothing to be done to avert the wrath of the *Bunyip* once provoked, so the tales serve to warn travelers to be mindful at the lagoon and to obey various prohibitions not to pollute or greedily consume. This demon embodies the unlimited fury of nature's retaliatory powers, which can even cause an annihilating deluge.

VODYANOI
Russia

The *Vodyanoi* is a male freshwater species whose primary residence is at the utmost depth of millponds. He has been sighted as an old man with a greenish beard all covered with muck, or sometimes covered with scales. It is also said that he is half-fish, half-man, and some insist they have seen a tail. Most say he never comes all the way up to the surface of the water, and that he rarely moves from his site — usually near the dam or mill wheel. He is considered responsible for all local drownings. Further, if anyone attempts to retrieve a body for burial, the act invites retaliation.

LORE

The *Vodyanoi* is said to be a fallen angel cast into the water by the Archangel Michael. He lives in a shining underwater palace with exquisite furnishings and chandeliers and considers himself a property owner in charge of all the many fishes and spirits of his pool or pond. It is said that when a new mill is built, the *Vodyanoi* will seek revenge by taking at least one human life because it tampers with his habitat.

The *Vodyanoi* is reputed to have a single-minded purpose: to drown human beings. The only people he maintains a special relationship with are the miller and a few fishermen. The miller has been suspected of sorcery and of making a pact with the *Vodyanoi* (akin to the Devil in some local opinions). He is said to dine with him in his underwater palace on occasion.

DISPELLING & DISARMING TECHNIQUES

To avert human sacrifice, local folk use a chicken or a black rooster in rites of propitiation, and the *Vodyanoi* is usually placated. It is said that crossing oneself before diving in will lessen any problems that may arise on a close encounter. Fishermen make offerings of bread, salt, vodka, and tobacco to ensure his help, for the *Vodyanoi* is easily aggravated and can punish them by hiding all fish and ripping up their nets.

MBULU
South Africa

The *Mbulu* is an amphibian river species of the Zulu people who appears human at first glance. But a careful look reveals scaly skin and a long, extraordinary tail that has at the tip a mouth with very sharp teeth and a will of its own. When the *Mbulu* comes out onto land, it is notorious for following people down lonely paths and whispering softly in their ears.

LORE

Once there was a widow who after tragically losing her children, all but one, lost her will to live. She gave her only living daughter a stick and sent her off to her uncle's house, instructing her to tap the ground outside his house with the stick. The mother promised that all her possessions would rise from the earth. She said farewell; she planned to end her own life.

The girl reluctantly left home. When she had gone a little way, she looked back and saw her mother's house burning. She knew her mother had set fire to the house intending to immolate herself, and that she could do nothing to help. She continued walking on, keeping to a path on the bank of a river. She soon encountered what she thought was a man sitting on a rock, who announced that whoever got wet when walking near the water must go in to bathe. Then he thrashed his hidden tail on the water so hard that water splashed the girl in the face. Obediently, she went in the river to bathe. While she was in the water, the *Mbulu* took her clothes and put them on. When the girl came out of the water and asked politely for her clothes, the *Mbulu* told her he would return them as soon as she was dry. Trustingly, the orphan walked on with the *Mbulu* at her side and, later, again asked for her clothes. This time the *Mbulu* said he would return them when they arrived at the next village.

When they arrived at the village and the girl begged for her clothes, the *Mbulu* instructed her to tell everyone that she was his servant girl. The girl was afraid of the *Mbulu* now, for she realized she was dealing with a powerful and strange being. She obeyed him, so people imagined the *Mbulu* to be an important woman with fine clothes and her as his servant girl. They did wonder why his voice was so deep for a woman, but he said he had been quite ill.

After a while, the *Mbulu* married a man from the village, while the poor girl was sent to work in the fields. While working, she regained her voice and began to sing sad songs about her enslavement and adventures. A woman who worked near her finally heard the words of the song and made a plan to see if they were true.

Since it is known that the tail of a real *Mbulu* is always hungry, always hidden, and has a will of its own, the girl set a trap to expose the creature. She dug a hole and filled the bottom with milk, then demanded that everyone in the village jump over the hole. The *Mbulu*, posing as a wife, was naturally reluctant but had no choice as everybody was participating. "She" tried to jump quickly, but the tail was out of control. It couldn't pass up delicious milk and came out of hiding to drink. Outraged, the villagers killed the *Mbulu* and buried it in the hole.

The man who had mistakenly married the *Mbulu* married the girl. She had a child, and one day while it was playing a pumpkin grew from the ground where the *Mbulu* had been buried, and it tried to kill the child. The villagers hacked the pumpkin to pieces, burned it, and threw the ashes into the river. Finally rid of the threat forever, the girl regained her courage and set out with her husband and daughter and magic stick to visit her uncle. There she tapped her stick upon the ground and all her possessions rose as promised and she shared them with her family.

DISARMING & DISPELLING TECHNIQUES

Courage and alertness is called for with the trickster demon *Mbulu*, as well as a sophisticated knowledge of its habits and uncontrollable tail. As long as the heroine remained in victim mode, she was enslaved, but when she raised her voice in song, she was able to conquer the demon. As with many spirits, death and burial is not enough, for from the bones or blood of dark powers, other destructive forces or beings can often arise.

MERROW

Ireland

The *Merrow* — in Irish, *Moruadh* or *Moruach* — is a uniquely musical species of sea fairy that is believed to have been ancestor to certain human families living today on the western and southern coasts of Ireland. Its nature is one of profound attachment to mortal men, whom the *Merrow* enchants easily. They are always seen wearing red caps covered with feathers, which somehow endows them with the ability to dive to their undersea homes. Their music is heard coming from the depths of the ocean, or at times notes float on the surface. They can be seen dancing to it on the shore or on the waves. They are charming and seductive by nature but extremely vengeful if crossed. They are all daughters of kings who live beneath the waves.

LORE

It is said that the *Merrow* metamorphosed into the harp, the national instrument of Ireland, and became thereby an embodied musical essence. In Moore's *Irish Melodies* we hear the opening lines:

> *'Tis believed that this harp, which I now wake for thee,*
> *Was a syren of old, who sung under the sea;*
> *And who often, at eve, through the bright waters roved*
> *To meet, on the green shore, a youth whom she loved.*

The *Merrow* has been sighted in these parts as early as 887 C.E., when one was found cast ashore in the country of Alba (now Scotland). She was documented as being of extraordinarily large proportions: one hundred and ninety-five feet long, with seven-foot-long fingers and nose. She was whiter than a swan from top to tip. It is difficult to credit the accuracy of these described proportions with the frequent later reports of her charms and mortal matings.

In another early sighting, one of Ireland's ancient kings of the legendary Fomorians came within reach of several *Merrows* while sailing these parts as he heard them singing. He drew closer but unfortunately they tore him limb from limb and scattered him to the waves. It is hard to know what provoked them.

The male *Merrow* is quite deformed and unshapely, with green hair, a red nose, and tiny eyes. They normally stay underwater, where they keep the spirits of drowned fisherman and sailors in cages at the very bottom of the measureless sea. It is said that the females prefer human lovers to the male *Merrow*.

PONATURI
New Zealand

The Maori *Ponaturi* is a coastal species of malevolent sea fairies who live in the watery deeps. Their skin is greenish white with an unnatural inner phosphorescent radiance, and their long fingers end in clawlike talons. They can be seen ashore in the middle of the night and glow eerily in the dark.

LORE

Late one afternoon, a young boy was swimming with his friends. He was much too far out and the sea was rough in the rising winds. The other boys tried to warn him, but he only laughed. Then suddenly, he disappeared beneath the pounding surf. When he came up he was no longer laughing, and he seemed caught somehow. But by what? In the fading light they could barely see him and they ran off to tell his father. "He's drowning!" they shouted, and they all ran back to show him the spot. But now the waters were dark and oddly still and the boy was no longer there. Devastated, the boy's father plunged into the water. Deeper and deeper he went, the water crushing his chest as he searched for his son.

At the very bottom he saw a long shadowy form resting among the seagrass and mounds of shells. He drifted closer. It seemed to be a strange house, all covered with mysterious carvings, with no windows; it was a long, low dwelling that might hold several families. He circled the house in search of the entrance until he came to a door, and attached to the door hung the body of his drowned child. Shaken, he went inside. The house was empty but for a very old and frail woman who sat just inside the doorway. "Show me the people who stole my son!" he demanded.

The old woman decided to help him. She said, "This is the home of the *Ponaturi*. Do as I tell you if you want to avenge your son's death. First, cover all the cracks in the house and then hide yourself well."

The father of the drowned boy did as he was told. When, near dawn, the *Ponaturi* returned, he began to leave his hiding place to go after them, but the woman held her hand out: "Wait," she whispered. "The *Ponaturi* do not know the cracks of their house are covered, and when the new day is at its brightest, they will be tricked into thinking it is night. The light of the sun will kill them instantly."

The *Ponaturi* were soon fast asleep, and after a few hours the father made a loud noise. The chief was the first to awaken, and he asked if it was still day. The old woman replied, "No, you have slept long and it is nearly night." The chief said, "I will sleep a few more hours because I am still tired. Wake me then."

When the sun was high in the sky, the old woman awakened the *Ponaturi* in the darkened house. The chief asked, "What time is it now?" And the old woman answered, "It is time for you to get to work." When all the terrible fairies had gathered to leave, the father crept out of his hiding place, and opened the door very wide. The *Ponaturi* burst through the doorway and shot upward to the surface of the water. Powerful rays of sunlight flooded the house, and instantly they all died, swallowed by the light of the new day.

The father bid the old woman good-bye. He tore the terrible door to the house of the sea fairies from its hinges and took it with him. When he returned to the shore the villagers looked at the door in wonder: it held a wood carving so like his drowned child that it moved them to tears.

It is said that from this tragic drowning and from the brave father's descent to the dwelling of demons, the art of carving was transmitted to the Maori people.

DISPELLING & DISARMING TECHNIQUES

Like all demons, the *Ponaturi* have a fatal flaw, and humans can use daylight as a weapon. Like most demonic spirits the fairies are creative as well as destructive and can become a source of inspiration. The father's dive into their subaqueous dwelling allowed him to wrest a gift of art from those who took life. At a terrible cost he found an eternal secret and brought it up to the light of consciousness.

MOUNTAIN

Mountains have universally been considered the abode of the Divine; their highest peaks, often concealed in mist and clouds, are sacred sites of revelation to which only the holy may ascend. Mount Sinai, Mount Olympus, Mount Fuji, Mount Ararat, the Five Sacred Mountains of China, Mount Meru in Tanzania, Mount Kailas in Tibet — all have been places of contact with the Other World. As always, spirit-imbued territory holds terrible danger and is forbidden to mere mortals.

When lightning flashes and thunder rumbles ominously, the powerful mountain peaks are thought to be the origins of storms. The waters that crash down and pour into rivers are necessary to life itself, and when withheld their source must be appeased through sacrifice. Who can approach Mountain's awesome peaks? It is clearly off limits to ordinary human beings. If cliffs, gorges, and avalanches don't scare a person off, the Mountain holds demonic spirits in great abundance to warn a daring climber. The spirits can appear as lights beckoning from a precipice and lead him to death, or they may loosen a rock underfoot or above his head.

Active volcanos erupt in fiery display of the Mountain's connection to subterranean worlds, where the dead reside. Mountains also hold treasure — minerals and gold — that belong to the chthonic beings deep within the earth, who are often very reluctant to part with it. Many demons are associated with mining activities.

Paracelsus, the Renaissance magician, physician, and alchemist, trained in metallurgy and mining, believed the various demons were there to guard treasure so that it would not be revealed all at once to careless human beings.

In ancient China, mountains, the intermediary forms between Heaven and Earth, were worshiped collectively as deities. It was high in the mountains that Taoist wizards gained supernatural powers and learned the secrets of medicinal herbs for longevity and even immortal life. There are several mountains in the East that are sites of pilgrimage to this day.

In Europe, the early Church knew there were abundant shrines to pagan gods in the mountains — and what terrain could be less hospitable to humans except perhaps the sea? So the Roman Empire claimed that the Mountain habitat belonged to the Devil himself. Formerly home to nature spirits, the climate changed. A huge new population of malevolent fairies hatched. The word *alp* ("elf" in English) means both "mountain" and "demon of the mountain" and expresses our ambivalence about wilderness — that mixture of reverence, awe, and terror which informs the multitude of demonic images and fierce lore of the Mountain habitat.

WHO'S WHO IN MOUNTAIN

HUWAWA	Mesopotamia
TENGU	Japan
HULDREFOLK	Norway
ABATWA	South Africa
YUKI-ONNA	Japan
PATUPAIREHE	New Zealand
TOMMY-KNOCKERS	North America
KISHI	Angola
GWYLLION	Wales
MAHISHA-ASURA	India
YUNWI DJUNSTI	North America
DUERGAR	Great Britain
MOUNTAIN FAIRIES	China
AKVAN	Ancient Persia
YAKSAS	Nepal
WHITE MONKEY	China

HUWAWA
Mesopotamia

Huwawa, an ancient guardian demon, was appointed by the
Sumerian storm god Enlil to watch over the Cedar Mountain
forest, located in the coastal mountains of Syria. *Huwawa*
appears in *The Gilgamesh Epic*, the best known story of its
day (circa 1600–2000 B.C.E.) and the model for much of later
Western hero literature, written in Akkadian in Old Babylon
but based on earlier Sumerian legend. *Huwawa* is a creature
of colossal size. His massive gorgonlike face is composed of
ropy twisted coils of intestine and can strike terror into the
heart of the beholder. He has a snarling mouth of fire and his
breath kills. Some say he is a personified volcano associated
with the underworld. Some say he is a storm god. He is a virtually invincible guardian demon whose presence renders the
Cedar Mountain invulnerable.

LORE

One night in the palace of the Sumerian city of Uruk that Gilgamesh had built and ruled, Gilgamesh's friend Enkidu had a nightmare, the meaning of which he could not decipher. Concerned, Enkidu and Gilgamesh made offerings to the sun god Shamash, who revealed the meaning to them: the heroes' mission was to kill *Huwawa* and to cut down the seven cedars of the sacred forest that he guarded on Cedar Mountain to build a temple in Uruk.

Despite the misgivings of his community and his mother, Gilgamesh (part-divine, part-human hero) had weapons made, and set forth with Enkidu to the Land of the Cedars. They traveled northwest for more than two years over seven mountains to the edge of the world.

When they finally reached Cedar Mountain and beheld the towering evergreens lit by the sun, all their mighty deeds seemed suddenly minute. They felt small and vulnerable in this giant landscape, and as the sun descended and then vanished, they became afraid. Again they made a sacrifice to Shamash and waited for dawn. In the morning they called out to *Huwawa*, but he did not answer. They trembled in the utter silence.

Suddenly *Huwawa* appeared, roaring like a thunderstorm. The ancient cedars bowed at the sound. Gilgamesh was stunned by the horrid, vast head of the demon. In the terrible, fierce battle that followed, Gilgamesh employed the savage winds of Shamash to rage against the mighty *Huwawa*. Finally he stabbed him with his weapons and it was Enkidu who cut off the head of the creature to carry home in victory. Then, together, they stripped the mountain of cedar trees.

The duo returned home in glory, dressed in golden robes. Because of this shining attire, Gilgamesh attracted the eye of the goddess Ishtar. When he rebuffed her rudely, she took offense and sent the bull of heaven down to destroy him. The two men fought the bull and won, but now they had gone much too far. To teach Gilgamesh a lesson, Enkidu was killed by Enlil, who was the protector of *Huwawa*. Gilgamesh spent the rest of his days grieving, searching for Enkidu, and learning about the limits of human life and the meaning of mortality.

DISPELLING & DISARMING TECHNIQUES

The chain of tragic events in the narrative of Gilgamesh was set in motion by his arrogant act of killing *Huwawa* and chopping down sacred trees of Cedar Mountain. The feat that the hero chose, conquering nature itself, daring to go beyond limits set by gods to claim the wilderness his own, has great resonance in later lore and even in present-day concerns.

Look for the echo of *Huwawa* in the very nature of the later demon population of mountain habitat. Many settled here to guard sacred treasures against the hubris of the mortal interloper, and like the terrain itself, they are fierce and pitiless.

TENGU
Japan

The *tengu* comprise a class of high-flying demons, probably Chinese in origin, who principally inhabit cedar or pine trees in the mountainous areas of Japan.

The *tengu* are of two main types. The "higher *tengu*" has a human form, and wears the red robes of a bishop and a small crown; it has white hair, a red face, and is often seen holding a fan made of feathers; each higher *tengu* resides on its own mountain peak. The "inferior *tengu*" has small wings and sharp claws on the ends of its fingers and toes. Sometimes they are seen wearing small black hats and clothes made of leaves. They all have large, shining, mischievous eyes. They usually travel in flocks. All *tengu*, higher and inferior, have elongated beaklike noses.

The *tengu* shares several traits with the Chinese T'ien-

kou, who is sometimes described as a shooting star and sometimes as a mountain demon in the shape of a dog that came
from the sky in fire and thunder. In either version, the Chinese
demon has two wings and kidnaps and eats small children, and
it can readily shape-shift. Another close cousin of the Japanese
tengu is the Hindu supernatural bird, Garuda.

Tengu are generally believed to be the spirits of arrogant
or vengeful dead, and are well known for their malicious
delight in practical jokes. They tend to prey on Buddhist
monks, interrupting their pious work by strapping them to the
tops of trees, or by offering them delicious food that turns out
to be excrement. They also can appear as Buddhist monks and
lead other monks astray, always in an attempt to stop prayers.
They also appear to many travelers who get lost in the mountains.

Like fairies, the *tengu* enjoy stealing human children
and hiding them from their parents. When and if the children
are returned, they've usually been reduced to a confused state
and never fully regain their senses. At other times the lower
tengu are busy carrying out nasty errands for the higher *tengu*.
Because all *tengu* can endow their followers with supernatural
powers, the species has attracted a large group of worshipers
known as mountain priests, or *Yamabushi*, who claim to be
able to cure diseases and exorcise demons.

LORE

A Zen parable tells of a hunter who was in the mountains. He came across a snake killing a bird. Suddenly a boar
appeared and began to devour the snake. The hunter thought
he should kill the boar, but changed his mind because he did
not want to be a link in such a chain, and cause his own death
by the next predator to come along. On his way home he heard
a voice call to him from the top of a tree. It was the voice of a
tengu. It told him how lucky he was, for had he killed the boar,
the *tengu* would have killed him. The man subsequently
moved into a cave and never killed another animal.

DISPELLING & DISARMING TECHNIQUES

Understand the rules: *Tengu* own all the trees in the mountains and must be propitiated for any lumber taken. Historically, they have had frequent contact with woodcutters; in order to successfully chop down a tree, woodcutters offer rice cakes to appease the spirit. If not satisfied, the *tengu* play all sorts of vicious tricks, such as starting avalanches or causing ax heads to fall off handles.

HULDREFOLK
Norway

The *Huldrefolk* (hidden people) are fairies. They're invisible, so though populous, are hard to spot. Some say it is their hats that make them invisible; others report that the secret lies in a special coat. Whatever the reason, they are there at all times, living in another dimension, hidden behind a veil of invisible vapor. When, on rare occasions, this veil lifts, the *Huldrefolk* can be glimpsed. The males closely resemble miniature humans; the female *Huldre* wears a blue, green, or white dress, has a cowlike tail and a hollow back.

LORE

The *Huldrefolk* live very much like *Homo sapiens* in their parallel universe. They get married, have offspring, own homes, farms, and businesses. The *Huldrefolk* are said to be Adam's children, by his first wife, Lilith (see her in Domicile). It is said that when the Lord unexpectedly dropped by and asked Eve to show him the children, she hid Lilith's. The Lord asked her if she had shown Him all the children. She said yes, and He replied, "Let those not revealed remain concealed." This is why the *Huldrefolk* are still hidden from our view.

DISPELLING & DISARMING TECHNIQUES

When building a house, take care never to build on top of a *Huldrefolk* dwelling. Tap the cornerstone with a stick. The sound can alert the builder to an invisible residence just below. Another method is to sleep one night just outside the potential building site. It is said if sleep is disturbed another plot should be found. If uncertain, a possession, such as a hammer or saw, can be left overnight on the planned building site. The next day, if the tool is missing, it is said the *Huldrefolk* have given their sign. Without their permission, building a home over theirs is futile — the house will be torn apart or burned down. Some *Huldrefolk* are good neighbors if treated with respect. Others are malicious regardless of how well human beings behave.

The *Huldrefolk* are the owners of all wild game. To them, hunting and fishing is not sport, it's a crime. Many brave hunters and fishermen have obtained permission from the *Huldrefolk* to hunt, although some areas remain strictly off limits.

Huldrefolk are famous for their buried treasures. Look for a blue light. Underneath the blue light lie vast riches. But beware: *Huldrefolk* may also be down there. Furthermore, treasure hunting has been said to lead to terrifying visions.

There are two ways to take possession of a *Huldrefolk* animal without risk. The first is to throw a steel knife over the invisible animal. As steel sails above it, the animal will materialize and can be claimed by the human thrower. A circle drawn with ashes will also keep the *Huldrefolk* from being able to enter a chosen hunting ground. This method is a bit confining, because the person can never leave the circle again.

Most important to all *Huldrefolk* is peace and quiet, especially in the evening. When in the hills after sundown, whisper, put dogs indoors, and tape down the bells on cats and livestock so that they do not ring. If disturbed, the *Huldrefolk* will take deadly revenge.

Above all, when observing the *Huldrefolk,* watch the time. Stories are widespread of human travelers who have been invited to join the *Huldrefolk* for a quick dinner or celebration, only to resurface and find all their friends have grown old. It should be remembered these are fairies. Babies must never be left unattended when they are near. Human males must be cautious because a *Huldre* can appear as a beautiful maiden, but if she lures a fellow home, he is hers forever. Like all fairies, she needs human DNA to better her fairy species.

ABATWA
South Africa

The *abatwa* is a Zulu spirit species, considerably smaller than the common fairy, so small that they often hide under blades of grass and sleep in anthills. They live in the mountains and rocky hills, but they have no central village. They are nomadic hunters who follow the game, devour their catch in its entirety, and move on to the next kill. When the *abatwa* travel, it is said that they ride upon one horse, sitting from the neck to the tail, one behind another. If they do not find any game on their hunt they will usually devour their communal horse.

DISPELLING & DISARMING TECHNIQUES

The *abatwa* are easily offended and quickly enraged. Their most common response is to murder by poison arrow. But if it happens that one meets an *abatwa* while journeying through the hills and mountainous regions of Africa, the typical encounter would go like this: The *abatwa* will ask, "From where did you see me?" This is a trick question to which the honest reply "I am seeing you here right now for the very first time" will be fatal. The *abatwa* are wildly sensitive about their size. The lifesaving answer is: "See that mountain way back there? I first saw you when I was on that mountain." The *abatwa* is usually placated by the stature this suggests and such flattery earns a chance for escape.

Far more dangerous than encountering an *abatwa* is stepping on one. When stepped on, the *abatwa* will stab the hiker with the point of an invisible but deadly poison arrow, which causes an immediate and baffling death that will confound the coroner. When in *abatwa* country, visitors must wear shoes with hard, thick, impenetrable soles.

YUKI-ONNA
Japan

Yuki-Onna (Lady of the Snow) can appear as a beautiful — in fact, irresistible — maiden wearing all white, her skin pale, her breath like frost. She also manifests as a white vapor that blows through the crack in the door. Other times she is seen hovering over her victim, a floating misty essence. In all cases, through her glacial lips she sucks the life breath gently but inexorably from her victims' mouths.

LORE

One bitterly cold night two men, a master and servant, were traveling through a mountain forest when they came upon a cabin. A snowstorm had begun so they stopped to rest. Both men fell asleep, but the servant woke suddenly when snow blew across his face. He opened his eyes and saw that the cabin door was wide open. A woman in a white flowing dress floated to the center of the room. He watched in terror as the pale figure bent over his master and breathed a misty stream of white smoke into his mouth. Then she turned to him.

He tried to scream, but could not make a sound. Her breath stung his face. The woman told him quietly that she had planned to treat him as she did his master, but he was far too young and too handsome. She threatened him with death should he ever mention this incident to anyone. Then she vanished. The man called out to his master, but there was no answer. His master was dead.

The next winter, when the man was returning home to his village, he met a beautiful maiden named Yuki. She told him shyly that she was on her way to become a servant girl in the village. He took her into his house and soon they were married. She bore him ten children, all unusually pale. Then one night Yuki was sitting beside a lamp sewing. As the lamplight illuminated her beautiful white face, the man was somehow reminded of that dreadful night so long ago. "Just now," he said to his wife, "you reminded me of a beautiful, ghostly woman I saw years ago who killed my master with her icy breath . . ."

Yuki threw down her sewing and took on demonic size: "It was I, Yuki-Onna, who killed your master!" she raged. "You have broken your promise to keep it a secret. If it were not for our ten sleeping children I would kill you now!" She warned him never to hurt her children, and assured him that since she would always know his every action, if harm came to any of them he would die. With that, she turned herself into a mist and floated up through the chimney.

DISPELLING & DISARMING TECHNIQUES

There is nothing to be done in any inevitably fatal encounter with *Yuki-Onna* during a blizzard. However, when a male traveler attracts a spirit, there are certain things he must know. All supernatural wives come with a condition, which can be any of the following: never speak of her origins, never tell any other human being that she has supernatural powers, never look at her when she is in a transformed state (and always give her privacy and time to transform), or never open the basket she brought with her or touch some item she declares forbidden. Any violation of her condition will bring about her disappearance and also may have fatal consequence for the spouse.

PATUPAIREHE
New Zealand

The *Patupairehe* are Maori fairies who live in remote mountains and hilltops, places wrapped in dense fog. They look like tall, redhaired, exceedingly pale humans, but they are rarely sighted as they move only through the dark or the mist on foggy days. Like many fairies, they consider themselves guardians of the wilderness and all that lives within.

Often the *Patupairehe* take human lovers, whom they visit late at night. The male *Patupairehe* are expert flute players, and use their musical skills to arouse human women who happen to walk nearby. Those who fall under the spell of the *Patupairehe* seldom if ever return to their old selves. Albino children are believed to be offspring of such couples.

LORE

Once a man's wife was carried off by a *Patupairehe*. The man searched everywhere but could find only her footprints, which led far away into the hills. He asked the village wise man for help. The wise man performed secret ceremonies to cause the kidnapped woman to remember her human husband (for in the fairy world, humans never remember their ordinary lives), and told the man to go rub his house all over with red ochre, put some food on the fire, and wait. Meanwhile, in the mountains, the wife was affected by the wise man's magic, and she began to long for her human husband so much that she wandered from the fairy hills and headed for home.

The *Patupairehe* chief noticed she was missing and went after her. He followed her footprints until he came to the village. Aghast, he saw her hut covered with red ochre and smelled home cooking. Naturally, these sights and odors were *Patupairehe* repellents that set the fairy running back to his foggy mountain home. The man and his wife lived happily ever after.

The *Patupairehe* have been known to inadvertently help humans. One day a man passed a spot on the beach where he

saw the remains of fish that people had apparently been clean-
ing. Thinking it odd that anybody would abandon a catch, he
looked around for the fishermen. The beach was deserted.
When he looked closely at the footprints he saw they were
faint, as if they'd been made the night before. He wondered if
the fishermen were spirits who had been forced to leave
because of the approach of daylight. The man decided to
return to the spot that night to see if the mysterious fishermen
would return.

At midnight he hid and watched from nearby. There
they were, the *Patupairehe*, throwing their magic net to catch
fish. As they worked, the man unobtrusively joined them. He
was paler than most men, almost as pale as the fairies, so they
didn't notice him. He worked among them all night and
learned how to throw the spirits' net. Before dawn, the fairies
started to collect their catch and bring in the net. They worked
quickly, eager to finish while it was still dark. Each fairy ran
a string through the gills of the fish he claimed. The man kept
up with them, collecting fish for himself, but his string seemed
too short, and the fish would not stay on when tied. Seeing his
difficulty, the fairies helped him and soon taught him how to
string fish.

Just before dawn some *Patupairehe* realized that they
had been working with a human. At this discovery immediate
confusion and argument ensued, but the sun had begun to rise,
so they had to vanish. In their haste they left everything
behind. The man escaped safely in the morning sunlight and
he kept the fairy net. This was how the Maori learned to make
fishing nets and string fish and become great fishermen.

DISPELLING & DISARMING TECHNIQUES

Not only are the *Patupairehe* heliophobic, they are afraid
of fire, ash, and the color red. They are repulsed by food that
has been cooked in fire. All these are effective deterrents. If
tricked, they can teach supernatural skills and be inspiring.

TOMMY-KNOCKERS
North America

The *Tommy-Knocker* is an American mining species that seems to have originated in Staffordshire, in England, where they were known as just plain *Knockers*. The *Tommy-Knocker* stands about two feet high, the size of a three-year-old, and has a disproportionately large head, long beard, and weathered, wrinkled skin. Their arms are long and reach nearly to the ground. They wear miniature mining outfits, caps and boots, and carry mining gear such as pickaxes. They are usually invisible to the human eye, so it is only by the sound of their tapping, knocking, and working in various shafts nearby the human workers that one knows they are present.

They can be helpful or malicious, but they are always mischievous. This temperament can be hazardous in mine shafts. The *Tommy-Knockers* are believed to have originated as ghosts of men who died in the mine in the past. They work like demons all night long.

LORE

In northern England, home of the original *Knockers,* the spirits often served to warn of disaster about to happen by knocking mysteriously and alerting the miners to aberrant sounds. Once in a while they could be helpful, as in the case of "Blue Cap," a famous *Knocker* who appeared as a blue-flamed light that flickered through the mine, landed on a tub of coal, and mysteriously moved the heavy tub as if by the force of many laborers. But when playful or vengeful they would steal candles and hide tools and, at their worst, set the mine on fire.

Tommy-Knockers do not like to be seen by humans and often react with extreme volatility and capriciousness when they know they've been spotted. One story tells of a coal miner whose load so outdistanced the others each morning that his fellow workers wondered how. He never seemed tired or over-worked and when asked how he managed to do such a hard night's work, he simply shrugged. Some coworkers crept in one night to see what was happening, and there was their friend sitting smoking quietly in a shaft. When they peered over his shoulder they discovered a huge team of *Tommy-Knockers* working for him. The *Tommy-Knockers*, according to this report, wore tall red hats and used miniature mining equipment. Soon as the wee demons realized they'd been sighted, they turned on their mortal companion in a fury, perhaps thinking he told his friends about them, and within moments the entire mine erupted in flames.

Other *Knockers*, called *Coblynau*, haunt the mines and quarries of Wales and point out ore by pounding, or "knocking," on the walls. They are said to be half a yard tall, and hideously ugly. They imitate the miners in dress, and carry tiny work tools, picks, and lamps. They work constantly, but never get anything accomplished. If not treated with great respect, they are known to cause rock slides. Their German cousins are the *Kobolds*, demon miners who take pleasure in malevolent games and trickery, and the *Wichtlein* (Little Wights), tiny men with long beards said to be death portents. The *Wichtlein* announce death by knocking three times on the wall.

DISPELLING & DISARMING TECHNIQUES

There's no getting rid of *Tommy-Knockers* or their European counterparts. However, it is clear that when they choose to be helpful, one must respect their privacy and keep their presence a secret to avoid fatal accidents.

KISHI
Angola

The *Kishi* is a two-faced male hill species. His forward countenance is human in features and quite attractive. This is the face that tricks its female victim. The rear face is hidden by long, thick hair. It has the features of a hyena. Its waiting mouth holds long, sharp teeth, and a jaw so powerful it cannot be pried off its meal by any means.

It is the human face of the *Kishi* that insinuates itself as a potential boyfriend, and in addition the *Kishi* is a smooth talker, a great raconteur who lures with ease. He often attends village dances, invites his intended meal out to dinner, and when the time is right turns his head around and devours her.

LORE

Three sisters, after collecting water from the village river, decided to explore the land beyond. The girls knew it was dangerous to wander off beyond the boundaries of their village, but they forgot the warnings, and little did they know that the hills behind the river were inhabited by infamous *Kishis*.

The sisters spotted a house in the distant hills and walked there. While they looked around the outside of the house, the *Kishis* watched from within and waited for their meal to enter. Meanwhile the *Kishis* got dressed in their finest clothes, hid their hyena faces under their combed thick hair, and welcomed the girls to their home. The sisters went inside and dined with the *Kishis,* but the youngest sister did not eat. She sensed that something was terribly wrong.

After the meal the *Kishis* played music for the sisters, and when night fell, the girls were shown a room in which they could sleep. When all was quiet in the house the youngest sister whispered, "I have seen their other faces. They will surely eat us. We must go *now!*" So all the sisters climbed out the window and ran away. It was just in time, because when they looked back they saw a terrible blaze. The *Kishis* had set the house on fire, hoping to roast the girls while they slept.

Later, when the *Kishis* looked through the ashes, they did not find their human meat. They realized the sisters had escaped and ran after them, hoping to catch them before they reached their own village. Meanwhile the girls arrived at the river but found it had risen during the night and was too deep to cross. They quickly climbed a tree. The *Kishis* spotted them and, enraged and snarling, roared that the sisters would never escape. The *Kishis* now revealed their hideous hyena faces, and as they pushed the tree trunk with their powerful bodies, the sisters shivered in the branches.

As the tree began to sway back and forth, the girls knew they would fall. The youngest sister spied an eagle flying in the sky and called to it for help. She offered it chickens to eat if it would help them. The eagle swooped down, picked up the youngest sister, and brought her safely to the other side of the river. The eagle returned for the other girls, but alas, one of them was too heavy, so he had to drop her into the river below and she was carried off. Before the eagle could reach the other, the tree gave way and the last sister dropped into the arms of waiting *Kishis* below. She was never seen again.

DISPELLING & DISARMING TECHNIQUES

Note that the one sister who lived to tell the tale never ate in the land of the demon. She was not seduced by his illusory civilized form and saw the wild carnivore within. When traveling in Angola, one must be as wise as the youngest sister.

GWYLLION
Wales

The *Gwyllion* (from the Welsh *gwyll*, which denotes gloom and darkness) are female spirits who live in unusually treacherous mountainous areas. They are haglike in appearance and are identified by their distinctive, hair-raising laughter. One notorious *Gwyllion* is described as an old woman wearing ash-colored clothing, an oblong four-pointed hat, and an apron over her shoulder, and carrying a pot in her hand. She cries "Wow up!" as she passes her victims, a signal of distress. Variations of this are "Wwb!" or "Ww-bwb!"

When travelers first lose their way at night, they often come upon the *Gwyllion*, whom they generally mistake for a kindly old woman who will lead them back on the right path. But after following these malicious spirits for a while, they hear that dreadful cackle, and then it is always much too late.

LORE

Once a traveler in the mountains realized he was on an unfamiliar path and feared he was getting lost. As night fell, he spied a woman not far off and called loudly for help. He received no answer, and assuming she was deaf ran toward her. But as he did, she seemed ever farther away. At last, exhausted, he stumbled to the ground and, looking about, found himself in completely unknown territory. It was then he heard the old woman cackling. Her laugh was awful, the telltale sign of a *Gwyllion*. Shaking, he pulled out his knife and held it high over his head. The steel blade flashed in the moonlight. It was the one sure repellent and it worked. She instantly disappeared.

DISPELLING & DISARMING TECHNIQUES

In bad weather, the *Gwyllion* might enter a human abode to get warm. During such a visit, the *Gwyllion* must not be offended or great harm will later come to the family. Clean water must be provided, and, as a courtesy, all metal knives must be hidden (unless flashed as a last resort). When outdoors, traveling in company is a good idea. It is usually only solitary travelers who have *Gwyllion* (or other demonic) encounters.

MAHISHA-ASURA
India

Mahisha-Asura is one of the epic demons of Hinduism and is found in the *Markandeya Purana* (c. 300 B.C.E.-500 C.E.). His basic form is of a buffalo, but he is a champion shape-shifter who has been seen as lion, elephant, human, and, amazingly, has become a million multiples of himself. This instantaneous, illusory cloning once created a nearly invincible army that set all the gods into hiding for a while. *Mahisha-Asura* was born of a mother buffalo (*mahisha*) and father demon (*asura*). The water buffalo, known for its extraordinary lust, stupidity, sloth, and mud-bathing indolence, gave *Mahisha* his attributes, and his father, unusually malevolent, contributed his disposition. The buffalo is also seen as a symbol of Death.

LORE

Every *asura* (demon) knows he must die eventually, for although supernatural, he's not an eternal being. Aware of his mortality, *Mahisha* meditated for over a thousand years to gain the power to ask a boon of the god Brahma. When he had earned this right, *Mahisha* asked for immortality. He phrased his plea as a trick request: I want to live, he said, until defeated by a woman. He assumed if Brahma granted this request, he would be assured of immortality. His plea was granted, but the seeds of destruction are always planted by one's own action, and *Mahisha* had radically underestimated the female gender.

Having won what he thought was immortality, *Mahisha* decided to take over the universe. He gathered all demons, and he went out on the battleground to win the heavens. He was so formidable and his army of millions so determined, that the god Indra went to enlist the support of the major three gods: Brahma, the creator; Vishnu, the protector; and Shiva, the destroyer. Thus all the Hindu gods became engaged in this cosmic war. After an initial, mind-boggling skirmish, *Mahisha* pulled his illusory cloning trick. Finally, with much roaring, earth trembling, and cosmic dust flying, the gods all finally made a getaway. They knew they could never defeat this raging buffalo demon and his armies. *Mahisha* ruled the heavens and tyrannized the world while the displaced gods, in hiding, plotted to overthrow his evil rule and win back the world for the forces of Good. But how? They remembered his fatal flaw and decided to send a woman. But where would they find such a goddess?

Devi is the Great Goddess and in her wrathful form is known as Durga. She is also called Nanda Devi, who is believed to dwell near Nepal, on the peak with her name in the Himalayas. Devi, the Great Goddess, was created from the powerful communal emanations of the gods and from that unnamed, unknowable Source of their own emanation. She was a vision of inexpressible beauty and was described as the Sublime Warrior Maid. She had eighteen arms; each held a weapon. Devi wore all the rainbow's hues, was clothed in a red gown, and was seated on a lion. She embodied the energy of the entire universe.

Rumor of this luminous new presence quickly spread to the demon camp. Devi was so described as to waken *Mahisha's* appetite. In his arrogance, he decided he'd marry her if she was all they said. He sent a messenger to convey his wishes to Devi. She said in reply: Tell him he will die. The radiant Goddess explained that she was there to guarantee his destined end. *Mahisha* was finally forced to confront her threats. He tried killing her lion with his mace. He was nearly crushed. Slow-witted and coarse, he wondered if perhaps she just didn't like buffalos, and if another shape might tempt her into a change of heart. He metamorphosed to human form. Dressed up and well groomed, he tried another marriage proposal. "Vanish!" she commanded, "Or die."

Mahisha, unable to fathom how a woman could reject him, persisted until the frustrated Goddess whammed him with her mace and discus. Then he resumed his buffalo shape for a snorting, roaring, no-holds-barred fight. *Mahisha-Asura,* using his illusion-making powers, transformed himself into an elephant and the Great Goddess cut off his trunk; then he shape-shifted to a lion and she slew him, but a demon rose from his neck; then he became a human man whom she killed with arrows. Meanwhile the millions of demons fought her and she sliced them to pieces, but demons in pieces can fight on with missing heads or limbs. The whole world was a raging battlefield. The blood flowed for nearly a century. *Mahisha* threw trees, and finally he ripped up mountains and hurled them at her like pebbles in his rage.

With her eighteen arms and weapons, Devi stood her ground. She saw through each of the demon's illusory shapes until finally she drank a bit of the elixir of the Divine life force, jumped up into the air and landed on *Mahisha-Asura* just as he was transforming from human to buffalo, and chopped off his head. She stood calmly on his body as he turned back into a buffalo. And he died.

DISPELLING & DISARMING TECHNIQUES

Order was restored to the universe in this cosmic myth by the Goddess who saw through all the illusory forms of the brutal tyrant *Mahisha-Asura*, one of the most powerful mythic evil forces of Hinduism. Although this is a battle of the gods, the model is set for the human being: to disarm and dispell such brutality, it is necessary to see through it to the beast beneath and to vanquish it, not for one's own sake but for the sake of others.

YUNWI DJUNSTI
North America

The *Yunwi Djunsti*, or "Little People," of the Cherokee is a fairy species, about two feet tall with long dark hair that reaches to the ground. They are said to wear white clothes, but tend to be invisible to the naked eye. Other than their size, supernatural status, and invisibility, they are very much like the Cherokee themselves: they speak the same language, sing similar songs, and even design their social structures in an identical manner.

There are four varieties of *Yunwi Djunsti*. One kind lives in rocky cliffs and hard-to-reach craggy mountainsides. They make their homes in the rocks, sometimes with many chambers and always with well-swept floors. The second variety make their homes outdoors in rhododendron patches. The third live in scrub brush. The fourth reside out in the open. The four varieties differ in levels of malevolence. The Little People in the open air and scrub brush are said to be unusually mean, while the other two varieties can sometimes be helpful if treated nicely.

Ordinary humans rarely see the *Yunwi Djunsti*. It is considered bad luck to see them and is always a portent of death. However, twins can see them and frequently speak with them. Certain conjurors can even capture them for hard labor around the house. Often, though, the species is so arbitrarily mischievous, delighting in tripping people, making household items drop and break, and wreaking general havoc, that even the most powerful conjuror may be forced to put them back where he found them.

Sometimes the *Yunwi Djunsti* get travelers lost in the mountains, and they often lure children away from their families. As in most fairy abduction situations, time spent with the Little People leaves the victim insane. One little boy was with them for weeks and upon return he behaved like a wild creature. Time spent with the *Yunwi Djunsti* can often lead to death. Sometimes, for no apparent reason, the Little People pick on one person and make his livestock sickly, ruin his roof, and generally make his life a misery. Conjurors have to be called in to help.

Sometimes the Little People bother travelers by throwing invisible sticks and stones at them, or pushing them down a mountain trail or off a cliff. One rock held caves so chockfull of *Yunwi Djunsti* it became quite famous and people came from far away to drum on the rock and listen to the creatures inside dance and sing. But all fairies resent disturbance, and one tourist kept it up too long, until finally a horde of Little People came out and fell upon him.

DISPELLING & DISARMING TECHNIQUES

It is bad enough to see any Little People but far worse to speak about it. Often it is after the telling that the victim dies. It is usually fatal to enter their homes and harmful to disturb their privacy. It must also be remembered that if a human being finds a lost object in the mountains, it is always the property of the Little People. Permission must be obtained to take it. Because the Little People are invisible, it is easy to forget that they are eavesdropping, but they hear every single word said about them.

DUERGAR
Great Britain

The *Duergar* is a populous species of solitary fairy that leads travelers astray by means of a flickering torch. He stands about one foot tall, wears a lambskin coat, moleskin shoes, and, as a hat, a piece of green moss stuck with a large feather. This is a malicious creature who believes the hills are his alone, and wants only to cause harm, mischief, or death to trespassing human beings.

LORE

Once on a dark evening, a young man attempted to cross the hills. He had lost his way just before sunset, and by night-fall was trapped in the middle of nowhere. He knew he was many miles from where he was supposed to be, and had no light to guide him. He decided to stop for the night to avoid getting even more lost. As he was about to sit down, he saw a flickering light in the distance. Thinking it might be the house of a shepherd, he walked in that direction.

When he finally reached the light he saw a small hut, with a roof of thick sod. He entered. Between two stones, there was a small fire on the floor that he was most happy to see. Near the fire was a pile of kindling and on the other side two huge logs. The traveler put some small sticks on the fire and lay down to rest. But soon as he had begun to doze off, the door opened and a tiny man entered silently and stared darkly at the intruder. The man stared back and knew he was looking at one of the infamous *Duergars*, and that under no condition should he offend him. Everybody knew that the *Duergar* had a hair-trigger temper and could do great damage when enraged. So the sensible young man kept still and did nothing but stare back at the scowling creature, keeping his gaze as neutral as possible.

The fire died down and the man grew cold but dared not move. Finally he began shivering and had to put some twigs on the fire. No sooner had he finished than the tiny *Duergar* picked up one of the huge logs, four times his size, and with a meaningful glance at the young man broke it in two like a toothpick. Clearly, this was a silent challenge to the man to break the other log, but instead, he remained motionless for the rest of the night.

When daylight came, the *Duergar* vanished, as most demons do. The hut and fire also disappeared. The traveler now saw that he was perched on the edge of a steep precipice. If he had leaned over to grab the "log" as the *Duergar* intended him to do, he would have certainly fallen to his death and not lived to see daylight.

DISPELLING & DISARMING TECHNIQUES

Travelers are always in great danger when hiking alone and the best *Duergar* protection is to know his habits. Suspended action while waiting for daylight is a most effective although difficult technique to master.

MOUNTAIN FAIRIES
China

Mountain Fairies are dainty, beautiful, and irresistible. Popular tales abound of travelers to the mountain terrain who come upon a bevy of maidens and are invited to stay. Fed on hemp, and quite blissful, they remain with the fairies for what feels like a short week. When they begin to grow bored with vacation and ask to return home the fairies usually release them readily. It is to their astonishment that these men find upon their return that families and relatives and neighbors have all long since become their ancestors. There is no more place for them in this worldly, time-worn plane, so up they go again to find their home with the spirits.

Mountain Fairies are not usually malevolent and are included in this Guide for their radical relationship to Time as we know it. Just as mermaids pull their human lovers under without any real sensitivity to human need for oxygen, so does the fairy pull her lovers into her near-eternal dimension without any regard to their lifespan. As long as they stay with her, they remain "alive." Some say these enchanted human beings are actually dead but do not realize it.

China has numerous fairies in all its mountains, flitting like butterflies. The mountains are a habitat where reality shifts and worlds appear and vanish like clouds. Some of these fairies are seen as *shen*, spirits of nature, and they embody sunshine, clouds, rain, mist, and delicately imbue all these phenomena.

China has Five Sacred Mountains: Mount Tai, of the East; Mount Hua, of the West; Mount Heng, of the North; Mount Song, of the Center; and Mount Heng, of the South. It also has Mount Kunlun, a Cosmic Mountain. China has three contributing spiritual traditions that look at mountains in different ways. To the Confucian, the mountain is an image of the Emperor, the unmoving highest ruler; to the Buddhist, the mountain is a habitat in which to gain enlightenment and from which to view emptiness; to the Taoist it is an unworldly refuge and a place of harmony, and in later Taoist sources it is the ultimate site to attain the goal of Immortality.

In all China's mountains, Time is as different as the view.

Taoist wizards live there and practice until they can give up mortal food altogether and eventually become the Immortals. What they feed upon is fairy food, the "elixir of life," made of cultivated crops of sesame, coriander seeds, peach tree gum mixed with cinnabar, elixir of gold, and powdered ash of mulberry, along with hemp, and most important, the fruit of a Tree of Life, which only bears fruit once every three thousand years.

LORE

Wang Chih was a traveler in the mountains gathering firewood when he came upon a few old men playing chess. He put down his ax and joined them. They gave him a stone to place in his mouth, and when he did, he lost all appetite and thirst. And so he played for a while. After some games, one of the other players said that perhaps it was time for Wang Chih to return home. He turned to get his ax but it was only dust. He left and returned to his village to find that many, many centuries had passed. So he returned to the mountain and practiced Taoism until he himself became an Immortal.

One of the Eight Immortals, named Zang Guo, had a white mule that he could fold up in his wallet and then take out and reactivate with a dab of spittle. It would transport him thousands of miles a day.

Taoist wizards are able to conjure *shen* (spirits) and control them, use the medicinal herbs of the mountain for longevity, rise above clouds, become invisible or shape-shift into the form of a beast or insect, and, after seven hundred years of life on earth, ride to heaven on a dragon's back and rule spirits. If they become one of the Immortals, they can fabricate banquets from thin air. Magical wine is poured from an unending source, and fairies from the moon can be conjured for a song and dance and then turned back into a chopstick. They can visit the moon itself before the night is through.

DISPELLING & DISARMING TECHNIQUES

To attain such powers takes a human lifetime of hardship, ascetic practice, in the heights of the unworldly isolated mountains. Despite the charm of the tales and the *shen*, such dimensions are not for beginners.

AKVAN
Ancient Persia

Akvan — "Evil Mind" — is an important Persian *div* with unlimited powers and incredible strength. He has the typical demonic wide mouth, fangs, and horns. He wears a traditional short skirt, his not quite hidden tail flashing warning as to his nature, and has curved, clawlike toenails on his wide flat feet.

Akvan can be found in the Persian epic poem, *Shah-Nameh (The Book of Kings)*, written by Firduasi for the Sultan Mahmud of Ghazna in 1009. A *div* is an evil spirit whose intent is to do harm to humans, spreading lies and destruction for the sheer pleasure of it. But *Akvan*, one of its very large, powerful species, has little intelligence and is mercifully predictable — he will always do the exact opposite of whatever is asked of him.

LORE

Rustem, the hero of the *Shah-Nameh*, was barely recovered from an important encounter with the much larger but similar-looking species, Div Spid (White Demon), whom he managed to quell in the mountains of Tabaristan. While Rustem slept, exhausted from his latest battle, *Akvan* came upon him in a surprise attack. Certain of his victory, *Akvan* asked which kind of death the hero might prefer. Would he rather be thrown from the mountaintop and be devoured by beasts on the rocks below, or perhaps thrown into the sea and be devoured by whales? Rustem, aware of *Akvan*'s quirky contrarian nature, opted for the mountain toss. He was thus thrown into the sea. He of course was a strong swimmer and quite able to navigate his way out of this soft landing — he swam safely to shore. After a remarkable career of dragon and demon quelling, Rustem's life was prematurely ended by an evil human king who lured him on horseback into a pit filled with spears. As Rustem died he managed to kill the king with his own bow and arrow.

DISPELLING & DISARMING TECHNIQUES

All demons have some area of weakness or fatal flaw and it is important to know it. In the case of *Div Akvan*, his reputation for always doing the opposite of what is requested is a lifesaver. If he were more intelligent he might vary his routine, but his slowness allows the traveler to trick him every time.

YAKSAS
Nepal

The *Yaksas* is a species of hirsute, wide-mouthed, fanged, and horned demons whose kingdom is called Kamrup. The epic story of Karunamaya, the Buddhist god of compassion and, in Nepal, also the god of rain and grain, is related annually by the Newars of Nepal at the chariot festival of Bungadyo. In the tale, Karunamaya must be wrested from the land of *Yaksas* to whom he has been born as the youngest of five hundred sons known as Lokanatha.

LORE

Once a king, a priest, and a farmer set out on a journey to Kamrup, land of *Yaksas*, on a desperate mission to bring Lokanatha, god of grains, back to their starving people. They soon came upon a huge and unmovable "man" asleep and blocking the mountain path. The king ordered him out of the way and told him of their urgent quest. "How can you dare to attempt to bring Lokanatha back without my permission?" the giant shouted angrily as he changed himself into a huge and threatening serpent. The priest realized that this spirit was the *naga* Karkotak, and he humbly asked his forgiveness, improvising that they had in fact come to ask his permission. The enraged *naga* continued to glare down at the trio, and the priest begged him not to be angry and praised him for being so adroit at shape shifting. "Can you also become very small?" the priest asked. Karkotak showed off by becoming the size of a single hair, whereupon the priest captured him in a pot, cast a spell, and subdued the spirit. Karkotak, helpless but impressed, said that he now realized how far superior in cleverness was humankind. The *naga* then swore allegiance and offered to aid the three travelers in any way he could.

Off went the quartet until they reached an impassable river. Karkotak shape-shifted into a very long bridge and the trio walked across his body safely to the far bank. After several days the group found themselves at the borders of Kamrup. There they camped and prepared whatever was necessary to make themselves acceptable to the *Yaksas*. The priest created a thousand goats, a thousand sheep, and a thousand buffaloes by throwing soybeans on the ground and transforming them with special incantations. The animals were fabricated in great quantity because the *Yaksas* were known to be meat eaters with excessive appetites.

The king then asked Karkotak to go on ahead, make himself tiny, enter the body of the *Yaksa* king, make him ill, and stay there until they arrived so they could cure him. Karkotak did exactly as he was instructed and the demon king soon grew very sick. Nothing could cure the pain in his stomach. When the king, the priest, and the farmer arrived in Kamrup, they announced that they were physicians from Nepal. The desperate *Yaksas* pleaded, "Please help our king, for he is dying!" The trio huddled over the sick *Yaksa*, and on the fifth day after the three began "treatment" with herbs, Karkotak left the king's body, according to plan.

The *Yaksas* had an exuberant and festive celebration. They ate all the animals the travelers had manufactured and drank vast amounts of wine to wash them down. After the feast, the grateful demon king asked what he could give them in return for their cure. They asked for Prince Lokanatha, the youngest son of the queen of the *Yaksas*. This request was met with howls of outrage, and the queen was beside herself with fury. Her eyes flamed, and it became immediately apparent that it was far too dangerous to remain in the demons' kingdom for another moment.

They escaped. But outside the borders, in hiding, they made a new plan — they would capture the spirit of the prince and take it home with them. Elaborate rituals were performed, then Karkotak was sent back to the castle with a bit of magical soot to smear upon the forehead of the child. Immediately, the spirit of Prince Lokanatha was seized with an urge to travel. The *Yaksa* doctor was called in, but the prince was so possessed that his spirit left its body in the night and flew in the form of a sacred bee to the hidden travelers.

The next morning, in the castle, the *Yaksa* queen discovered Prince Lokanatha's dispirited, lifeless body. She woke all the demons and they flew after the king, priest, and farmer. They retrieved the spirit of the prince, placed it back in his *Yaksa* body, and then viciously attacked the travelers who barely escaped with their lives, went back into hiding, and wondered what to do next.

The king thought of waging war, but because of the probable loss of lives on both sides, he decided war was not the solution. The priest called upon the deities of Kathmandu who intercede against Evil. The deities arrived and went with the quartet to speak to the *Yaksas*. Finally, they were able to subdue the demons, and after many more transformations on the road back, the fertile spirit of Lokanatha, also called Karunamaya, the god of rain and grain, was at last brought to Nepal, and the farmer planted rice to feed the people. Thus was the great nurturing and compassionate spirit seized without bloodshed from the land of the demons, where the brave travelers ventured to find him. And since those days, rain and rice and peace and happiness came to the Valley of Nepal.

DISPELLING & DISARMING TECHNIQUES

It should be noted that in the story of Bungadyo, the successful wresting of the Buddhist god of compassion, who is known by many names, from the midst of a demonic realm was possible because it was done for unselfish purpose and carried out with compassion.

THE WHITE MONKEY
China

The White Monkey, a remarkable twin of the Tikoloshe of South Africa (see him in Water), is a *shen* denizen of the mountains of China. He is huge and malevolent, and like many mountain demons, he lives in a cavern or cave. The *White Monkey*'s primary interest is stealing women. He has the advantage of being taller than the South African species and virtually unstoppable.

LORE

One time a traveler and his attractive wife were passing through unknown territory when the husband was warned that a local *shen* had been actively kidnapping females. Alarmed, the man hid his wife in an inner chamber of the house they were staying in, and he carefully guarded her each night; even so, the *White Monkey* managed to abduct her. The distraught husband went searching for her everywhere and traveled farther and farther into the mountains for weeks, to no avail. He was about to give up when he suddenly came upon what looked like a huge stone door. He knocked, and the door was opened by a fairy, who told him upon inquiry that his wife was held prisoner by the *White Monkey* who lived within. The man was instructed to come back the next day to the cave's entrance and to bring with him a very large supply of wine, ten dogs, and some strong rope.

The man returned with all these items and gave them to the fairy. Soon the *White Monkey* devoured the dogs, an obvious treat, and went on to drink all the wine, until he was in a stupor. The fairy then bound the creature with rope and called in the husband. He reported later that what he saw was an enormous white monkey bound up on a vast bed. Enraged, he killed the creature at once, and his harem of human females were set free.

DISPELLING & DISARMING TECHNIQUES

It is said that firecrackers are effective in routing this species and thus perhaps averting an incident like the one recounted here.

FOREST

Midway on our life's journey, I found myself
In dark woods, the right road lost. To tell
About these woods is hard — so tangled and
   rough
And savage that thinking of it now, I feel
The old fear stirring: death is hardly more bitter.
DANTE, THE INFERNO, CANTO I
TRANS. ROBERT PINSKY

The Forest, just a step beyond the boundaries of civilization, holds danger and mystery, wild animals that lurk in the thickets and secret paths that lead to invisible hosts. Sylvan spirits and myriad forms of fertile life breathe as trunks creak and a constant rustle, perhaps only the wind, alerts the traveler to the fact that he is never alone.

Hunters and cowherds on the edge of the woods since antiquity have often encountered demonic guardian species and forest fairies who play under toadstools and ferns. Pliny described trees that speak. In Asia blood has been seen oozing from felled trees, and in many cultures trees are considered either deities or abodes of demons. Night turns the darkness of the woods into the roof of the underworld, and as the demons emerge, the air becomes thick with them.

The Forest, which teems with life so vital to humankind, can never be cultivated. Cut it down and the consequences are soon fatal. Wander in it and risk the danger of getting eternally lost or devoured. The edge of the Forest is always the boundary between the wild and the domesticated, the animal and the human community. It holds its genius loci, who may appear as demonic guardian species of wilderness and wild creatures and attack trespassing hunters, mischievous fairies who sometimes visit nearby villages, and the many huge man-eating species that are an ever-present danger to the children and domestic animals of the villages.

The Forest is the favorite site of fairy tales, of ancient

rites associated with fecundity and with tree worship, of unexplained disappearances, of wild encounters and appetites, and of transformations, seasonal and personal. It is the haunt for libidinous ogres, dwarfs, and satyrs who constantly pursue women. It is a raw territory of mostly male predators, flesh-eaters, and cannibals.

WHO'S WHO IN THE FOREST

PAN	Greece
WINDIGO	Canada
KURU-PIRA	Brazil
BORI	West Africa
WOOD-WIVES AND SKOGGRA	Germany and Sweden
RAKSHASAS	India
RAVANA	India
LESHII	Russia
ELOKO	Zaire
ONI	Japan
KUMBHAKARNA	India
KAYERI	South America
DODO	Ghana
SHEDIM	(Judaism)
KITSUNE	Japan
KHABANDA	India

PAN
Greece

Pan ("all," "everything"), the son of Hermes and a nymph of Arcadia, is one of the world's ancient spirits, a god of woods and pastures, a guardian of flocks and of shepherds who gave him offerings of milk, honey, and lamb. He is immediately recognizable by his fawn-skin coat, his ruddy complexion, his goat ears, horns, beard, legs, and hooves. He carries a curved shepherd's staff, and plays his pipes.

    Pan is closely linked with the satyrs, a rough, shaggy, goatlike species with demonical natures associated with continuous orgies. Both *Pan* and the satyrs are associated with the pagan god Dionysus and the bacchanalia. These spirits of excess resemble the goatlike *shedim* and *seirim* (demons shunned by the ancient Jews) and contribute to the later image of the Christians' horned, hirsute, goat-hoofed Devil. *Pan* is also linked to the Italian Faunus, a mischievous woodland spirit associated with fertility and worshiped in ancient Rome; and to Priapus (whom *Pan* may have fathered), a god of fertility from Asia Minor whose symbol was the phallus. Altogether *Pan*, a powerful pagan spirit, is profoundly connected to the fecundity of both the woods and population.

LORE

Pan, free and untamable, was filled with and driven by wild insatiable lust. Though his advances were not infrequently rejected, and his nymphs metamorphosed to escape, his myriad sexual exploits were sometimes successful. One love affair with the nymph Pitys ended unhappily only when she was turned into a pine tree. Unremorseful, he pursued Echo, and as the nymph ran away from him made such hideous noises that a "pan-ic" spread through the forest and caused a group of frenzied shepherds to tear Echo apart, leaving only her voice.

Pan's famous pipes, the Syrinx, are named for another unfortunate nymph. *Pan* pursued the beautiful nymph Syrinx through the woods and nearly overtook her when she stopped at the water's edge and was transformed into a bundle of water reeds. As the wind blew gently through the reeds, there came an exquisite sad sound. *Pan* stood at the water's edge overwhelmed by his loss and the beauty of the music. Sorrowfully he gathered seven reeds and bound them together to create a pipe he called Syrinx after his lost love. The seven pipes were said to represent the seven spheres and produced sound that expressed all the harmonies of the universe. *Pan*'s music could be heard all over the woodlands of Arcadia.

Plutarch wrote that in the reign of Tiberius, a sailor heard a mysterious voice call three times: "The Great God Pan is dead!" It was supposedly at that very moment that Christ was born.

Pan is never seen in a final battle, and unlike other

archaic pagan spirits of this Guide, he never was actually van-
quished, just demoted, as his countenance became the Devil's
own. *Pan* lives on, and until the last pine (Pitys) tree has been
cut down, his music will be heard in all forests. Its notes res-
onate in many tales that follow.

WINDIGO
Canada

The Algonkian *Windigo* (or *Witiko*) is a seasonal, subarctic man-eating species. During the winter moons when food is scarce, there is a fear of the creature. With cadaverous body and a face out of an Edvard Munch portrait, highlighted with horrid glaring eyes, the *Windigo* have been described as giants with hearts of ice. Many who have been in close proximity to them have experienced chills and the sense that their own hearts were freezing over.

The *Windigo* use trees as their snowshoes and cover vast distances in a single step. As they travel from victim to victim, blizzards accompany them. Naked and gaunt, the entire species stalks the forests of the north in search of human flesh, lurking silently in the shadows of trees, tall as the old timbers themselves.

A *Windigo* has a scream that paralyzes its intended meal so that it cannot escape. Once it is upon its prey, a *Windigo* rips out vital organs in seconds. When sated, packs of *Windigo* have been seen playing catch with human skulls. It is a remorseless beast that will devour its own family. In the land of the Cree and Ojibwa, the *Windigo* are believed to have once been normal human beings who have become possessed cannibals.

The *Windigo* can infect the human, and therein lies the unique power suggested in the double meaning of its name. The root word is Algonkian for both "evil spirit" and "cannibal," so *Windigo* describes both a demon and a way of acting like one. Any person possessed by this cannibal spirit has literally become a *Windigo* and is probably incurable. Some people choose this transformation, others happen upon it. The latter cases are caused by being bitten, by dreaming of the *Windigo*, or by being involuntarily transformed by a malevolent sorcerer.

Voluntary *Windigo* are individuals who go into the forest, fast for several days, and offer their flesh freely to the species. A *Windigo* may adopt such a person as its own child.

The possessed human grows a heart of ice, becomes notably hirsute, has a craving for raw human flesh, and behaves like the demon itself, although he never attains the full height of the supernatural being.

The earliest sightings of this species are reported by Jesuit missionaries in the 1600s. The Hudson Bay Company diaries of the 1700s mention the species quite often.

LORE

Once, in the darkest depth of winter, a woman saw a father and daughter return to her village alone — without the rest of their family. She wondered what had happened to the others and became suspicious. She therefore made the entrance to her home slippery by pouring water on the threshold until it froze into a high sheet of ice. Then she went to bed. But instead of going to sleep she waited tensely with an ax in hand for their attempt on her life. Just as she thought, the daughter approached at midnight, and the old woman pretended to snore as the *Windigo*-possessed girl came closer and closer. Then, suddenly, just as the girl was about to spring for her throat, the old woman raised her ax and killed the creature. The father, who had been waiting outside, crept in. By then the old woman was able to escape and she hid to watch what happened next. She witnessed the *Windigo*-possessed father devour the corpse of his own daughter.

DISPELLING & DISARMING TECHNIQUES

The only known way to avert *Windigo* possession is to throw excrement at the creature. This confuses it enough for a small window of escape. If that method doesn't work, the next choice is to go immediately to a local shaman. If he cannot help, the last resort is to kill the possessed person, cut the body into pieces, and burn it to kill the spirit so that it does not infect others. Some say a silver bullet can also be effective.

KURU-PIRA
Brazil

The *Kuru-pira*, a guardian species of the Desana people, also known as the *boraro* because of his distinctive cry, has red eyes that glow like burning embers, and jaguarlike fangs. His ears stand erect. He is tall, of human shape with a hairy chest and huge, pendulous genitals. He has no knee joints, and thus has difficulty getting up if he falls. The *Kuru-pira* can be immediately recognized by his oversize long feet, which always face the wrong way. His heels are in front and his toes face the rear. *Kuru-pira* feet are fashioned to deceive: they point in the direction that the creature has just come from, leading victims directly into his path as they try to avoid him.

LORE

When a *Kuru-pira* attacks his victim, he emits his distinctive *boraro* growl. His roar is similar to that of a jaguar, only slightly more prolonged and considerably louder. A hunter once heard this chilling sound close by and leapt up a tree to observe. He knew the *Kuru-pira* can kill his victim by two methods: his urine is lethal, so he may urinate on his victim to kill instantly, or he may hold a person tightly until crushed. The hunter looked down grimly as he saw that the crushing method had been used on his friend, and he watched in horror as the *Kuru-pira* made a small hole in the dead man's skull and sucked out the blood and flesh, as one might suck out a lobster claw. He watched as the *Kuru-pira* closed the hole, blew up the emptied skin, and ordered the "man" to return home. The hunter was shaking with fear, for he knew he was next. They had taken too much game. He had warned his friend that the *Kuru-pira* kept careful count of how much game a hunter steals. When a hunter kills more than he can eat or carry, he puts himself in a dangerous situation, with little chance for survival.

"Boraaro!" sounded again, and the tree branch shook. The hunter fell to the ground, and as he crashed he remembered to do the only thing that would save his life: he placed his hands in the demon's footprints. The *Kuru-pira*'s legs stiffened and he froze, unable to pursue the hunter, who narrowly escaped. The fate of the hunter's friend was different. A shell of his former self, possessed by the spirit of the demon, he returned with a tobacco offering the next day and henceforth lived with the wild animals.

DISPELLING & DISARMING TECHNIQUES

The *Kuru-pira* can sometimes be appeased with tobacco offerings. Travelers in Brazil report that when they place their own hand in the footprint of the demon, its legs will stiffen and it will fall. As with many ogre types, the weakness is in their knees. One other well-known method is to step in the creature's track but face in the opposite direction. This will cause the *Kuru-pira* to lose his way. When followed by a *Kuru-pira,* run backward as quickly as possible, looking the demon in the face the entire time. It is techniques like this that confuse large, stupid demons worldwide.

BORI
West Africa

The *Bori* is a populous species of spirits who reside in various habitats of the Hausa people in West Africa. The forest *Bori* is often sighted in human form but with hoofed feet. However, *Bori* tend to shape-shift. They can terrify people by walking around headless or slither by like giant pythons, and appear occasionally in homes as a husband or a sister, play-acting apparently just for fun, until the real human walks in. Most people report that a *Bori* will leave a footprint in ashes like a rooster, which is the most foolproof way of discovering an impostor table companion. If a *Bori* is sighted in a group of average human beings, he will seem slightly weird and have oddly unfocused, dreamy eyes.

The forest *Bori* is never vicious unless offended, and with continual worship and sacrifice, it can be placated. However, a careless act, such as spitting or throwing water on a hot fire and causing a spark to fly into an invisible *Bori*, will aggravate him. Using a *Bori*'s name in vain can make one the focus of his malevolent attention. So terrible is the consequence of such focus that one prayer specifically implores, *"Allah ba su ganin nisa"* — "God, let their attention be attracted far away from me!"

A *Bori*, paradoxically, wants to be wanted, and when called will travel to his conjuror as quickly as the wind. The more his help is requested, the more it will offer assistance (at a price). There are certain instances when the help of a *Bori* must be obtained — when building a new house or starting a business, for instance, or attempting to heal certain diseases. *Bori* who offer help must be thanked with specific sacrifices. Each *Bori* has its special preferences for fowls, incense, song, and colors. It is imperative to remember which *Bori* likes what.

If a *Bori* becomes offended and can be neither placated nor escaped, its victim will be killed not by a sudden violent attack but by a slow sucking away of life force. In some cases a victim who feels this wasting away can be helped by a specialist with a charm or prayer to avert the specific *Bori* attacker.

Among the Hausa it is believed that every sickness or misfortune is caused by a specific *Bori*, and that each individual spirit can be placated through regularly held dances. The dances are performed by individuals who are believed to be frequently possessed by one or another *Bori*. The dances are accompanied by music and drums, and a specific song is used for each individual *Bori* who is invited to the dance. The dancer then becomes a spokesperson for that specific *Bori*. Over a hundred and fifty *Bori* guests are danced for at any one of these rituals. This is reportedly a good place to sight them firsthand.

DISPELLING & DISARMING TECHNIQUES

Iron repels *Bori*, so powerfully that even saying the word *iron* a few times will drive them off. Also it should be kept in mind that a *Bori* is a slave to his own name. Once its name is discovered, the repetition of it will make the *Bori* a virtual slave to the namer. Incantations with insults can be used to drive *Bori* away, but that is somewhat risky and praise is traditionally more effective in handling the sensitive *Bori*.

WOOD-WIVES AND SKOGGRA
Germany and Sweden

The *Wood-Wives*, a fairy species, can be found in old forests and dense groves. Petite and beautifully dressed, with long claws, they are often accompanied by violent whirlwinds. So intricately connected to the woods are these spirits that it is said that if a branch is twisted until the bark comes off, one *Wood-Wife* dies in the forest.

Hunters are the humans most at risk of attack by the *Wood-Wives*. In heavily infested forests, to get home safely, the hunters must first offer up part of their catch. But if propitiated, like many fairy species, they can be helpful. If, for example, a *Wood-Wife* asks a mortal to fix her broken wheelbarrow and the task is nicely done, the wood chips that she leaves as payment may turn into gold.

Like many ancient nature spirits, *Wood-Wives* abhor human hubbub: churches with their loud bells, and all destructive machinery in the forest, threatens their very existence. Most idiosyncratically, *Wood-Wives* detest the use of caraway seeds in baked bread. Since they are often lured from the forest by the smells of baking, they may approach people in their kitchens. It is in the cook's best interest to prepare an extra loaf for their visit. But *Wood-Wives* refuse loaves that have been pricked with a fork or punctured with a finger, and never accept caraway seeds. One story tells of a *Wood-Wife* who ran through the forest, screaming, "They baked me a caraway bread, it will bring that house great trouble!" And it did. The farmer and his wife soon lost their money and home, and fell upon hard times.

The Swedish *Skoggra* is almost identical in appearance to the *Wood-Wife*, but she is often sighted in prowl mode. When she encounters a lumberjack or hunter, she will often attempt to seduce them or, perhaps in a different mood, will cause them to lose their way.

LORE

A *Skoggra* had so enchanted a hunter that he made his way nightly into the dangerous woods for a tryst. But with each passing day he returned home looking paler, more tormented and haggard, until his friends decided something had to be done. They pleaded with him not to succumb, and the next night they held him back and struggled with him as the forest spirit called and called. They sat on him and held him down.

When he hadn't gone to her by the following night the *Skoggra* came to get him; closer and closer she sidled, calling to him as his friends held him tightly. He frothed at the mouth and was so out of control that finally his best friend went out with a gun and aimed at the spirit. A shot rang out and she fell to the ground. Immediately all the other *Skoggra* manifested from the darkness of leaves and branches. They sadly picked her up and carried her back into the forest. The man who shot her lost his eye, the very one with which he'd found her through his target sight. The eye simply vanished. But he felt that it was worth the loss to save the life of his friend.

DISPELLING & DISARMING TECHNIQUES

Herbs such as red verbena and St. John's wort can be used liberally to keep these forest spirits at a distance. Anything red, being said to be the color of the devil, repels. Steel and iron are often carried in the pocket to keep fairies away. Some say their retreat at the sight of these metals represents their attitude toward "progress" in general, and that as the centuries pass and industrialization encroaches, the species moves farther and farther into the small remaining pockets of wilderness.

RAKSHASAS

India

The *Rakshasas* (Night Wanderers) is a species of *asuras* (Hindu demons) who inhabit the forest of Lanka and appear in every conceivable shape and form but tend to extremes in height — they are either unusually tall or elfin. Many *Rakshasas* have potbellies and animal heads — elephant, horse, and snake heads being the most prevalent — with fanglike, razor-sharp, protruding teeth. Some are beautiful. According to other reports, their eyes flame and their tongues hang down at great lengths and they have horns. *Rakshasas* sometimes appear in human form, and they generally have red hair, huge ears, wide mouths that go virtually from ear to ear, and a single arm, eye, or leg — or perhaps three of each, never the usual two.

Rakshasas have been known to devour horses and human

beings, inhabit and reanimate corpses, and shape-shift into birds — vultures and owls, particularly — and, less frequently, dogs, deer, and even men (usually married men with the intent of deceiving their wives) and beautiful seductive women. They can enter a person by mouth while he is eating or drinking and are especially dangerous during pregnancy.

One type of *Rakshasa*, known as Pisacas, dwells in the town's water supply and can make people waste away. This type is frequently seen hanging about cemeteries because they are corpse eaters. They have an exceedingly gaunt look, their ribs stick far out, and their hair stands on end, as if they've had a bad fright.

DISPELLING & DISARMING TECHNIQUES

Fire is powerfully effective in Pisacas control. *Rakshasas* generally maintain a state of invisibility but are known to be found at places of worship, where they attempt to disrupt prayer, as this practice greatly upsets them; thus prayer is useful in driving them off. Some say that calling them "Uncle" will stop them in their tracks. However, they are powerful, and it was a female *Rakshasa*'s disruption of the prayers of a holy man that resulted in the appearance of awesome Ravana, featured next.

RAVANA
India

Ravana, king of all Rakshasas, has ten heads, twenty arms, and
fiercely burning eyes. *Ravana* is an almost invulnerable champion shape shifter, able to take forms as diverse as a rock, a
corpse, and a puff of smoke. *Ravana* can break mountains in
two with his bare hands and can create storms at sea. He is
known best for his ongoing battle with Rama, the god incarnate hero of the Hindu epic, *Ramayana*.

LORE

When *Ravana* was born, the universe filled with hideous
shrieking noises. His mother was the daughter of a demon
chief, and his father was a saint she had tempted in mid-
prayer.

Ravana gained power by asceticism and meditation for

thousands of years. When he'd earned enough to ask Brahma for a boon, he asked for immortality, which was not granted. After some negotiation, he was given protection from all elements, but he arrogantly scoffed at the idea of needing protection from human beings. And so *Ravana* became virtually indestructible. For instance, each of his ten heads grow back immediately if cut off. But he was not ultimately indestructible, because he had left a loophole.

Ravana was a tyrannical boaster and a womanizer, impulsively quick to fury and always overconfident. He had a huge harem and added to it frequently by seizing women by the hair and flying them through the air to his kingdom of Lanka. He was a demon who had everything, even a flying chariot, but he craved more. He was deeply envious of Rama, whose exploits were renowned.

Rama was a great hero, a god incarnate, living in exile in a forest with his faithful wife, Sita. One day Rama encountered and insulted *Ravana's* grotesque sister. This was the last straw. *Ravana* set a trap to get Sita alone. He waited until Rama was out hunting, and, disguising himself as a beggar, approached her hut. She was polite and charitable to him so he then revealed himself as the ten-headed handsome demon he believed he was. He invited her to go with him to Lanka and, with great charm, promised her anything her heart desired. When she refused his offer, he seized her by the hair and dragged her to his flying chariot. Before Rama returned, Sita was in Lanka.

Sita, the beloved, faithful, and utterly devoted wife of Rama, imprisoned in *Ravana's* palace, steadfastly resisted the demon. He tried every way to make himself attractive to her, but she ignored him, and wept for Rama. *Ravana* grew increasingly bitter with each rejection. He finally threatened to devour her whole if she would not succumb, and left her to think it over.

Meanwhile, Rama searched everywhere for Sita. Finally his devoted servant, Hanumat (son of the wind god), discovered Sita's whereabouts, assumed the form of a cosmic monkey, and in one step crossed over the sea to Lanka. Then, shrinking to the size of a tiny monkey, Hanumat sneaked into the walled garden to tell Sita that help was on the way.

Despite the numerous and fearsome Rakshasas who populated the forest of Lanka (now Sri Lanka), Hanumat was not afraid. He gathered his countless troops of flying monkeys to build a bridge of stones across to the island. Rama crossed over the bridge into enemy territory and there he waged awesome battles against the forces of *Ravana*. Hanumat and the troops destroyed the royal gardens, threw boulders, and set fire to the kingdom. There was much shape shifting, illusion, gore, smoke, and roaring until finally *Ravana* and Rama faced off. As Rama's arrows struck *Ravana*'s ten heads they each popped right back and the demon roared triumphantly. Finally, Rama, using a supernatural arrow of the god Vishnu, struck the demon in the heart, which was not indestructible. And that was how *Ravana* met his prophesied end by the hands of a mortal.

It wasn't over forever, of course. *Ravana* was only living out one of three demon lives as punishment for a past-life deed he had committed when he was a celestial gatekeeper and refused entrance to the sons of Brahma because they were not properly dressed. (See another incarnation of *Ravana* as Hiranyanakashipu in Domicile.)

LESHII
Russia

The *Leshii* (*les* is "forest" in Russian) is a guardian species that is generally thought to be the genius loci of the forest — an ancient spirit and a tricky shape shifter. The *Leshii* have been seen as a tall man covered from head to foot with black hair, worn uncombed and wild. He has also been seen with cloven-hoofed feet, a tail, small horns (like the Devil), carrying a club or whip, indicating his status as master of the forest and all animals within it. He will occasionally take the shape of a bear, a bird, or more commonly a wolf, but sometimes a friend or even a mushroom. When the *Leshii* appears as an ordinary peasant his shoes will be always worn on the wrong feet. And his eyes glow.

The *Leshii* is endlessly mischievous. He removes sign-posts. He calls out to travelers in familiar voices and lures them into unknown parts of the forest until they are hope-lessly lost. He has been known to appear as a creature tiny as a blade of grass, or become a gigantic ancient tree. In the latter case, a run-in with a *Leshii* leg will seem at first like bump-ing into a sturdy, hair-covered tree root. The spirit is volatile and at that point may decide to help out or tickle his prey to death. He may also be heard weeping when a favorite tree is felled.

Russians who have reported sightings are people who routinely use the forest for work or passage. Hunters, wood-cutters, and cowherds often see the *Leshii*. They all leave him a little something for protection, and frequently cowherds make pacts with the species so as to avert harm to their herds.

LORE

The *Leshii* often keeps grazing cows from wandering too far into the forest and falling prey to a hungry wolf. Sometimes the cowherds make "special arrangements" with the *Leshii* to keep their cattle safe. They take off the cross they wear around their necks and hand it to the forest spirit, then they swear loyalty to the *Leshii* and give him their communion wafer instead of swallowing it. These pacts cause the cowherd to be looked upon as a person with occult powers. Once a cowherd who lived on a remote farm innocently showed kindness to a *Leshii* disguised as a passing traveler. He allowed him to spend the night, gave him supper, and refused payment for the lodging. The *Leshii* offered a "herdsman" as protection, telling the cowherd that his cows would be safe from then on, all he needed to do was drive them out from the gate in the morning and wait for their return at night. He warned him never to go out to their grazing ground. This went on for years until the cowherd's curiosity got the better of him. When he got to the edge of the forest, he saw an extremely tall old woman acting as herdsman, and when he said good morning to her, she nodded, shrank to nothing, and then vanished before his eyes.

Other tales reveal that the *Leshii* does steal babies who are left by themselves when their parents are out picking mushrooms. Even small children who wander off may be picked up by the *Leshii* and not returned — at least for a long while. In one story, a baby stolen from the cradle was much later returned as a favor. She had grown to be a beautiful young woman and the parents were grateful. This was an unusual case. Most reports are dire. The *Leshii* victim is often a woman who goes to the forest alone or whose husband is away. One such young woman was walking in the woods and found a beautiful necklace. Without crossing herself, she pocketed it, and later put it on. She heard a voice say, "You have something of mine." But she did not heed the message. Soon the *Leshii* himself appeared in the shape of a man and said, "Since you did not return what you found, now take me too." From that night on he appeared whenever her husband was away, and soon she began to waste away until finally she died. In other cases, when the woman is held captive in the woods, she returns mute, wild, and covered with moss.

DISARMING & DISPELLING TECHNIQUES

When encountering the *Leshii* in the Russian woods, one must immediately turn all clothing inside out. Put the left shoe on the right foot and the right shoe on the left. This usually outsmarts the species. The sign of the cross is always effective. If he does not vanish, a fire will often work. The *Leshii* fears fire. Drawing a magic circle around the campfire is also said to be helpful. A porridge offering, such as kasha, is highly recommended and blini can work at times to avert trouble. The eccentric spirit also will leave laughing if a good joke is told.

To conjure a *Leshii*, take several branches of young birches and make a circle with their tips pointing to the center. Enter. Face east. With one foot on the stump of a tree, say, "Uncle Leshii, ascend. Do not come as wolf or as a fire, but come in human form." The *Leshii* will appear for work — but remember, its service is given only in exchange for your soul.

ELOKO
Zaire

The *Eloko* is a people-eating dwarf of the Nkundo who lives in hollow trees in the dense rain forest of central Zaire. The *Eloko* is hairless but is covered with a coat of grass that grows over his face and body; his clothing is made of leaves. *Eloko* eyes are like fire. They have snouts, clawed fingers, and although very small, their jaws can open wide enough to consume an entire human being. Their remarkable power is in their music. The *Eloko* bewitches its victims by ringing tiny magical bells while walking — camouflaged — through the forest. The bell is also associated with the god of death. The *Eloko* may have originated as one of his retinue.

LORE

Once a hunter brought his wife to his hut in the woods, but had to leave her there to return briefly to his village. He warned, "If you hear a bell, do not answer, whatever you do, for if you listen to the bells, you will die." With that he left.

All day the wife sat alone and wary in the dense, dark forest, silent until just past twilight, when she heard the exquisite sound of delicate bells. Their music grew slowly, coming closer, filling her ears and the air all around with an irresistible ringing, until at last she could no longer control herself, and called out: "I am here. Come here and get me!"

The *Eloko* immediately appeared, tiny and green with leaves and grass. "You called to me," he said, "and I came for you." The poor woman was delighted to see the leafy creature who had bewitched her with his bells. She cooked a large meal of fish and bananas and graciously offered it to him. The *Eloko* said he could not eat the food because he ate only human flesh. "Give me part of you to eat," he commanded. "You are a big and delicious woman."

The enchanted woman agreed and gave the *Eloko* a piece of her arm. He roasted her flesh over the fire and ate it quickly, then he vanished. The woman, in terrible pain, covered her wound with leaves. When her husband returned he found her lying on the ground and moaning and asked what had happened. She said only that she had a sore, but begged him not to take her bandages off.

Again, when daylight came, the man had to leave his wife in the forest alone. Again she heard the bells, and again called out to the *Eloko*. He appeared instantly and she was happy. She offered him fish, but he asked for one of her buttocks. Obediently the woman gave her flesh to him and he disappeared. The woman's pain was intolerable and she cried out in anguish. When her husband came home he warned her that she would die if she remained there, but she told him to go away. "You are a fool," he told her. Then the husband took his weapons and pretended to set out, but he hid nearby.

Soon came the bewitching bells and the *Eloko* appeared again, but this time the husband crept close to the hut and shot an arrow at the *Eloko* just as the creature was about to take the woman's liver. As the *Eloko* was struck by the arrow, it caused him to slip and fall over the woman, and its knife killed her instantly. The man threw a spear through the body of the *Eloko*, and then cut off its head. He carried it into the village to show everybody what had really happened in the forest to his poor enchanted wife.

DISARMING & DISPELLING TECHNIQUES

Although certain amulets and fetishes may avert the spell of the *Eloko*, only professional hunters with magic powers can safely travel through the forest. The bells of the *Eloko* are impossible to resist. This cautionary tale is a warning never to leave a wife alone in the forest and for all ordinary people to remain in the familiar, civilized village.

ONI
Japan

The *Oni* is a splendid species, and probably the most popular in Japan. His body is pink or blue, his face basically human but grotesquely flat, with a mouth that runs ear to ear and a third eye. He has three toes and three fingers on each hand. The fingers and toes end in talons. He often walks, but he can fly and he has horns. *Oni* range in size but maintain these features.

Excessive in their behavior, all *Oni* drink and eat too much, randomly abduct young women, and are revoltingly uncouth.

These demons are always present when disaster strikes, and are also associated with disease. They bear the souls of the wicked to the underworld. On the last day of the year a special ceremony called the *Oni-yarahi* is held to expel the *Oni* and the misfortune that they represent from the coming year.

LORE

Once a sweet young bride was abducted by an *Oni* on her way to her own wedding. He manifested as a dark cloud and when the sky had cleared the bride had vanished. He brought her to his mansion for a wife. The girl's mother bravely went forth to find her daughter, and soon, with the help of a priestess, she located the home of the hideous *Oni*. When the mother was certain the *Oni* was out, she knocked on the castle door. The girl was overjoyed to see her mother again and embraced her, gave her dinner, then hid her in a massive stone chest. The *Oni* soon arrived home and had a fit of temper when he smelled a human on his premises. The quick-thinking girl placated him with some improvised news: "I am pregnant!" she announced. Elated, the *Oni* called for all his dogs to be killed as a feast and for a lot of sake. He got roaring drunk, and finally passed out. As he snored, the girl unlocked the stone box and fled with her mother. The women took a boat from the *Oni*'s supplies and started to cross the river.

The *Oni* awakened to find his wife gone. He discovered that the boat was missing, and in a monstrous fury strode to the edge of the water. He saw the women disappearing into the distant horizon. He did what any *Oni* would do under the circumstances: he began to drink the river dry. The small boat that was carrying the mother and daughter started traveling back to the mouth of the *Oni* as if on the end of a long strand of noodle. In desperation the two women prayed to the priestess for help. They were answered by a quick piece of tactical advice. They turned to face the nearing shore and together they lifted their kimonos and exposed their privates. This completely unexpected sight caused the *Oni* to laugh uproariously until all the thousands of gallons of water spewed from his mouth back into the river. He rolled around in a fit of hilarity while the little boat sped off on the rising waters and carried the women to safety.

DISARMING & DISPELLING TECHNIQUES

This *Oni* story demonstrates a childlike weakness in the impulsive, larger-than-life demon varieties. Despite their great powers, they are so preoccupied with satisfying excessive bodily needs that their intelligence is diminished. They remain vulnerable to human trickery and ingenuity. Shocking an *Oni* is a good way out of a bad situation. They can also be given tasks, such as counting holes in a sieve, that keep them distracted and occupied while the victim escapes. Throwing dry peas about in four directions, done at the *Oni-yarahi* ceremony, chases the *Oni* away.

KUMBHAKARNA
India

Kumbhakarna, the gluttonous Rakshasa brother of Ravana, standing 420,000 meters high, is the tallest known demon in the world. His colossal stature alone would have made him invincible, but fortunately for humankind when *Kumbhakarna* opened his mouth to ask for a boon from Brahma, he was tongue-tied midsentence by a goddess. All he could manage to say was: "I want . . . to sleep!"

All the gods breathed a sigh of relief and Brahma happily agreed to his request. He arranged for the mighty *Kumbhakarna* to sleep for six months at a stretch and awaken for only one day at a time. Whenever *Kumbhakarna* awakens, he is naturally ravenous. Like a cosmic bear who has been hibernating, the demon eats everybody and everything anywhere in his neighborhood (which covers a wide territory). He can eat a city's supply of food in a gulp along with most of its citizens. His drinking habits consume the produce of thousands of vineyards.

LORE

In the forest of Lanka, Ravana needed his brother's help to fight Rama in his last epic battle, so he sent his army in to awaken *Kumbhakarna*. They fed him herds of cattle and rivers of wine before he would even stand up. Finally the demon yawned loudly, stretched, stood, and was ready for battle, but he was still hungry. He swallowed many troops of Hanumat's army (they were all delicious flying monkeys) before Rama was able even to wound him. So powerful and brute a force was *Kumbhakarna* that he was able to go on fighting even after he'd been cut to shreds by *Rama*. Only small, torn remnants of his limbs endured, but the fierce body parts hailed damage upon the forces of Good. Finally Rama sliced *Kumbhakarna*'s head off with his sacred arrow and that was the end of the vast and gluttonous sleeper.

(At least it was for this lifetime. He and his brother Ravana have one more cycle to go as demons for acting too hastily as bouncers at the celestial gate before they are free. See Hiranyanakashipu in Domicile.)

KAYERI
South America

The *Kayeri* is a seasonal species of the Cuiva people, best observed in the rainy months and generally dormant in sunshine. It wears a blue-green hat, sometimes yellow, and when in the shape of a human male is quite tall and strong and has two wives. *Kayeri* live under the ground in deep caves and rise to the earth's surface through the holes made by ants. All mushrooms in the forest are aspects of *Kayeri*, as are ficus tendrils, the agouti, and the *unkuaju* plant.

Kayeri usually can be found hanging about the base of tall trees. They eat nothing but cows, which they chase at night through the fields. When farmers complain of missing cows, it is said that a *Kayeri* has taken them home to eat under the earth with his two wives.

Whenever a *Kayeri* is killed, all the others become very upset, and when the beating of sticks against trees is heard, that means something has angered them. It is said that the *Kayeri's* distinctive cry is: "Mu, mu, mu."

LORE

Once there was a man who was about to set off on a hunt. His two daughters begged to go with him until finally he consented, and they set off together. As they walked into the forest, the girls laughed and made a lot of noise. The father warned them to be quiet as there were a number of ant holes on the path, which could mean there were *Kayeri* about. They walked on and on in search of deer until the girls grew tired and decided to return to camp. They bid their father good-bye, and started back. "Beware of the Kayeri," he warned, for the demon was known for his lust and particularly for abducting very young women.

After a short time, the father's dog managed to catch a deer, and he cut off the best parts and carried them home. When he arrived, he asked his wife where the girls were. The wife said, "They have not yet returned." The man, suspecting the worst, ran back where he'd left them, and there he heard a cry in the distance. "That must be my daughters screaming!" he realized, and headed quickly in the direction of the screams.

Sure enough, the *Kayeri* was walking west with the girls thrown over his shoulder. The girls scratched, bit, and poked him to no avail. Then the girls saw their father, and he signaled to them to cover the *Kayeri*'s eyes. He then shot the demon in the kidneys with an arrow tipped with bone. The *Kayeri* dropped the girls, screamed "Mu, mu, mu!" and jumped into the river and turned into a stone. All around the father and his daughters came a terrible sound: a host of *Kayeri* were beating trees with sticks. The human family ran for their lives and made it safely to camp to report this cautionary tale.

DISPELLING & DISARMING TECHNIQUES

Beware the *Kayeri* in rainy season, as the father told his daughters. Be alert wherever ant holes seem conspicuously abundant, and as a weapon, carry a special arrow tipped with bone.

DODO
Ghana

The *Dodo* is a rapacious male species of the Hausa people that hides in trees waiting to pounce on unsuspecting forest travelers. He can take any shape, but is often sighted as a snake, or an animal with a keen sense of smell, sometimes even a giant covered with long hair. He is always ravenously hungry for human flesh. Some believe the *Dodo* is the spirit of a dead man who vengefully prowls the forest grabbing living mortals.

LORE

Once there were two women who were at a stream fetching water. One woman was pregnant, and the other, out of envy, threw dirt into her pot while her back was turned. The spiteful woman left, and the pregnant woman found her jug much too heavy to lift. Just then a *Dodo* came by and offered help. She accepted gratefully. He told her that if her child were a boy it would be his friend, but if it were a girl it would be his wife. The woman, eager to get her jug home and desperate for help, agreed to his conditions.

Later the woman gave birth to a girl, and her rival went and told the *Dodo*. He waited. The girl grew up and a marriage was arranged. The promise to the demon was forgotten. But on the wedding day, the rival went to the *Dodo* and told him what was going on. The *Dodo* set off for the wedding, and when he arrived he announced he had come for his promised wife. Ashamed, the poor mother had to explain the debt to her husband. The husband asked, "Whose horse is this?" and, as it belonged to the wife, he said, "Give it to the *Dodo*." The *Dodo* took the horse and ate it whole, but he still demanded the bride.

The husband then offered his wife's cattle and the *Dodo* swallowed them whole. They gave the *Dodo* all their food, but that was not enough. "Have the guests!" the husband cried. And the demon did, but still he demanded the bride. The ravenous *Dodo* ate everyone, including the father. Alone, the virtuous young bride trembled and cried out for help. A knife fell from above, and naturally the demon ate it, cutting himself in half. All the guests, her father and mother, the cattle, and the horse came out, as well as the bridegroom, and the girl was happily married after all.

DISPELLING & DISARMING TECHNIQUES

The only two things that can stop a *Dodo* are running water, which it cannot cross, and a deus ex machina like the one the bride produced.

SHEDIM
(Judaism)

The *Shedim* is a hairy and horned wild species of Jewish demons. They are said in the Talmud to eat and drink like human beings and have basically human features, but with lolling tongues and wide mouths. (Compare the *mazzikin*, who are often invisible and always harmful, and the *lilin*, who are winged; see Lilith in Domicile.) The *Shedim* are referred to in the Bible as unclean spirits and were later relegated in folklore to woods and various other uninhabited places.

LORE

Once in a small village in Russia lived a hunchback who could no longer stand living with his mean, hunchbacked twin brother and so set out on his own. He found himself in the forest alone, and since he was tired and it was very late, he lay down to sleep. At about midnight a loud commotion nearby woke him up and he saw a large party of *Shedim* dancing and making a great noise.

As soon as the *Shedim* saw him, they grabbed him and pulled him into their wild dance. Scared, he did exactly as they did, making the same sounds and attempting the same leaps and wicked steps. They were delighted and invited him back. But when they sensed his hesitation, they demanded a pledge. He offered to leave various items of clothing or possessions, but they would have none of it. "Give us your hump," they said in unison. Then, with no more fuss, they took it and disappeared. The man was so pleased to be humpless that he proudly walked back to his village to show off his new physique. His envious twin brother demanded to know how he had gotten rid of his hump, so he recounted the tale.

The twin brother set out to do exactly the same thing. He found the forest, lay down to rest, and waited for the dancing *Shedim* to begin their festivities. Midnight came and so did they. He joined them and skipped, leapt, and kicked and yelled as had his twin. Again they were delighted. They said, you kept your word, and they returned his pledge. When they had vanished the twin found himself with a hump on his back and now another on his chest!

In Japan a nearly identical encounter was reported: Once there lived a good old man who had a large wen on his cheek that was quite disfiguring. He went off into the woods one day to cut some firewood, but it began to rain, and he sought shelter in a hollow tree until the storm passed. It rained for a long time, and then it was nightfall when suddenly there arrived, close by, an entire pack of Oni.

They were horned, fanged, and hairy, of various sizes and shapes, and all grotesque with their usual three eyes and three toes apiece. He was relieved that they didn't see him in his hiding place. Soon they began a rowdy evening of dancing and demonic noisemaking. They drank too much and feasted gluttonously and danced some more and were so absorbed in their activities that the man was caught up in their high spirits. He went out to join them and executed some amazing high kicks and twirls. The demons were favorably impressed. "Come back tomorrow night," they insisted, and to be sure, they demanded he leave a pledge till then. They took his wen and sent him home.

He was handsome again. Word of what had happened immediately spread around town. Now, his next-door neighbor, a mean and envious type, also had a wen, and of course he decided to copy his wenless friend's adventure. So he did. And the Oni showed up and he joined their dance. But he was as untalented a dancer as he was mean and envious, so the demons were disgusted with this boring, clumsy performance. "Here," they said. "Take your pledge wen back and don't ever return!" The nasty neighbor now had two wens, one on either cheek. And the forest demons had vanished.

DISPELLING & DISARMING TECHNIQUES

Usually spitting three times will drive away the *Shedim*, and also making a gesture known as "to fig" (bending the thumb and inserting it between index and second finger, then making a closed fist) will powerfully repel and infuriate the *Shedim* (but can provoke retaliatory gestures). Both

Shedim and Oni usually show merciful vulnerability to human trickery.

Usually it is best not to play with Others, and joining a fairy ring almost always means never going home again. Eating food in the Other World also makes a return trip impossible, yet in these stories the human travelers seem somehow immune to the fate of dancing and drinking encounters. The focus in these tales (well known in many varieties throughout Europe) is on the nature of the human visitors. Motive matters. The goodhearted and guileless disarm the demons and exit in much better shape than the malicious or miserly.

KITSUNE

Japan

The *Kitsune* are wild fox demons known to do terrible mischief, to possess humans, and to take their shapes. In fact, the *Kitsune* is rarely seen in its original shape, but often appears as a bewitching young woman. It shape-shifts by a stroke of its fire-shooting tail. It then puts on a human skull, turns around, and bows to the Big Dipper. If its skull does not fall off, it turns into a beautiful maiden, its most successful form. It is a wanton animal and will in time deplete the energy of its victim and go on to the next. The *Kitsune* came by way of China, where it is called *Huli jing* (see Domicile) and is considered a lewd, canny supernatural creature capable of great damage. Long ago some mischief makers went around cutting off women's hair at night. This act was attributed to the

Kitsune, and from then on foxes were believed to cut women's hair when assuming their shape — perhaps as some sort of pledge. They are also associated with shaving men's heads as pranks.

LORE

One gentleman of fifty came upon a group of captivating females in a restaurant and joined them to drink sake. He left with one, spent the night with her, and when he awoke the next morning, she had vanished. He realized that the entire group had been foxes and that he'd been targeted because of his own lascivious nature. But it was too late. He wasted away and died thirty days later. In other tales the dinner date drinks too much wine and reverts to her fox shape, leaving her escort shocked but safe.

So widespread is the mischief of the troublesome *Kitsune* that there is an annual festival called *Kitsune-okuri* (fox-expelling) that takes place in Totomi province on January fourteenth. A mountain priest leads a procession of villagers, who each carry straw foxes and straw dolls to the mountain outside town and there bury the straw foxes. The ceremony is believed to avert all *Kitsune* pranks (such as their well-known habit of using human voices to lure wayfarers and casting spells over people) for the coming year.

The *Kitsune* have engendered many expressions, and perhaps the most well known is *Kitsune-no-yomeiri* (fox's wedding), which describes the aberrant phenomenon of rain occurring during brilliant sunshine. It is said that any time this sight occurs, a fox bride is going through the woods to the house of her fox groom.

Another eerie sight is *Kitsune-bi* (fox fire). It is said to be caused by a mysterious emanation, like a fireball that the fox breathes through his mouth or creates with his magic tail, or perhaps by a group of torch-bearing foxes leading a wedding procession of foxes. The light appears at twilight and then simply vanishes. The most extraordinary of all demonic fox powers is *Kitsune-tsuki* (fox possession; see Psyche).

Note: The *Kitsune* spirits are not related to the white foxes who serve Inari (god of rice). The white foxes, invisible to mortals, are messengers for the god of rice and appear as good servants of this god in all depictions of Inari shrines.

KABHANDA
India

Kabhanda is a Rakshasa of uncommon appearance in the Hindu epic *Ramayana*. Due to a fight with the god Indra, he was dealt such a terrible blow that his head was driven down into his torso. In the same battle Indra took another swipe and cut off his legs. So *Kabhanda* appears as an enormous, barrel-shaped, hair-covered entity. He has eight arms, each one mile in length, and he walks around on them in spider fashion. His face is located mid-torso, where his wide, fanged, typical Rakshasa mouth grimaces from his belly, and his one eye stares menacingly from mid-chest. His body ends at his shoulders and he has no neck.

LORE

The hero Rama was en route to Lanka to rescue his wife, Sita, from the palace of the demon Ravana. He was just about ready to leave the forest when he ran into *Kabhanda*. The enormous barrel-shaped creature slithered toward him like a huge spider and blocked his path, rearing up and peering menacingly out from his belly at the hero. Unafraid, Rama attacked him and gravely wounded him. *Kabhanda* then weakly pleaded with Rama for a favor: he begged Rama to burn him alive. Rama granted his request. Instantly, from the ashes, *Kabhanda* rose to his next life as a good spirit. He graciously returned the favor Rama had done for him by releasing him from a life as a demon. They left the woods together and went to Lanka. In his new form and life, he aided the hero Rama in his final battle with the terrifying Ravana.

DISPELLING & DISARMING TECHNIQUES

This transformation is unusual in its immediacy, but it expresses the potential for good inherent in many supernatural demonic spirits and is typical of many Hindu demons who can serve out a lifetime as *asuras* warring with the gods and then in another become gods warring with demons.

DESERT

> One often meets men in the African deserts who
> belong to quite a peculiar human species and who
> suddenly disappear from sight.
>
> PLINY, *NATURAL HISTORY*, VII, 2

The Desert is vast, inhospitable territory — traditionally referred to as wasteland or wilderness — with no fixed signposts, and frequent mirages that make for difficult traveling. Dunes eerily shift, sculpting a transient landscape where past and present can be buried in a sudden sandstorm. It is a habitat of extremes where space and time as we know it are erased; map and compass are often useless; and the human traveler feels awe, intense dread, and amazement.

Desert spirits are as plentiful as grains of sand and have lived through the millennia without any regard for humankind. They imbue each rock and plant of this archaic strata. Many were the first beings, here long before people, or Good and Evil, and they continue in a nondual universe of their own. In Aboriginal lore, Dreamtime beings traveled here and their energies remain, creating a map of sacred places for those people who came after. In Native American lore the ancestral spirits also formed the geography of sites where ceremonies are still performed. Ancient nature deities were buried here by later peoples who occupied the landscape, and powerful demons, devouring spirits, and tormentors were banished in antiquity to desert wilderness.

The mysterious nature of the Desert, with its unpredictability, challenge, and power, is reflected in or perhaps embodied by its demonic population of exotic djinn, whose intriguing tales entertain nomadic peoples. Entire invisible, prefabricated spirit cities can suddenly appear and just as suddenly vanish. Other demons manifest as natural phenomena such as sandstorms. Many call out in familiar voices and lure the traveler from the caravan, then provide a ghoulish ending.

For visionaries who have deliberately walked through the desert wilderness, it is the site of their most powerful encounters. It is here Jesus was tempted by Satan, and St. Anthony assailed by demonic hordes for twenty years. For all travelers to this most ancient place, the journey requires formidable strength, preparation, and spiritual power.

WHO'S WHO IN THE DESERT

SUREM	Sonoran Desert
SET	Sahara Desert
AZAZEL	Judean Wilderness
IBLIS	Arabian Desert
DJINN	Arabian Desert
SHAITAN	Arabian Desert
GHOUL	Arabian Desert
DEVALPA	Arabian Desert
MIMI	Arnhem Land, Australia
ST. ANTHONY'S DEMONS	Sahara Desert
PALIS	Arabian Desert
MAMU	Great Sandy Desert, Australia
AHRIMAN	Iranian Desert
NAMARRGON	Arnhem Land, Australia
HO'OK	Sonoran Desert
SATAN	Negev

SUREM
Sonoran Desert

The *Surem*, about three feet in height, are considered to be the precursors of the Yaqui people. The *Surem* were nomads who did not know sickness or death and who could communicate with animals and plants, with which they lived peacefully in the wilds. The little people moved about and carried a lake with them, rolled up like a carpet, and whenever they needed water or fish, they would unroll the lake and fish in it. The time during which they lived this way was called the *yoania:* an ancient, nondual, unitary world when all being was psychically interconnected, an enchanted time before the Spanish came, a time that preceded Christianity.

The *Surem* can still be found today living in a concealed parallel universe that remains in the *yoania*, an "uncivilized" world that exists in wilderness, in wastelands, and in the sacred tale of the Talking Tree, which is still told at certain festivals.

LORE

The *Surem* were a peaceful people living in ancient times when one day a Tree (some say a stick) began trembling and vibrating and made strange undecipherable noises. The villagers went to seek the help of a young sea hamut (wise woman), to act as a kind of oracle, for she understood the unknown language of the Tree and was able to hear its message. Some say it was God who spoke through the Tree, but "God" was unknown to the *Surem*. The young wise woman told the people what the voice prophesied, that soon there would come an entirely new way of life. It would be brought by people who called themselves *padres* and they would teach the *Surem* about "good" and "evil," about something called baptism, about marriage, and also about cultivation of seeds, and with these ideas would also come death to all people and to animals and plants. The villagers listened carefully to the message, and then half of them chose to stay and continue into the future, and half chose to leave before the future came.

The two groups held a feast and a dance of farewell as they parted. To this day the place exists: the place of the last dance.

Those who stayed became taller and eventually became Yaquis who married, cultivated the earth, lived, and died. The others went underground to form a world of their own. They remained *Surem* who live to this day in the *yoania*. Some say they walked into the sea and live under it; others say their world is under the earth. Some became so small they appeared as ants. Some people say they all are seen as ants to this day. The *Surem* took all their powers with them under the earth, and in far-off desert places and caves.

DISPELLING & DISARMING TECHNIQUES

Seekers can travel to the distant *Surem* places to receive these powers, but not without dangerous consequences for those who find them. The *Surem* are still manifest in many ways even for those who do not travel to contact them. They are associated with *seataka*, an inborn power of intuitive intelligence that can be used for good or evil. It contains within it the gift of precognitive power, clairvoyance, "second sight," and is seen in people who have a profound connection to the natural world. The gift of healing is also considered to be inherited directly from the *Surem*.

SET
Sahara Desert

Set, called Typhon by the Greeks, is one of the most ancient and powerful Egyptian deities. He has a tough, camel-like profile, a reddish complexion, squared-off upright ears, and ramrod straight posture.

Set represented the negative aspect of the sun, and over the millennia came to stand for all forces of moral and physical darkness. Ra, the sun god, represented by Osiris, the father, and Horus (his son and symbol of the rising sun), often appears with *Set*, expressing the double nature of the deity. In ancient Egypt *Set* grew to be known primarily as the destructive force of the southern sun, whose deadly rays create unbearable heat and drought that turn earth into uninhabitable stony wasteland.

Set was also considered the thief of the rays of the

beneficial sun, so the setting sun was under his control, as was the part of the year from the summer solstice to the winter solstice when the rays of the sun are weakest and crops cannot grow. He was also the agent of earthquakes, storms, and other natural disasters that upset the natural order of things. *Set* was also a god of war.

All Egyptian gods and demons have body-double animals. *Set*'s representatives were the crocodile, hippopotamus, pig, tortoise, serpent, antelope, and turtle. He was also associated with the ass. Some of these animals were notably sacred, with shrines in ancient Egypt, and the powers attributed to them were a mix of good and evil. The amphibians and reptiles were regarded with fear and suspicion because of their ability to live on land and in water, and all animals that roamed *Set*'s realm, the desert, were regarded with ambivalence. To drive *Set* away, certain offerings of these animals were made on special holidays and always under the full moon. These rituals were essential in ancient Egyptian religion.

LORE

Set was always envious of his glorious brother, Osiris, the mythic founding king of Egypt who gave its people laws and religion. After creating this civilization, Osiris went off to influence other nations, leaving his faithful wife Isis to rule in his absence. When Osiris returned, much later, his brother *Set* was waiting for him. In an radical act of sibling rivalry, *Set* tricked Osiris into lying down in a wooden chest, which *Set* and his seventy-two helpers slammed shut and threw into the Nile. The river carried the chest (with Osiris in it) to the sea. Poor Isis roamed the entire world looking for her husband. *Set* claimed ignorance and refused to help.

Isis finally found the chest. She carefully hid the chest in a tree. The tree, however, was cut down, and made into a pillar of the house of a king. Again Isis tracked it down and asked for it back, but *Set* was a step ahead of her and got to it first. In the dark of night, *Set* removed the chest from the pillar and took the body of his brother out of the chest. He cut up Osiris's body and scattered his parts throughout Egypt.

Ever faithful, Isis patiently traveled all over, picking up the pieces, trying to put her husband together again. Eventually Isis located the phallus of Osiris and, with the help of magic incantations, managed to become pregnant with her husband's child. She gave birth to Horus, who was fated to avenge his father's murder.

Set attempted to thwart Horus's growing up — at one point a scorpion bit the child and killed him, but Isis, with more magic, was able to revive her son. With the protection of other gods, Horus was to grow to manhood and challenge *Set*. In *The Book of the Dead*, the fight between Horus and *Set* is the classical fight of Light and Good versus Dark and Evil. Horus triumphed over *Set*, but just when he was about to do in his father's murderer, Isis intervened. She felt mercy for her brother-in-law. And so the influence of *Set* is still felt and Horus's battle continues to be waged on earth.

AZAZEL
Judean Wilderness

Azazel was king of the *seirim*, an ancient species of goat-like spirits. Although some say "Azazel" was simply the name of a place near Jerusalem, others say that it referred to an archdemon who dwelled in the desert. In ancient Jewish custom, on the Day of Atonement, two goats were brought to the tabernacle. One goat was sacrificed for Yahweh, the other was laden with the sins of the people and taken to the wilderness for *Azazel*. He is spoken of in Leviticus 16:8:

> And Aaron shall cast lots upon the two goats; one for the Lord, and the other for Azazel. And Aaron shall bring the goat upon which the Lord's lot fell and offer him for a sin offering. But the goat on which the lot fell for Azazel, shall be presented alive before the Lord, to make atonement with him and to let him go to Azazel in the desert.

As this passage shows, *Azazel* was as important in ancient Judaism as Satan came to be later in Christianity. *Azazel* represented the powerful evil supernatural adversary to the Lord. *Azazel* appears in the Apocryphal Book of Enoch as an angel fallen from heaven because he lusted after mortal women. On earth he then established himself as a corrupt archdemon teaching unrighteousness. In the Book of Enoch he is charged with revealing eternal secrets to humankind. God responds to this charge by sending angels to bind *Azazel* and imprison him in the desert in a place called Dudael. He is to remain there until the Final Judgment.

Eventually, *Azazel*'s notoriety seemed to fade away, and his place was ultimately usurped by Satan (the Adversary, in the Book of Job), whom the New Testament takes up as its most important fallen angel.

In Islamic lore, *Azazel* is also mentioned as a fallen angel who lusted after mortal maidens. His name becomes interchangeable with Iblis, and then Iblis becomes the archdemon of Islam.

IBLIS
Arabian Desert

Iblis, the spirit of doubt, is a fallen angel of Islam, a powerful subversive spirit, and the chief of all djinn, with an army of *marid,* a vicious and powerful class of djinn. He is closely related to Azazel.

LORE

According to one account, *Iblis* was a powerful angel who refused to bow before Adam at Allah's command. When asked why, *Iblis* replied, "I am better than he; Thou created me out of fire, and him Thou created out of clay." *Iblis* was, as the Q'uran describes him, "puffed up with pride" and believed himself to be far superior to a mere human being. For this disobedience he was cast out of heaven. "Get thee down out of it," said Allah. *Iblis,* the fallen angel, pleaded for clemency and begged not to be cast into the dark pit, but to be given respite until the Day of Judgment.

Iblis was given respite, and then he said he would sit in ambush for humankind, and tempt this usurper Adam and all his sons, and see if they truly remained loyal and good. He was sent forth "despised and banished" and told he would eventually go to hell with all who followed him, condemned to haunt ruins and eat unblessed food until Judgment Day. He became the King of the Shaitans (Satans).

In another version, before the creation of humankind, Allah sent down his angels to destroy the djinn (who had been created from the intense heat of the desert winds and lived as a race of beings for twenty-five thousand years but had begun to flaunt Allah's laws). The angels managed to kill or disperse most of the djinn and to capture *Iblis.* They brought *Iblis* up to heaven, where they educated him in their ways, and *Iblis* quickly gained stature there. Meanwhile, the surviving djinn united to form a new nation. *Iblis,* despite his angelic status, was still hungry for power and flew down to the nation of the djinn and became their king. They called him "Azazel," Lord of the Djinn.

DJINN
Arabian Desert

Djinn, an ancient, Islamic, invisible, illusion-casting species
who live for centuries, can manifest in any form and travel
anywhere instantly. Like the Greek daimon, they are spirits of
an intermediate nature between humans and angels. It is said
in the Q'uran that they are an ancient species who were created before humankind from smokeless fire. The *Djinn* have
no bodies of their own but are masters of illusory disguise.
However, because the *Djinn* are made of fire, when they manifest in human form they have flaming eyes, which are set ver-
tically in the head, not horizontally as human eyes are. Aside
from human form, certain *Djinn* also appear in the shape of
black dogs or snakes or toads or black cats. They are considered the cause of violent sandstorms, whirlwinds, and shooting stars.

Although *Djinn* inhabit ruins, wells, kitchen fireplaces, and public baths, their favorite abode is the desert. Some believe *Djinn* live just under the sand in organized towns and only rise to the surface to harass humans. Some have heard music from *Djinn* "villages" — campsites like human nomadic abodes — which suddenly appear and then vanish in the blink of an eye. When journeying through the Arabian desert it is necessary to call out to the *Djinn* and ask their permission to pass by. Each place has its own resident spirit, its ancestral genius loci, and one addresses it respectfully. If answered by a sudden whirling pillar of sand, it is wise to turn back at once.

LORE

One day King Suleyman (or King Solomon), who had great powers and a formidable magic ring with jewels given him by the angels, used his art to gather the multitudes of *Djinn* around him, for he wanted to see what they looked like. He conjured them to come into his presence, and as they poured forth in vast numbers, the earth trembled. When they became visible to him he reported that he saw legions of aberrant creatures, some two-headed, some fire-breathing, and then many thousands in the shapes of fantastical hybrid animals with the head of a cat and body of a dog and hooves, or with heads on backward. With his magic ring held high, he watched as they bowed to him, for he could subdue all but *Iblis*. King Suleyman used his magic for the powers of good, and he soon had a legion of *Djinn* building for him, diving for pearls, collecting jewels, and mining minerals. No human could craft metal like the *Djinn*, and their fabulous rings play a part in many tales.

It is said that for each human born, a *Djinni* (singular) is also born. He is a kind of supernatural twin who tempts the human being from birth to do the wrong thing. He is always present, as are the angels the human has to guard him. The *Djinni* can change form. If a black cat were to enter the house at night, he might actually be the twin *Djinni* of a member of the household, and if he is hurt by his human twin, the human will inflict harm upon his own self as well. The result of such an event is insanity. Along this line it is said that if a human unknowingly eats *Djinn* excrement, his intelligence shoots up immediately. Thus the proverbial expression, "He has eaten *Djinn* dung [*goh-e-djen*]!" of a very bright child.

All *Djinn* are closely intertwined or involved in human affairs. Like fairies, *Djinn* steal human babies and substitute their own. They also indulge in petty demonic acts like pushing people down stairs, making them yawn uncontrollably, spilling their milk, and giving them nightmares, but these are minor annoyances compared to the serious maladies that *Djinn* are known to cause, such as epidemics, convulsions, insanity, and death.

In the Q'uran, chapter 72 is named for the *Djinn*, and there it is said: "And some of us are the righteous, and some of us are otherwise. We are sects differing." It says in this chapter that some *djinn* have surrendered and they are not harmful, and some have deviated, and the latter will go to hell.

DISARMING & DISPELLING TECHNIQUES

Since all *Djinn* are invisible and plentiful as sand, they are considered to be always present and listening — reputedly they know every language — so care must be taken when discussing them. One must never inadvertently injure them by throwing water on a fire — they often rest in ashes. A stone thrown in the desert may injure some invisible *Djinn* offspring and force retaliation. Any black cat, black dog, or snake might be a *Djinn*, and therefore these animals must be treated with respect. Never sweep at night, for obvious reasons.

Fortunately there are many documented ways of keeping the malevolent *Djinn* away. The first method is to recite the protective *bismillah* "in the name of Allah." To eat without reciting the *bismillah* is virtually an invitation for *Djinn* to lurk in the food, where they may be ingested along with the meal. The prayer is effective at other times when it's known *Djinn* are near, such as when turning off a lamp at night or stamping out a campfire.

Djinn loathe salt. When used in food, salt will keep them

away, as will salt sprinkled on the floor, carried in pockets, in shoes, tucked under the pillow, or thrown up in the air at night while out walking. Since *Djinn* are attracted to human blood, salt is a necessary ingredient at such events as circumcision, the slaughtering of animals, or childbirth.

Djinn also abhor loud sounds. They are afraid of pins, needles, silver, iron, and steel. Successful exploitations of this fear include wearing a metal ring, keeping a knife under the bed, stringing a nail around the neck, or adding a coin to the bathwater. *Djinn* are repelled by strong odors; in particular the smell of tar drives them off at once.

If *Djinn* should get inside a human, a cure must be found to drive them out or the person will become insane. Many of the disarming techniques above can be used to expel the creatures. Tar, for example, can be used on the body, in addition to the inhalation of smoke or incense along with specific incantations. Salt is usually put under the pillow of anybody who is ill. Most often, the recitation of sacred words is employed, as are charms written by people skilled in such things. Often the charms are written in the *Djinn*'s native language, far more ancient than our own. One interesting cure involves preparing a meal (salt-free) for the *Djinn*. The ill person, in order to stimulate the *Djinn*'s appetite, eats a morsel while the *Djinn* watch hungrily from within, then exit the human body to enjoy the rest of the meal. The meal should be placed far away from the patient for best results.

SHAITAN
Arabian Desert

The *Shaitan* (Satan) is a type of djinni created of fire by Allah. While djinn behavior can be moderate or mischievous and members of the species have even converted and become good, the *Shaitan* is invariably evil. Iblis is the king of the *Shaitan*, and, like Iblis, the entire function of the *Shaitan* is to lead humankind into sin by temptation. They manage this by creating illusions in the minds of humankind — enthralling visions of pleasures to be had by committing various sins — and they are endlessly imaginative.

The *Shaitan* eat dirt and excrement and have a notable aversion to water. If one forgets to wash after supper and goes to bed with unclean hands, they may be licked to bloody stumps by morning. Forgetting morning ablutions results in unclean tempting thoughts sent by the *Shaitans* throughout the day. Many of the species look exactly like human beings, although they can shape-shift into animals or inhabit corpses. Some possess people. Some tempt people to do evil. Some take the shape of seductive women to lure travelers.

LORE

It is said that each man has his own guardian angel and his *Shaitan*. In that most favorable aspect, the *Shaitan* is like the Greek daimon and is said to inspire all great poets. The *Shaitan* is inspiration itself and is always connected to poetry and to art. One traveler en route through the desert was suddenly seized by two invisible spirits and transported to their leader. The *Shaitan* leader turned out to be the composer of a famous poet's work.

A huge population of *Shaitans* was accidentally released by fishermen in Morocco from bottles that had the seal of Solomon on them, which accounts for a sudden increase in their numbers.

Once there was a very poor old fisherman who cast his net early one morning and pulled up a strange vessel with a seal on its lead cover. Hoping the vessel might contain something precious, he pried open the lid. A dark smoke arose, slowly at first, and eventually covered all the sky, then formed itself into a massive presence who glared at the old fisherman. "Prepare to die," the spirit said. "I will kill you, and one favor only will I grant you, which is that you choose the method of your death." The fisherman, frozen with fear, asked how the spirit could treat him so, as he had been his liberator. The genie (or djinni), who was a *Shaitan*, answered that he had been sealed in the bottle by King Solomon, whose rule he refused as he had refused the will of heaven, and while in confinement he had first sworn to aid any human who delivered him by giving him riches, making him a monarch, and granting him three wishes of any sort. But after three hundred years had passed, he angrily arrived at his current resolution, to give the person only a choice of how he wanted to die.

The fisherman, having recovered his wits, and desperate to save not himself but his family from ruin, spoke quietly to the towering demon: "Do you swear that you were in this vessel, for I cannot believe that such a grand figure as yours ever did fit in such a container. In fact, I cannot even believe your oath but only my eyes, so I could only believe you if you are able to reenter this vessel." The challenged demonic creature dissolved again into smoke and collected himself slowly within the vessel until he was entirely contained. The fisherman clamped the lid shut upon him and cast him into the sea, resolving to warn all other fisherman by his tale to beware of opening any vessel and thus releasing a wicked spirit.

DISARMING & DISPELLING TECHNIQUES

Most important is the species' aversion to fresh water, which will stop them from all activity. The bone of a hare also works against them. A white cock will keep the *Shaitan* away. It is also said that the door can be shut against the *Shaitan* at night, for they cannot open a shut door. They cannot open water bottles or oil containers that are shut tightly or take the covers off jars, so keeping food enclosed in a sealed vessel will keep the demons out. In the case of the fisherman, it was presence of mind that saved the day, and the classic trick of diminishing demons by containing them. This also works in the case of Madame White (see Water), and the Naga Karkotak in the case of Yaksas (see Mountain).

GHOUL
Arabian Desert

Ghoul ("destroyer") is the most malicious species (along with the *ifrits* and *marids* who make up the wicked army of Iblis). He is often sighted with matted shaggy hair that hangs over his eyes, and he shape-shifts endlessly, but in all forms maintains hooves as feet. The *Ghouls* commonly transform to ox, camel, or horse and often appear in human form. They light fires at night to deceive travelers and they call out "Good evening!" as if they were human. A *Ghoul* specialty is singing like a siren, so sweetly the traveler will be lured to their camp, and then, once gotten alone, the *Ghoul* will show its claws, rip apart its prey, and devour it whole. However, he can be generous if treated well. If a wayfarer cuts his hair and grooms him so he can see well, he'll go out of his way to help that person. The Si'lats, female *Ghouls*, are hideous, and they operate in the same carnivorous ways, but again have a generous side: if a human nurses at the breast of a Si'lat she will treat him as one of her own.

LORE

The *Ghoul* frequents the Valley of the Angel of Death, which is in the salt desert on the road from Teheran to Qum. One messenger was sent out but came back without having delivered the message because he saw two *Ghouls* on the horizon, and when they evaporated at daybreak, he was certain what they were and knew he should not proceed.

DISARMING & DISPELLING TECHNIQUES

It is said that if one loosens the belt of one's trousers, the *Ghoul* will stay away. A *Ghoul* can be killed in one blow. But, beware: a second blow will bring it back to life.

DEVALPA
Arabian Desert

The *Devalpa* usually appears as an innocent, decrepit old man who stands weary and sighing at the edge of the road. As people pass by, he pleads to be taken on their shoulders. If anybody is good enough to pick him up, he will shape-shift immediately: yards of snakelike legs erupt from his scrawny abdomen and wrap around the bearer. His rescuer in a death grip, the *Devalpa* imperiously commands, "Work for me!" If the good samaritan chooses to live, he will do so for the rest of his life as a slave to the *Devalpa*.

LORE

The *Devalpa*'s most prominent role is in the famous story of Sinbad the sailor. Shipwrecked, Sinbad ran across a pathetic old man whom he assumed was a fellow castaway. The old man weakly signaled Sinbad to carry him across a brook. Sinbad charitably hoisted him up on his shoulders, and then, midstream, felt the scrawny legs grow powerful around his neck. He glanced at the legs tightening around him and saw that they were covered with rough black skin. Horrified, he tried to shake the old man off, but the terrible legs squeezed him into unconsciousness.

When Sinbad awakened, he found the "old man" still crouched on his shoulders. The *Devalpa* commanded him to walk. Sinbad was now in the position of being the old man's camel and trudged on for weeks while his rider picked fruit from the trees above as they passed. This relationship grew more and more unbearably burdensome each day.

Eventually Sinbad came across some grapes, which he fermented into a potent wine, whose effects allowed him to forget his desperate situation and lent him a drunken levity. The *Devalpa*, noticing the effect of the wine on Sinbad, commanded him to pour some of this beverage for him. The captor gulped down the drink and soon began to relax his grip on Sinbad's neck. As he drank more, the tentacle limbs slipped off slowly, and soon the creature lay drunk on the ground. Sinbad picked up a heavy rock and dashed his brains out.

DISARMING & DISPELLING TECHNIQUES

Wine is the downfall of many demons. Their excessive nature always causes them to imbibe too much and fall into an unconscious stupor. This permits the hero to bind them, kill them, or escape. (See Asmodeus in Domicile, Oni in Forest, and the White Monkey in Mountain.)

MIMI
Arnhem Land, Australia

The *Mimi* are an ancient family of Aboriginal fairylike spirits who have concealed themselves within rocks in the Arnhem Land plateau of Australia for over ten thousand years. The *Mimi* are described as having such extraordinarily thin and elongated bodies that they cannot venture out on windy days because the wind would cause them to break in half. Hunting is reserved for still days. The tall, fragile beings wear bunches of leaves to cover their genitals.

Never seen by modern travelers, they were glimpsed by Aboriginal medicine men long ago when people could still see spirits. They are assumed to still inhabit the rocks, upon which they have left images of themselves and their activities. All *Mimi* have keen hearing and can detect when a human wayfarer is nearby. When the *Mimi* hear someone coming they run to the rocks, blow on them, and the rocks open up like magic doors to allow the *Mimi* to enter and hide. Certain noises that one hears in this area are the concealed *Mimi* moving around inside their homes. Some *Mimi* are friendly to humans, many are antagonistic, and none are dependable.

The *Mimi* are said to be fond of dancing and singing, and some say they taught the Aboriginal ancestors how to write songs and to dance. They also are said to have taught the art of cave painting, in which their self-portraits are rendered on the stone walls, along with drawings of other ancestral spirits. *Mimi* keep wallabies, pythons, and certain types of kangaroos as pets as a human might keep dogs. They hunt and eat wild kangaroos. If anyone injures a tame animal, it may be a *Mimi* pet and serious consequences will ensue. Injuring a tame kangaroo or wallaby may lead to madness or death.

The *Mimi*, on calm and breezeless days, are skillful hunters, and very adept at hunting kangaroo. It was in fact the *Mimi* who taught the Aboriginal ancestors how to hunt and prepare kangaroo meat.

LORE

Long ago, when the *Mimi* were not as utterly invisible as they are now, special people could see them, and one man was even invited to visit the camp of the *Mimi*. Food and women were offered to him, but he knew that if he accepted, he might turn into a *Mimi* spirit himself. He waited until the *Mimi* were asleep, then he escaped and ran back to his human camp. He could hear the angry *Mimi* call out to him. He told everybody of his encounter. He apparently learned magical things from the *Mimi*, because he became one of the first powerful Aboriginal healers.

One can mistake a *Mimi* for a similar-looking, unusually thin species of ancient evil spirits called Nadubi, which inhabit the same space and have existed from the same time period. They have magical spinelike barbs that stick out from their knees, elbows, wrists, and head, and will use them against Aboriginal travelers, especially those traveling alone. They stalk the desert at night, are always ravenous, eat meat raw, and steal honey. To be shot by the invisible barb of a Nadubi is almost always fatal.

DISARMING & DISPELLING TECHNIQUES

Humankind has learned many creative and healing arts from the *Mimi*. However, as with all fairy species, certain prohibitions prevail and no dining is permitted. Encounters with these powerful species must be left to professionals.

ST. ANTHONY'S DEMONS
Sahara Desert

St. Anthony's Demons are some of the most illustrious and illustrated of the many desert species. They appear in every imaginable hostile animal shape.

LORE

St. Anthony of the Desert was born into a prosperous Egyptian Christian family early in the fourth century C.E. When he was about eighteen years old, his parents died, leaving him in charge of a young sister, a luxurious home, and acres of arable land. Six months later, while walking past a church and reflecting on how little value the Apostles placed on material things in their commitment to Christ, he heard a voice from the door: "If you would be perfect, go, sell what you possess and give it to the poor, and you will have treasure in heaven." (1 Cor. 15:42).

Anthony immediately went home, gave all his possessions to the poor, his sister to the care of nuns, and from that day on devoted himself to spiritual practice. He began his training by studying under solitary ascetics who lived outside his village. He worked for enough money to buy bread, always giving the excess to the poor. He was inspired by the ascetics' devout commitment to prayer, their compassion, and their practice of fasting and sleeping on bare ground.

It was about this time that Anthony received his first visit from the Devil. Seeing Anthony so young and determined, the Devil tempted him with visions of his own past: a loving sister, delicious meals, all the comforts of home and wealth. But Anthony only prayed harder. The Devil harassed him day and night, put foul thoughts into his mind, and one night even shape-shifted into a young women who made sexual advances.

In the days that followed, Anthony stayed up all night, vigilantly on guard. On days that he didn't fast, he ate only once per day, after sunset, and only salted bread and water. He slept on the bare ground, and did not wash or anoint his body with oil. Anthony chose that his flesh would suffer so that his soul would grow strong. He tried to live each day as a possible last day. In this way he battled temptation for the salvation of his soul.

In a step to escape temptation, Anthony moved to the ancient tombs outside the village. He selected a tomb and had a friend lock him inside. One night the Devil came with many demons and whipped Anthony until he fell to the ground. He knew it was the demons who beat him so harshly, for no human was capable of inflicting such pain. Luckily, the next morning his friend returned to the tomb to bring bread. Seeing Anthony lying wounded, he picked him up and carried him to the village. There Anthony was watched by the villagers, but that night, while all slept around him, he woke and asked his friend to carry him back to the tomb. Despite his weakened state, he was carried back, and locked inside again.

That night the demons returned in the form of lions,

wolves, scorpions, bulls, bears, and leopards. Each powerful animal beat him senseless. Wounded in body, but still strong in mind, Anthony called them cowards who needed numbers for their strength. He challenged them to beat him, saying the Lord would protect him. The demons were forced out by a beam of light that miraculously shone down into the tomb. Anthony was cured of all his pain.

It was soon after, on his way into the desert, that Anthony saw a silver dish on a lonely road. He knew it was a demon in disguise. As soon as he said this aloud, the "dish" vanished. As he continued onward, "gold" was thrown down in his path, but he simply stepped over it and never looked back. As he wandered deeper into the desert, he came upon an abandoned fortress. It was here that he took up residence, locking himself inside.

Anthony remained alone inside the desert fort, seeing no other people, for twenty years. Whenever his acquaintances stopped by, they remained outside but could hear the voices of many demons harassing Anthony behind the tall walls. The voices told Anthony to leave the desert, that it was their domain, and no place for weak ascetics. The friends called to him in alarm, but he told them not to fear, for demons were powerless to hurt those who did not fear them.

The demons groaned, whispered, screamed, and muttered for many years, during which time Anthony gained followers as word spread of his struggle. They set up tents all around his demon-infested abode and wouldn't leave. Twenty years after Anthony locked himself into solitude, they tore his door down, and Anthony came forward. He showed no physical decline. He seemed in perfect form, his soul immaculate, years of wisdom on his face.

Anthony was not angry that his followers broke down his door, and from that day he became their teacher. He became St. Anthony: a healer, a performer of miracles, though he claimed no knowledge of any medical practices. Anthony is believed to have died in 356 C.E., leaving many followers in the desert.

DISARMING & DISPELLING TECHNIQUES

Noise and friendly laughter are traditional demonic repellents. The isolation of saints and scholars seems to invite demonic encounters, which are utilized by these extraordinary voyagers for the purpose of transcendence.

PALIS
Arabian Desert

The *Palis* is a potentially deadly foot-licker species that attacks its victims at night when they're sleeping in the desert. He licks the soles of their feet until their blood is gone. There is no known description of the species' appearance.

LORE

One night, when the caravan stopped at a lonely place and all were about to retire, a wise wayfarer advised his mates to beware the *Palis*, for he was sure the demon was lurking nearby. They asked him what this creature did, and as they lingered around the campfire he told them its awful habit: "This demon is a footlicker, and he will lick the soles of your feet until all your blood is gone. Before you wake up, you'll be drained. This has been the fate of many." The travelers heeded the precautions he advised and each made sure to lie down with the soles of his feet touching the soles of a fellow traveler's feet.

When the *Palis* arrived, smacking his lips in anticipation, he noticed no soles at all. He walked in circles again and again, around large forms with a head at either end. He was utterly baffled. He continued walking around and around searching for the soles of feet, which was how he always began his meal. He muttered, "I have traveled to over a thousand valleys, but never before have I seen humans with two heads!" Finally, the demon was exhausted by his circumambulation, and the sun began to rise. The pale light signaled his hasty departure.

DISARMING & DISPELLING TECHNIQUES

Like many of these single-minded species, the *Palis* hasn't an ounce of intelligence and can be easily tricked. Although the sole-to-sole method is the best known for this species, salt should also be kept close by as a repellent.

MAMU
Great Sandy Desert, Australia

The *Mamu* (sometimes called *Gugur*) are malevolent man-eating demons of the Aboriginal people who roam the desert. The *Mamu* have been around since ancient times. They are adept shape-shifters and have been sighted as "friends," fellow travelers, small birds, and even inanimate objects. They are described as very tall, with huge pointed heads and bloody fanged teeth. The males carry large clubs with which they strike their victims.

LORE

A hunter who happened to be out alone had caught an animal and was carrying it over his shoulder back to his resting place. He looked down on the ground and saw a stone blade in the sand. He picked it up and trudged on. Later, after he built a fire and laid his food out to cook, he began to sharpen his spear with the stone. But this stone suddenly changed into a *Mamu* and cut his throat. The *Mamu* dined on the man, mixing him with the game that had been roasting.

In another tale, a *Mamu* went about disguised as a young man. He used to sit on top of a sandhill and wait for solitary human travelers. Once an old man came by. The "young man" asked the old man to tell him stories of the Dreamtime, and offered him some kangaroo meat. The older man ate some of the meat and then lay down to sleep. That was the end of him. The next day the same "young man" went to another hill, sat down, and waited until another traveler came by. But this traveler happened to be a wise man and he recognized the *Mamu* in disguise. He was asked for stories and offered meat, but when the man took the meat he saw a mouth of teeth in it, so he only pretended to eat the meat, and he lay down to rest. Later, when the *Mamu* wasn't looking, he threw the "kangaroo meat" into the flames, for he knew the meat was actually the *Mamu*'s wife in disguise, and when anyone swallowed the meat she would bite at their heart and laugh, saying, "I'm not meat!" Then her husband *Mamu* would devour them. That was the fate of the first traveler, but this wise man outsmarted the *Mamu*.

DISARMING & DISPELLING TECHNIQUES

Dogs can sense when *Mamu* are nearby and will bark loudly. A circle of fire, many companions, and dogs barking will keep this desert demon away. Children must be taught never to leave the circle of fire after dark, for obvious reasons.

AHRIMAN
Iranian Desert

Ahriman, spirit of destruction, head of the evil empire and all the *daevas* ("demons" in Persian lore), was a primordial spirit who arose as the independent counterforce of Ahura-Mazda, who in the religion of ancient Persia was the eternal God, the Wise Lord and Spirit of Good. The realm of *Ahriman* is the desolate wasteland of the desert, although he is also seen sometimes in hell.

LORE

Unlike Satan or Iblis, *Ahriman* has never been one of a host of angels. He has never been beholden to the wishes or command of God or of Allah. He was originally an equally powerful force to the god of Goodness. Although his reign is not eternal, and in the end he will perish like all villains in narratives and the good will ultimately prevail, he is here for a long time. During his stay, he will seduce mortals into worshiping him whenever he can.

According to Zoroastrianism, Ahura-Mazda created the universe as well as the twin spirits Spenta Mainyu (the spirit of Light, Truth, and Life) and Angra Mainyu (the spirit of Darkness, Deceit, and Death). The battleground of the war of these two created spirits is our terrestrial world. Over time, Ahura-Mazda and the spirit of goodness Spenta Mainyu merged to become the eternal God who is all good and light, order and truth — that which opposes *Ahriman*. It is *Ahriman*, the force of Evil, who is responsible for all things antithetical to Good. The battle between these two has been predetermined to rage for a specific amount of time. The time is divided into eras, each of which lasts thousands of years. After the fourth age of these eras, there will be three saviors who will destroy the forces of Evil. Eventually Ahura Mazda will triumph and the new world will be restored to his rule. But this will be later. The world we inhabit now is divided between Good and all the powers of darkness: demons, disease, death, and miseries.

In another version of the origin of *Ahriman*, he was one of a set of twins. The other was Ohrmazd (a contraction of Ahura Mazda). They were born to Zurvan, a preexisting Creator who pledged that his firstborn would rule. *Ahriman* ripped open the womb to be first in line. Zurvan, bound by his promise, tempered the length of time that *Ahriman* could rule the world. After a prescribed time, Ohrmazd's turn will come and all will then be transformed under a reign of goodness and light. But during his rule, *Ahriman*, the demon of demons, created harmful animals, biting creatures, disease, unhappiness, poison, death, drought, famine, and several notable demons called Evil Mind, Tyranny, Enmity, Violence, Wrath, and Falsehood. He created a particularly repugnant female demon named Az, and one dragon.

In one tale, *Ahriman*, ruler of the desert, had a son named Zohak and wanted to train him to be as evil as possible. He suggested to Zohak that he kill his own father and when the boy did, *Ahriman* (who of course had not really been killed) installed himself in disguise as a chef in the palace. There he prepared the flesh of animals to further corrupt the boy. His son so enjoyed the dishes that he wished to reward the chef. *Ahriman*, disguised as cook, asked only that he be allowed to kiss the young man's shoulders. His wish was granted, after which he immediately vanished. Snakes began to sprout from the spots he kissed, and when Zohak chopped them off, they grew back. *Ahriman* then entered disguised as a physician to help the lad. He told Zohak that he had to feed the snakes with human brains daily. Zohak did as he was told, and so became the pride of his archdemon father, *Ahriman*. He ruled for a thousand terrible years until he was finally destroyed.

DISPELLING & DISARMING TECHNIQUES

When dealing with demonic forces of this order, and with the attributes of evil so clearly defined, the traveler is asked to choose.

NAMARRGON
Australia

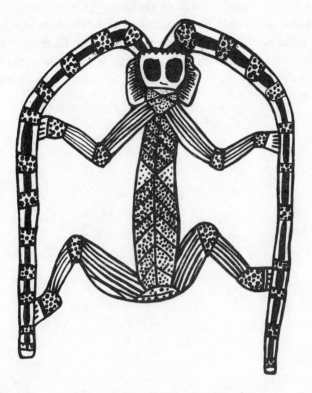

Namarrgon, or *Mamaragan* (Lightning Man) is an ancient, volatile, and belligerent Aboriginal spirit who lives in Arnhem Land.

LORE

In the dry season *Namarrgon* stays in a water hole that is to be avoided. Should anybody throw a stone, or drink from that water hole, or even so much as riffle the surface, he would rise up and destroy them with a flash of lightning. He would cause flooding and drown whole villages. During the monsoon season he travels in the air and roars in the clouds overhead. It is his arms and his legs that are the flashes of lightning, and as he strikes the ground, destruction is instantaneous. Some say he throws stone axes down to create the flashes of light.

Namarrgon terrified the Mimi spirits and the Aboriginal people with his displays of power, which can be seen throughout the sky, which cause so much damage, destroy camps, and kill so many people. He has fathered many children who have all taken on the shape of a spectacular insect, flaming orange and blue, that mates in the early rainy season. Sorcerers were sometimes able to enlist the help of *Namarrgon* in their magic.

HO'OK
Sonoran Desert

Ho'ok is a legendary demon of the Tohono O'odham (The Desert People). She was human in appearance, all but for her hands and feet, which are animal claws. The *Ho'ok* was a fierce man-eater who carried off small children and babies, which she killed and ate. She lived in a cave in the land of the Tohono O'odham, whose center is the Baboquivari Mountain, where their Creator and Elder Brother I'itoi lives, and whose vast range is millions of acres of desert extending down into Sonora from what is now called Tucson.

LORE

Once a beautiful young woman sat by a pond and was quietly weaving when she saw a red kickball pass by. It was the kickball of the youngest of two brothers who were competing in a race to see which one would win her in marriage. The girl quickly hid the ball beneath her skirts, while the young men raced over to see who won. They asked her if she'd seen a kickball, but she said she had not. After they left, the girl went home and told her family what had happened. They prepared a sleeping mat for the bridal pair to be, for the tradition was that the bridegroom would sleep for four nights at the home of the bride and then take her to his house, but she waited to no avail — the bridegroom did not appear. After four nights the time was up. Meanwhile, the special ball, which was made by the sun of red dust, had disappeared into the womb of the young woman.

Time passed and a child was born, but it was a strange child and it had the hands and feet of an animal. As it grew, it became fiercer and it attacked and hurt the other children. Finally the mother had to take the child, *Ho'ok*, away from the community. She led the child out to the desert and told her to go in search of her father. She pointed to the heat waves rising up in the distance and said that *Ho'ok* should travel in that direction to find her father. *Ho'ok* traveled south, following the mirage all the way to Mexico, but then she saw the heat waves again, rising up in the north. She began to travel in that direction.

Ho'ok walked on and on but could never reach the heat waves. As she walked, the sun began to disappear behind a mountain. *Ho'ok* came across a cave and thought that perhaps her father lived there, although he was not at home. She searched again the next day, and again slept in the cave that night, and finally made the cave her home. From there she set out every night to find babies and children to eat.

The people went to the home of I'itoi, in a cave on the west side of Baboquivari Mountain, to ask his help. I'itoi appeared as a tiny old man but was extremely powerful. He told the people to hold a dance and he invited *Ho'ok* to the ceremony. He prepared a special tobacco with a sleeping drug of certain flowers and he gave it to her to smoke. After four days and four nights of this smoking and dancing *Ho'ok* finally fell into a sound slumber. Then I'itoi carried her to her own cave and sealed it with a door. The people had already placed firewood within the cave and now I'itoi set it on fire. *Ho'ok* awoke and slammed herself against the walls of the sealed cave until the mountain cracked open. I'itoi jumped upon the crack and sealed it shut with his foot. *Ho'ok* perished within.

This was not the end of the story, however, for from the smoke of the fire a menacing hawk was born that I'itoi once again had to quell, and even later, from the bones of *Ho'ok* were born other creations. The footprint on the cave of *Ho'ok* is still visible today. Near Pozo Verde in Mexico are grounds where the villagers believe the final ceremony was held. It is used today as a shrine.

SATAN

Negev

Satan, a fallen angel, is also known as Lucifer, Sammael, Asmodeus, Mephistopheles, the Devil, the Adversary. "What is thy name? And he said my name is Legion, for we are many" (Mark 5:9).

Before his famous temptation of Jesus in the desert, this archdemon had only slowly evolved into the powerful, independent entity called *Satan*. He first appeared (in the Book of Numbers) when God sent "a satan" on His behalf as a messenger to let Balaam know what he had done wrong. "The satan" then appeared in a starring role in the Book of Job, but he was not yet a single personality. "*The* satan" means adversary, obstructor, or accuser, but is not a proper name. He was simply present in a large divine assembly of angels and became the catalyst for the story of Job by suggesting that Job was good and pious only because he was rewarded for this with a nice life. What if, suggested the satan, he were to be tormented and miserable; would he still be loyal? He gained God's approval to put Job under adverse circumstances to see whether man's true nature was good. Under the worst trials Job remained true. In this harrowing tale, the satan never acted as an independent agent, but was subject to the will of God.

Much later, in rabbinical writings, *Satan*'s origins began to be linked to Eve and the apple incident. Also it was here that the satan was mentioned as a powerful wicked angel known as Sammael, "chief of the satans." Objecting to God's creation of man, Sammael led a plot against humankind and traveled to earth, using the serpent to start the Fall by tempting Eve. For this, he and his follower angels were cast out of heaven, just as Adam and Eve were cast out of Eden.

During the apocalyptic era *Satan* was interchangeable with Azazel of the desert. By then *Satan* had developed twelve wings (the other angels had six) and a distinctive profile: he exists only to wreak destruction in the mortal world and to bring humankind to an end, and he wars with God to become the subject of worship.

Satan does not "possess" people as the "unclean spirits" do, and is not "cast out" as these demons are throughout the Gospels. He is seen more as metaphorically "entering the heart" of a person who turns to evil and thus to *Satan*, not because he is sick and possessed, but because he allows himself to be tempted. The human being, then, is an instrument of the Devil and does his bidding for the Kingdom of Darkness. *Satan* is the personification of Evil.

At the time of his encounter with Jesus in the desert, *Satan* has become the Devil (*diabolos* = Slanderer), under whose direction all malevolent spirits work. As chief of demons, and god of our terrestrial world, he rules the Kingdom of Darkness and subsumes all evil powers. He can influence mankind on a daily basis and can cause illness via his army of demons. By now he alone is responsible for tempting people to evil action, for the envy of Cain and his fratricide, and for the deception of Eve. He can transform himself into infinite shapes, can even appear as an angel of light and brilliance, for he's the great Deceiver.

LORE

After Jesus was led by the Spirit into the wilderness, he fasted for forty days and forty nights, and he was hungry and *Satan* arrived to tempt him. "If you are the Son of God, tell these stones to turn into loaves." Jesus replied that man does not live by bread alone. Next, *Satan* took Jesus to Mount Seir, a height from which he could glimpse in an instant all the kingdoms of the world in all their splendor. "I will give you all this power and glory," he said. "Worship me, and it shall all be yours." Jesus declined the offer and said that Scripture said, worship God alone. "Be off Satan," Jesus said, and in one version of the story his decline of worldly power was enough to quell *Satan*.

According to Luke, the story continues: *Satan* then took Jesus to a parapet of the Temple in Jerusalem and challenged him to hurl himself down as a test to see if he was really guarded by angels. For the third time Jesus declined, saying, "It has been said: You must not put the Lord your God to the test" (Luke 4:12).

It was then *Satan* left him, "and angels appeared and looked after him" (Matthew 4:11).

DOMICILE

Perhaps because the Domicile was, and in many cultures still is, the site of childbirth, marriage, and death — the most important events in the human journey, are surrounded with ceremony and spirits good and evil — or perhaps because the foundation of each new home rests on ancient spirits' own subterranean abodes, or perhaps for reasons known only to the mysterious spirits, demons and fairies are always closer than the neighbors. The home is crowded with spirits. Each must be approached with caution, amulet, talisman, or sometimes a professional exorcist.

At times the various Domicile species set up house in uninhabited ruins, or dwell outside the main house of farms, in outhouses or barns. Many enjoy the entrance of a dwelling; they lurk at the threshold to harm or help residents, and they often pounce on visitors, especially those who do not observe prescribed entry rules. The bedroom houses succubi and incubi (female and male demons who come via dreams or arrive disguised as spouses for sexual play with humans) who are very active at night and cannot be stopped by closed shutters or doors. Supernatural wives are often revealed (too late) in this room by sudden aberrant or violent behavior. Marriage itself can be threatened by subversive species who engender animosity between couples. And then, each night, any sleeping human, after a hard day, might be the victim of a Mare attack. Children, especially before christening, are most vulnerable to attack in the nursery, a popular habitat for certain fairies and some malevolent demons.

There are also the genius loci to consider, for they have always lived here and must be fed nicely and propitiated or they can make life unlivable. Then there are the species under the dwelling, who might be anybody's ancestors and need placating. (Until a few centuries ago in Germany it was common practice to bury a live child in a sealed room beneath a home-to-be as a sacrifice to those dangerous spirits who might be displaced. This ensured their goodwill.)

Disease demons, before antibiotics, were considered agents of fever, headache, and fatal illness. They were also the personifications of plagues. Prophylactic species can be found perched on window ledges facing out. Their apotropaic images ward off disease species from flying attack. The kitchen, because of potential food spoilage but also its cozy stove, seems to attract hordes of demonic helpers and fairies.

The welcome mat may attract unwanted visitors; all in all, it is the Domicile that universally holds the most variegated population of demons, fairies, fallen angels, and subversive spirits of any habitat.

WHO'S WHO IN THE DOMICILE

CROUCHER	Babylonia
ASMODEUS	(Judaism)
CHANGING BEAR MAIDEN	North America (Navajo)
DOMOVOI	Russia
HIRANYAKASHIPU	India
LILITH	(Judaism)
CHANGELINGS	Great Britain
PAZUZU	Babylonia
ISITWALANGCENGCE	South Africa
LIDERC	Hungary
AL	Armenia
FOX FAIRY	China
MARE	Norway
KITCHEN FAIRIES	China
FAIR LADY	Hungary
NISSE	Norway

CROUCHER

Babylonia

An ancient descriptive lament about demons of the domicile goes:

> *Doors do not stop them*
> *Bolts do not stop them*
> *They glide in at the doors like serpents*
> *They enter by the windows like the wind.*

The *Croucher*, an entrance demon, is one of the invisible *rabisu* ("the ones that lie in wait"), a species that makes its presence so deeply felt that it instantly causes the hair of any mortal to stand on end. This is how all *rabisu* are depicted, by their effect, so hair-raising as to be indescribable. We can only claim to represent them by the words and images in all amulets, talismans, and incantations used against them.

Ancient people of Babylonia believed that multitudes of evil spirits filled all space of all habitats. They were an abundant population, described categorically as *utukku, ekimmu, gallu, alu,* and *rabisu.* The first two are departed spirits of the dead who cannot find rest and do harm, especially around graveyards; the third is a devil in the shape of a bull who wanders around the streets at night; the fourth is another community specter in the shape of a black dog. One can avoid all of these by staying home. But staying home will not prevent a run-in with a lurking *rabisu* like the *Croucher,* an embodiment of evil who lies invisibly in wait for its mortal victims at the threshold of each house. When God says to Cain, "Sin crouches at the door," He may be referring to an always present evil force (or inclination) that waits there, ready to pounce.

Other *rabisu* have also been seen perched atop roofs, ready to pounce on newborn humans. In ancient Rome people shot arrows at the roof to protect pregnant mothers (especially vulnerable) from these invisible demons. In Syria there is a roof demon called the *bar egara,* who leaps on men when they leave home for work. Clearly it is at the threshold where one must be especially alert for spirits.

The door itself holds tremendous powers — in Rome the two-faced door god Janus watched both the entrance and exit, and in China there are two door gods to protect each entrance. In many cultures the front door is painted with special colors or signs and is adorned with various depictions of ancestral spirits, or carries an amulet to touch when passing through, such as a mezuzah. An ancient Babylonian warning to evil spirits was shrill as a present-day burglar alarm:

> He who endeavors to injure the columns and the
> capitols, may the column and the capitol stop his
> way!
> He who slides into the young oak and under the
> roofing,

He who attacks the sides of the door and the grates,
May the talisman make him weak like water!
May it make him tremble like leaves, may it grind
   him like paint! May it leap over the timber, may
   it cut his wings!

If that doesn't stop them, apotropaic statues might. Kings placed statues of powerful demonic spirits at the entranceway of their palaces, paying them homage in part to placate them but also to enlist their help against other less powerful species. To this day in many cultures one takes off shoes prior to crossing over the threshold, and a groom still carries his new bride across it to avoid unlucky consequences.

LORE

One night in the town of Posen, a young man, apparently a thief, forced his way into the locked cellar of a stone house on the main street. The next morning he was found dead on the threshold of the house. After this incident, the family who lived in the house were attacked nightly by spirits who threw their belongings about and did so much damage they were forced to move out. The house stood abandoned for years, but the activities extended to affect the entire community. Nobody in town could do a thing to stop the nightly fracas, and so finally the *baal shem*, famed rabbi of Zamosz, was sent for. He forced the demons to reveal their names, and it turned out they believed the cellar was their property because a previous owner of the abode had relations with a demoness who bore him many children. As heirs, they resented the human intruders. Furthermore, their population had so increased in number (as is the case with demons worldwide) that they were spilling out into the town. The case was brought before a rabbinical court. The demons had papers that substantiated their ancestral relationship, but despite their prior claim, the case was decided in favor of the humans. The demon heirs were told to evacuate their home. The *baal shem*, by powerful exorcism, was able to send them to the wilderness. The case of the dead thief on the threshold was solved by the subterranean family he had accidentally unsealed.

From a nineteenth-century Shanghai newspaper report:

In China, to prevent a bride's feet from touching the threshold, a red cloth was placed over it, and she was lifted from the sedan chair to her bedroom by attendants. Upon this particular occasion, when the sedan chair arrived to take the new bride to her future house, her friends looked into the sedan and were shocked to find a huge snake in the chair. They warned the bride not to get in, but she ignored them. When she got in the sedan chair, she saw on the seat not a snake but a strange knife. She tucked it into her trousseau box. After the ceremony, when the new couple was alone, she told the groom what had transpired. He asked to see the knife, and so she took it from the box and handed it to him. As soon as he picked it up his head fell off. She screamed and aroused the household. They accused her of murder. When the magistrate was called, he asked to see the weapon, and as soon as she showed it to him, *his* head fell off. She remained unharmed. It was the talk of the town. They called her the "demon bride."

DISARMING & DISPELLING TECHNIQUES

Shutting the door works against some demons but imprisons others. They should always have a way out. In Jewish lore it is suggested that a small hole in the door will allow them egress. A mezuzah properly attached to the doorpost can help. In some cases crossing oneself helps, and maintaining special alertness at the entranceway to any house, and staying in good company, the kind that produces human laughter and friendly noise, may chase them off.

ASMODEUS

(Judaism)

Asmodeus (*Ashmedai* in Hebrew, meaning "evil spirit") is the undisputed king of the demons of Hebrew lore. He has three heads that face different directions. One is the head of a bull, the second the head of a ram, and the third the head of an ogre. He has the legs and feet of a cock and he rides a fire-breathing lion. All of these animals are associated with lust, which is his specialty. His other power areas are wrath and revenge. He wreaks havoc in households and produces enmity between man and wife. His favorite place is the bedroom.

Asmodeus is said to be the son of Naamah and it has been said that he is husband of Lilith, the queen of the demons. By name he is clearly connected to an ancient Persian demon of wrath, Aeshma. The cock feet of Asmodeus (and later, the Devil) can be traced back to a Babylonian belief in the cock as an important divinity of night to whom sacrifices were made and indicates the powerful stature of this demon. In Christian lore *Asmodeus* retains his hybrid shape and powers and is also known as Sammael, one of the fallen angels, and at times becomes interchangeable with Satan. *Asmodeus* represents one of the Seven Deadly Sins — Lust (see Psyche).

LORE

In the apocryphal Book of Tobit, *Asmodeus* fell for Sarah, a young Persian virgin. He wanted her all for himself, and in a short course of time he killed every one of poor Sarah's seven bridegrooms on their wedding night before they lay with her. She was suspected of sorcery and she prayed for Divine intervention. At that very time, the pious, blind Tobit prayed for help for his family and sent his son Tobias to Media on a mission to recover some silver he'd loaned long ago to Sarah's father. God heard both prayers and sent the angel Raphael to help. Tobias was escorted by the angel Raphael in disguise as an old man named Azarias. While camping beside the river Tigris, Tobias caught a large fish and Azarias taught Tobias to save its heart, liver, and gall. The latter cured blindness, he said, and the heart and liver could be used to cure a person plagued by a demon or evil spirit. The angel then instructed Tobias to propose marriage to Sarah despite her femme fatale reputation, and to follow his instructions. Tobias did as Azarias told him, and on his wedding night with Sarah, Tobias burned the fish's organs as prescribed and the smell drove *Asmodeus* away from the bridal chamber. It all worked out happily for the couple. However, the demon's reputation for the destruction of marital bliss continued on for centuries.

Asmodeus is also famously associated with King Solomon. In one story the king had grown arrogant and transgressed the Ten Commandments by having a thousand wives, so the Holy One sent *Asmodeus*, king of the demons, to sit on his throne. *Asmodeus* was able to usurp the throne by stealing and using Solomon's magic ring. Solomon roamed the streets saying that he was the real king of Israel, and everybody thought he was insane. Finally, Solomon's mother and one of his wives discovered that *Asmodeus* was an impostor; the demon left tracks in ashes with his telltale cock's feet. Solomon was found and was returned to the throne, where he ruled with even greater humility and brilliance.

In another version of the tale, it was King Solomon who initiated the ordeal by engaging *Asmodeus* in a philosophical discussion about the nature of reality and illusion, during which *Asmodeus* tricked the king into giving him his magic ring (inscribed with the name of the Almighty). Then *Asmodeus* threw the ring into the sea, and immediately King Solomon found himself in another life, wandering about as a beggar. He worked for many years in hard labor, and after an arduous time of trials, he became a cook in the kitchen of a king. One evening he was preparing a fish that turned out to hold in its belly the very ring that *Asmodeus* had thrown into the water. He placed it on his finger and again became King Solomon. He awakened in his own bed within the same moment that he'd left but with new insights gained from a "lifetime" away. From then on he became an even wiser and humbler king and judge than he had been before.

DISARMING & DISPELLING TECHNIQUES

> To discover demons, spread ashes around your bed
> at night and in the morning you may see if any foot-
> prints, like those of a cock, are there.
> — The Talmud (Berakhot, 6a)

If *Asmodeus* is found in the bedroom, the heart and liver of a special fish can be placed on an incense-burner and roasted for the terrible aroma. The type of fish is known only to angels, so the next best thing is any pungent-smelling herb, such as garlic, or strong-smelling smoke from incense — or burning tar, which is always an effective repellant (see Djinn in Desert).

CHANGING BEAR MAIDEN
North America (Navajo)

Changing Bear Maiden, the quintessential demonic female of the Navajo, is first glimpsed as a model housekeeper. She is a gentle, beautiful virgin, an orphan, who can be seen in the kitchen preparing meals for her twelve good brothers. When next seen, she is filled with wrath and the spirit of revenge and has shape-shifted into a lethal she-bear.

LORE

Changing Bear Maiden lived with her loving brothers, twelve skilled hunters and excellent providers. The sibling family lived in harmony until one day *Changing Bear Maiden* became the object of the notorious trickster Coyote's desire. After many tests, she agreed to marry him, much to the horror and resentment of her brothers. Her nature changed as she fell under the control of the seductive, lusty Coyote.

One day the brothers were going off to hunt and tried to leave Coyote behind. He begged them to bring him along on the hunt, and at last they gave in. After a while they could no longer tolerate his mischievous ways and sent him home with some meat. They instructed him to go around the forbidden canyon, and not to cut across it, but Coyote did not heed their warnings and was killed before arriving home. The story of his demise is recounted in many ways, but the brothers were not responsible.

It was night when the brothers arrived home. Coyote had not yet returned. Their sister asked where her husband was. The brothers answered that they had warned him not to enter the canyon, but that he probably had and may have been harmed. "What have you done with him?" *Changing Bear Maiden* asked angrily, in a voice her brothers had never heard before. She was certain that they had killed her husband and was filled with rage.

Before they went to sleep that night, the brothers sent the youngest to hide and watch their sister. He saw her rise up and face the east, then, moving the way of the sun, she turned and faced the south, west, and north. Then *Changing Bear Maiden* pulled out her right eyetooth and replaced it with a large tusk. She then did the same with her left eyetooth. He then saw her remove her lower right and left canine teeth and replace them with tusks made of bone. No sooner had she begun to pull her teeth out than hair began to sprout from her hands, and as she continued, the coarse shaggy hair spread over her arms and legs and body.

The youngest returned to his brothers to report what he had seen, and was sent back to the hiding place to view more. His sister continued to move in the direction of the sun, pausing to open her mouth at each direction. Her ears grew and began to wag. Her nose changed into a long snout. Her nails turned into large claws. The youngest brother watched until dawn and then went back to report what he'd seen to his brothers.

As he spoke, a she-bear suddenly rushed past the lodge and followed the trail that Coyote had taken the day before. At night she came back wounded, and they all watched from a hiding place as their sister who had been a bear walked around her fire removing arrowheads from her body. The next morning a "she-bear" rushed past the lodge, and again returned bleeding and spent the night magically healing her wounds. This continued for four days and four nights, until she had killed all those responsible for Coyote's death. Meanwhile, the brothers, fearing for their lives, fled. They left the youngest brother at home. When they were gone, the Wind came to help the youngest brother dig a hole under the center of the hogan, and from this dug four tunnels, each branching off in one of the four directions.

When morning came and *Changing Bear Maiden* returned and found that her brothers had all departed, she poured water on the ground to see which way they had traveled. The water spread out to the east. She rushed off toward the east, overtook the brothers who had gone in that direction, and killed them. Again she poured water, and for the other three directions, found her brothers and killed them. Finally she poured water and it sank into the ground. *Changing Bear*

Maiden quickly dug downward, and there she found her youngest brother hiding beneath her. She greeted him, and told him to come up. She held out her finger for him to grab, but the Wind warned him not to accept her help but to climb out of the hole by himself.

The youngest brother climbed out of the hole and walked toward the east while *Changing Bear Maiden* tried to lure him into the deserted hut. But the Wind warned him not to enter so he passed on. His sister then asked him to sit facing west so that she could comb his hair, but the Wind warned him not to do it because it was late in the afternoon, and he would not be able to see her shadow. He was advised to sit facing north.

When they both sat down, and as she touched his hair, he could see her shadow transform as her snout grew longer, and he could see the shadowy wagging of her ears. The Wind told him to get up, and pointed out the plant in which *Changing Bear Maiden* had hidden her vital organs. The boy ran to the plant (despite many obstacles that sprung up from the ground) and he could hear her lungs breathing in the plant before him, and shot his arrow straight into the plant. The bear/woman fell to the ground, with a stream of blood flowing in two directions. The Wind told the boy that the two streams of blood could never meet, for if they did, his evil sister would be revived.

The brave brother cut her breasts off, threw them into a piñon tree that had never borne fruit, and they became pine nuts; her tongue became cactus, and her vagina, the yucca fruit. He cut off her head and it became a bear and walked off into the woods, first promising only to attack to protect its species. The Wind helped him revive his siblings. They all built a new hut. Then the youngest brother went off to live at a place called Big Point on the Edge, which is in the shape of a Navajo hut, where he still is believed to reside today.

DISARMING & DISPELLING TECHNIQUES

It is the youngest brother who, with innocence, courage, and unselfishness, acts as hero in this tale and finally transmutes the body parts of the destroyed demoness into useful and nurturing animal and vegetable life. Often the sheer animal energy of the demon lives on after the quelling and must be dealt with later. Sometimes the remains must be burned or reburied and sometimes, as in this case, they seed and create good things.

DOMOVOI
Russia

The *Domovoi* (*dom* means "house"), like the genius loci of the Greeks, is considered a guardian spirit, and is referred to as "Grandfather" behind his back. Shy, and not given to public appearances, the *Domovoi* is rarely seen but is heard nightly in odd groans and creaks. When he does scurry out from behind the stove and across the kitchen floor at night, he is usually covered with fur, and has been mistaken for the family cat or dog. This is his most frequent form, but once in a while, when he has shape-shifted into the guise of master of the house, he has been seen as a doppelganger. Reports of sightings of the *Domovoi* as a very old man with a beard are also frequent.

When the *Domovoi* is not in the kitchen, he'll wander into the stable. He even grooms the horses in the middle of the night in a sort of fairy-helper way. He is fond of horses and cows and can converse with them fluently.

The *Domovoi* is usually a domesticated presence, vital to the intrinsic health of any household. But, like all demonic species, he is volatile, impulsive, and subversive by nature. When a *Domovoi* is aggravated by homeowners, or thinks he hasn't been paid proper respect — if, for example, there's salt in his porridge offering, dishes left in the sink, or simply no special treat left out for him — he can quickly erupt in a violent tantrum. He throws pots at the head of household. He spreads manure all over the front door and stoop. He ties horses to the stalls so they cannot get to their food and slowly starve to death. The *Domovoi* can do all this and more in a fit of excessive spirits, without any obvious provocation.

LORE

Once the *Domovoi*, well known for braiding the manes of horses, took to braiding a maiden's hair each night. She never even owned a comb, but always looked quite lovely. He told her never to unbraid her hair or to get married. But one day she decided to marry and to comb her long hair. On the morning of her wedding the bride was found dead.

The *Domovoi* is a powerful house spirit, and at night his cold hand upon one portends death. He also sometimes chokes people fatally while they sleep. Despite this, his warm soft touch at night always signals future good fortune.

The *Domovoi* is believed by some to have been a fallen angel, hurled to earth from heaven by the Archangel Michael. While other spirits landed in forest and water, the *Domovoi* landed in the house. Two subspecies of the *Domovoi* are the Bannik and the Ovinnik, both vicious and dangerous. The Bannik is the spirit of the bathhouse and has been known to peel the skin off visitors. The Ovinnik often burns down barns and generally waits until the owner is within. The *Domovoi* is always better behaved than his demonic close cousins, for the ancient guardian role from which he came deeply influenced his temperament and he is inherently protective. He simply demands extreme loyalty.

DISARMING & DISPELLING TECHNIQUES

The *Domovoi* is considered with the usual ambivalence toward such powers. His goodwill and protection is sought, however, so he is never averted or dispelled but can be disarmed by offerings of kasha, tobacco, and juniper. Since it is almost impossible to get rid of the creature, it's best to learn to live with him. If the family moves, it is best to formally invite him along and bring some of his stove coals. To not do so will make future life miserable. He will avenge himself on the departed family as well as the new one.

HIRANYAKASHIPU
India

Hiranyakashipu is a powerful cosmic Hindu asura (demon) of
the threshold, which is the sole place, "not inside and not outside," where he is vulnerable. He is huge, horned, and has the
demonic appearance of a Rakshasa with large animal ears,
clawed feet, and a tail.

LORE

Once there were two gatekeepers of the celestial world
who refused entrance to the two sons of Brahma, the Creator,
because of the way they were dressed. The sons happened to
be sages and worthy of enormous respect and were so infuriated they cursed the gatekeepers to fall to earth and be born
in the mortal world as demons. The curse was later modified
to a finite period of three demon lifetimes (many millennia),
after which the two would again ascend to the celestial world.

The gatekeepers made their first demonic appearance on
earth as the brothers Hiranyaksha and *Hiranyakashipu*. On
the day of their birth, the earth trembled and a comet
appeared on the horizon. As they grew they spread terror
everywhere. The first brother, Hiranyaksha, met his death in
a deluge of his own creation when he was killed and the world
was saved by the gods.

Hiranyakashipu lived on, determined to avenge his
brother's murder at the hands of the gods. He took up eons of
austerities to earn the *tapas* (superhuman powers) necessary
for a battle. When he had finally accumulated enough power
to demand a boon from Brahma, he tried to word it cleverly:
"I seek the following boon: that I not meet my death at the
hands of gods or created beings, and through no weapon of any
kind, and not on earth or in the air, and not at day or night or
inside or outside my house!" And Brahma said: "Let it
be so!"

Thinking himself utterly invincible, *Hiranyakashipu* let
loose a reign of terror, tormenting both sages and ordinary
humans. He said that all must henceforth worship him alone.

Meanwhile, back at his mansion, his wife had a baby. Despite all paternal training, the boy refused to bow to evil or follow in his father's footsteps. *Hiranyakashipu* attempted to kill the saintly child three times, but each time was thwarted by divine intervention. Sure that the child would grow up to be good (unlike his other serpent son Hrada), *Hiranyakashipu* made one more effort to do the boy in, and nearly succeeded. As he sat just outside his house with a raised knife and the boy on his lap, Vishnu could stand it no more.

Vishnu, in the terrible incarnation of Man-Lion, appeared. Sitting cross-legged on a small pile of hay at the doorway to the demon's mansion at twilight, the Man-Lion, not on the earth nor in the sky, and at a time that was not day nor night, neither inside nor outside, destroyed the hideous in-betweener, *Hiranyakashipu*.

Of course, this was only one lifetime, and *Hiranyakashipu* had only two reincarnations to live out his sentence before ascending to the celestial world again.

LILITH

(Judaism)

Lilith is the most important Jewish femme fatale of the succubus species (female demons who engage in erotic activities with male humans while they sleep) and the only spirit of her gender referred to in the Bible. It is only a brief mention, following a description of a wasteland inhabited by jackals and hyenas: "And Lilith shall repose there" (Isaiah 34:14).

Ancient tributaries to the powerful *Lilith* point to her major roles, all associated with night, with seduction in the form of a temptress-succubus, and by the Middle Ages, also with the death of human infants. Her biblical mention may have been intended to refer to ancient Babylonian demonesses called *lilitu* (female night spirits) or to the Sumerian wind demon Lil (wind). Also, the word "night" in Hebrew is *lilah*, and the screech owl, *lilit*.

There was an Arabian demon (Um Es Sibyan) like *Lilith* with infants. She had the body of a c' chest of a camel, and a human face, and flew nig like a bird — *warh-warh-warh*. The cry was a d to any child who happened to hear it unless the parent repeated the preventative *tchlok-tchlok-tchlok* continuously until the demon had passed by. Another source of her combined attributes was the Greek Lamia, whose children by Zeus were killed by Hera and who for revenge became a child-killer and joined the Empusae, the demon daughters of Hecate who lay with sleeping men and sucked their vital forces until they died.

Lilith can be sighted in the home, an ironic habitat for her, given her fiercely antidomestic attitude. *Lilith* is seen flitting through the Talmud, her long, lustrous black hair shining in the moonlight, her eyes aglow. There, she is mother of all the *shedim* (demons) and, apparently, the wife of Adam before Eve, based on the commentaries arising from the phrase "Male and Female He created them" (Genesis 1:27). In the eleventh century, *Lilith* appears in a popular book, *The Alphabet of Ben Sira* (based on an apocryphal text called *The Wisdom of Ben Sira*), as the first wife of Adam.

LORE

In this tale, God created *Lilith* as a companion to Adam, not after Adam or from his rib, but at the exact same moment and from the same dust. God created her so that Adam would not be alone. But *Lilith*, who insisted she was made from dust just as her husband was, felt she was equal to him and would not behave in a submissive or subservient manner. Their stormy relationship culminated with *Lilith* refusing the missionary position and insisting on being on top. Adam wouldn't hear of it and forced her to submit. *Lilith* flew away that very night and was soon in a cave, cavorting with hordes of demon lovers. It is said that these promiscuous couplings produced a hundred demons a day, called the *lilin*. Some say that *Lilith's* offspring singlehandedly account for all demons alive.

Adam complained that he'd been abandoned. "Lord of the Universe, the woman thou hast given me, has fled from me." The Lord sent (before Eve was created from Adam's rib) three angels named Senoy, Sansenoy, and Semangeloff to tell her to come back. *Lilith* was enraged. She replied that not only would she never return to domestic life, but she would henceforth attempt to take the souls of human infants away. However, she finally agreed that if confronted with an amulet that bears the names of the three angels and the words "Out Lilith," she would not do any harm. As Adam and Eve propagated the human race, *Lilith*'s fame spread, as did the recitation of the charm against her.

Lilith became the antagonist of so many tales that she appears under various names, like Agrat bat Mahalat, who rules 180,000 malicious spirits, and who enjoys tempting single Talmudic scholars with her luxuriant long shining black hair; she slips under their sheets and provokes relentlessly erotic dreams and nocturnal emissions. In fact, perhaps one of the best ways to catch a glimpse of *Lilith* is to practice asceticism and scholarship in solitude for a while.

Lilith reportedly wound up marrying Asmodeus (the demon of Wrath and Lust) around the thirteenth century; a number of tales from the Middle Ages show them as a couple. She also appears as the companion of an evil spirit named *Sammael*, an alternative name for both Satan and Asmodeus; they are seen in the dark as two black dogs roaming the empty streets.

In one famous tale *Lilith* was sent to tempt King Solomon as he studied Torah. As soon as she manifested, the Hebrew letters flew up mysteriously from the pages. This immediately alerted the king to danger. When he looked up from the Book he saw a strikingly beautiful dark-haired woman in his room. Half tempted, but very suspicious, since none of the doors to his room were open, he grabbed the woman by the arm and dragged her over to a mirror. She had no reflection. With her illusory appearance stripped away, she vanished at once. The Hebrew letters returned to the Book. King Solomon returned to his studies.

DISPELLING & DISARMING TECHNIQUES

In an ancient Aramaic charm used against *Lilith*, a writ of divorce is served on her, and she is commanded to go forth stripped. The stripping of this demoness somehow erases her power, as when one strips an officer of his stripes or strips someone of their "dignity." Perhaps removing her illusory garb shows her for what she is in the same way as King Solomon did by dragging her to a mirror. Mirrors are excellent household diagnostic tools because no demon has a reflection, but tricking a spirit into standing in front of a mirror is difficult because they all know they have no bodies. For the nursery, the amulet inscribed with the names of angels, Senoy, Sansenoy, and Semangeloff has been used effectively for a long time.

CHANGELINGS
Great Britain

Changelings are fairies, often described as pale, big-headed, mentally retarded, or deformed human babies. In actuality they are not human at all. In order for fairies to successfully steal human babies (as they often do) and take them down to the subterranean Fairyland, they must leave in the crib either carved wooden substitutes or elderly, feeble, washed-up fairies who pretend to be human infants. Especially at risk of being stolen are those babies not yet named or baptized, and all those left alone and unguarded.

As they grow older, *Changelings* are notorious for playing pranks, such as stealing milk, or playing music that forces people to dance against their will, and breaking valuable household objects. It is difficult to tell if one's own baby is a *Changeling*, but in Hungary, England, and parts of Africa, children born with teeth are suspected. If it's been behaving like a *Changeling* — breaking things, being quite naughty, or speaking in a precocious manner — a parent can try to trick it into disclosing its identity.

LORE

A woman who suspected her child might be a *Changeling* was so upset she didn't know what to do. She just knew that the weird-looking thing in her house was not her own sweet babe. She told her neighbor about her suspicions and the neighbor gave her some advice. She sat the baby down in a chair in the kitchen, and then she carefully boiled some water and then threw in eggshells, discarding the eggs. The *Changeling* suddenly asked: "What are you brewing?" Of course, the spoken words themselves were advanced enough to send a chill through the mother. "I'm brewing eggshells!" she replied calmly as she could. "Oh!" the *Changeling* exclaimed, "In the fifteen hundred years that I have been alive, I have never seen anyone brew eggshells before!" When the mother then turned to destroy the now proven supernatural creature, she found instead her own innocent babe asleep in its place.

In some versions of this tale (told in France, Germany, and Japan) the *Changeling* simply bursts into laughter at the eggshell boil, instantly vanishing, leaving the human child in its stead. Unfortunately, getting rid of the *Changeling* often resulted in abusive practice. At times mothers were advised to whip the *Changeling* until a fairy appeared who would say, "Do not beat it, I've done your child no harm," and then shamefacedly return the real baby and take her own back. Many suspect children were put onto red hot shovels, or beaten, all in an attempt to force the "fairy" to return the "real child."

DISPELLING & DISARMING TECHNIQUES

To guard a baby against fairies in the Scottish Highlands, whisky mixed with earth was fed to the baby as its first food. Metal was also used to ward off fairies, such as hanging iron crosses, scissors, and knives around the crib, pins stuck in the infant's clothing, or laying the father's trousers across the cradle, or surrounding it with a circle of fire. Salt on the head or sprinkled around the room was also believed effective. Some placed the cradle in the center of the floor. In northern Scotland a custom was to wave the Bible three times over the child to represent the Holy Trinity. In addition, the sign of the cross was drawn on the floor of the nursery.

In Ireland a charm was made from old horseshoe nails, hen excrement, and salt that scared away the *Changeling* and brought the human baby back. Worldwide Christian *Changeling* prevention is baptism.

PAZUZU
Babylonia

Pazuzu is a hybrid creature, with the feet of an eagle, the paws of a lion, the head of a dog, the tail of a scorpion, and four wings. Half his head is skinless and the skull is exposed. He has a deathlike grimace. *Pazuzu,* or rather the image of him, would be found perched in the window of any ancient home, facing outward.

The powerful demon is said to have embodied a dread pestilence believed to have been carried by the southwest wind, even the deadly wind itself that swept over the Arabian desert, a scorchingly hot and withering wind — a killing wind. The presence of such an apotropaic image as *Pazuzu* in the window of a home is clearly meant to ward off others of his own kind. Some idea of the incredible power of these ancient demons can be heard in the following conjuration against them, which the Guide recommends saying aloud for full effect:

They are seven! They are seven!
In the depths of the Ocean, they are seven!
In the heights of the heavens, they are seven.
They come from the Ocean depths, from the hidden retreat.
They are neither male nor female.
They have no spouse. They do not produce children.
They are strangers to benevolence,
They listen neither to prayers nor wishes.
Vermin come forth from the mountain,
enemies of the god Hea,
They are agents of vengeance of the gods,
raising up difficulties, obtaining power by violence.
The enemies! The enemies!
They are seven! They are seven. They are twice seven.
Spirit of the heavens, may they be conjured.
Spirit of the earth, may they be conjured!

The demons are dreaded, utterly impervious to pity, benevolence, and so alien as not to have any sympathetic connection with human beings. The conjuration is not specifically addressed to one or another demon, because one never knew which of the demonic spirits might be the agent of the disaster. *Pazuzu*, grotesque as he is, was only one of a terrible crowd of like spirits who bore disease to households in ancient times. He was powerful enough to be employed to avert others.

LORE

Pazuzu has come down to contemporary lore via Hollywood, which brought him into the body of a child in *The Exorcist*. He was not seen and had only a small speaking role, but it was memorable. During an exorcism, the camera closed in on the face of the child, and the baritone voiceover of *Pazuzu* startlingly came from her mouth, answering the exorcist's request, "Tell us who you are." He replied, "Pazuzu."

This was actually quite odd, as prior to this role he was known only for pestilence, never for possession.

DISPELLING & DISARMING TECHNIQUES

The use of terrifying demonic images at the door and in the window to avert species is used to this day in China, where mirrors on the roof are used to deflect evil spirits who try to perch there. The idea is that when demons approach and see their own image, they will be so repulsed or terrified by it, they'll fly elsewhere. In this tradition, spirits can see their own reflections. In Jewish folk tradition a warding-off technique is to write on the door of the house, "So-and-so is not at home." In Nepal a technique is to get up very early in the morning, knock on somebody's door, and when they say, "Who's there?" reply, "Headache with fever," and quickly run away, thus transferring illness to another household. Presumably they can try the same transference the next morning.

ISITWALANGCENGCE
South Africa

Isitwalangcengce (Basket Bearer), a Zulu spirit, is much larger than most domicile species. He resembles a hyena, but has an extremely wide head, shaped rather like a basket. The Basket Bearer lurks about near the house waiting for women and children to return from the market with meat. Typically, the *Isitwalangcengce* snatches the meat and hurls the child into his basket-shaped head for a later meal. It is believed that the Basket Bearer enjoys human brain. He arrives at this delicacy much like a seagull: he throws his victims onto rocks to break the skull open, and leaves the other body parts behind.

LORE

Once a man outwitted a Basket Bearer by gathering small sticks from trees as he was being carried away in the basket. Slowly, passing trees and quietly snapping off twigs as he went by, the man piled wood in the basket until the load seemed heavy enough to substitute for his own body so the Basket Bearer would not notice his absence. Then he reached up to a tree, held on to a limb, and slipped out of the basket. *Isitwalangcengce* kept going, unaware that he was carrying mere wood, assuming that the load was the man himself. When the Basket Bearer arrived at the rocks and dumped out his contents, he found no man, just a bundle of wood.

The Basket Bearer was enraged, and rushed back to the man's village to retrieve his meal. Unable to find the man, he grabbed a young girl. However, the man who had escaped had told the entire village how he had managed to outsmart the demon as soon as he returned. The girl had listened carefully and she knew what to do. The demon fell for the same trick, and presumably moved on to easier hunting ground.

DISARMING & DISPELLING TECHNIQUES

As the tale shows, for all their ferocity, many demonic species can be easily outwitted by *Homo sapiens*, and often be overcome entirely by tricks that wouldn't fool a human child. If caught by an *Isitwalangcengce*, there is no known amulet to protect any human. One must rely on wits alone while they are still available.

LIDERC
Hungary

The *Liderc* appears in three striking variations: a flickering light, a demonic household helper, or an incubus. In its ignis fatuus form it is a *Lidercfeny,* which is often a death portent seen shining mysteriously just over the roof of the household that will be struck. The household helper *Liderc,* called a *Mitmitke,* appears as a featherless chicken. It may arrive on its own or be hatched from an egg incubated under the armpit. It carries out tasks for its master. Unfortunately, it carries out tasks too quickly and efficiently and always wants more to do, until eventually it incessantly begs its master for new chores. This variety of *Liderc,* who can shape-shift to human form, soon becomes a household pest. If not given tasks, it will eventually destroy its owner.

The third variety of *Liderc* is the prevalent incubus species that appears when a lover is absent for too long. This opportunistic demon lover enters the house via the chimney as a flame (connecting it with the flickering light type). He literally loves his victim to death, returning night after night until, after excessive copulation (demonic energy and stamina being traits of both the obsessive household *Liderc* and the incubus), the human lover wastes away to nothing and dies.

This variety of *Liderc* can manifest as a fiery person, or flame, or even a star, rather like the Bulgarian Zmej. It appears in a shining sky carriage and makes stops to cohabit with mortal women who afterward also often waste away.

LORE

Once there was a young widow who wept constantly for her departed husband, grieving her loss, until one night, a *Liderc* arrived in the form of a star. When it began landing directly above her house, and everybody in town saw the star vanish every night, rumors began that she was with a *Liderc.* Her father warned her that if this gossip was true her visitor was an unclean spirit, and she would waste away. At first she denied that she had a lover, but her father said she was looking paler and paler every day, and when she finally admitted it, her father insisted that she at least look to see if one of her visitor's legs resembled that of a goose. "If so," he said, "hide the boot he wears on his other leg." She looked, as her father told her, and lo and behold, her lover had the leg of a goose. So she hid his boot. This so infuriated the *Liderc* he turned into flame and never returned. The widow was sick for a very long time afterward, but she finally recovered.

Another tale of the *Liderc* lover is about a young wife whose husband has left for the army. She was miserable until one night, without so much as a door opening, her "husband" appeared to comfort her. These visitations continued for a while, until one day the young wife confided in a neighbor that her husband visited her regularly, appearing in uniform. The neighbor told her it was impossible that this visitor was her husband and that he might be an unclean spirit. The neighbor was a wise woman and advised the wife to scatter ashes at the door and examine her visitor's footprints the morning after. That was how she discovered his one goose foot just in time, for she too had begun to wither away.

DISPELLING & DISARMING TECHNIQUES

To stop a *Liderc* lover from entering via the bedroom door, one can tie a door handle with a cord used to hold up trousers. This makes it impossible for him to enter. If he has already arrived, hiding his boot and thus revealing his origins will stop him from returning. The last strategy (to employ when the *mit-mitke* shape-shifts to human form) is to follow the *Liderc* to church, and expose him to the entire village by looking at him in a significant and knowing way. This will blow his cover and he'll vanish immediately to save face. The household-helper *Liderc* cannot be gotten rid of, only kept busy. But one can give it impossible tasks — like bringing home sand or water in a sieve. The only other way is to stuff the creature into a hole in a tree trunk. There are no means to avert the portent *Liderc*.

AL
Armenia

The *Al* is a species of terrifying half-human, half-animal creature with brass fingernails, long snakelike hair, a fiery single eye, iron teeth, and the tusks of a wild boar. The *Al* carries iron scissors. Whenever it wears a pointed hat covered with small bells, it becomes completely invisible. *Als* live in damp places like the stable or sandy wet areas on the road or unclean corners of the house. But their awful deeds are done in the nursery.

Als (perhaps from the Babylonian *alu,* a family of evil spirits shaped like a black dogs) began as disease-carrying demons and evolved into a gruesome specialty. They attack pregnant women, strangling them and their unborn children and pulling out their livers. They also attack and steal newborns up to seven months of age, and are said to cause miscarriage as well.

LORE

In the beginning God gave Adam an *Al* for a companion but the *Al*, made of fire, was not compatible with Adam, made of dust. Then God created Eve. This infuriated the envious *Al*, who has been out to destroy women ever since.

In Christian legend, St. Peter encountered a grotesque being with iron teeth and tusks sitting on the roadside in a sandy wet place, and asked him to identify himself. The creature replied: "Call me *Al*." He went on to describe his activities. "I strangle the mother in childbirth and pull out her liver. I steal the unborn infant and carry it to our demon-king."

DISARMING & DISPELLING TECHNIQUES

To keep the *Als* away, one must put many iron utensils, pots, knives, and other objects all around one's body. When pregnant, a woman must sleep with a piece of iron under her pillow — a sword or knife will do. A pin may help. In some lore sticking a pin in the blouse of an *Al* will make it a slave. There are also special prayers that can be uttered during childbirth to discourage an *Al* from attacking the liver or a newborn.

FOX FAIRY

China

The *Fox Fairy* (*huli jing*) is considered highly dangerous and held in awe. It was believed to be the *shen* (spirit) of the dead and has been seen rising from graves. The *Fox Fairy* often shape-shifts into a tempting, wicked young woman, or an old man or scholar. In fact, the female *Fox Fairy* has an affinity for scholars (as they are reputedly unusually virtuous) and will attempt to seduce them whenever possible. The *Fox Fairy* is after the vital essence of its human lover during orgasm, and will steal it away. Lovers eventually become consumptive and waste away to nothing. The *Fox Fairy* moves on.

The *Fox Fairy* can also shape-shift into the semblance of a person long dead, and as that person haunt houses and terrify mortals. It has also been known to appear in the guise of somebody who actually lives far away. It is seen as a clever trickster, a cunning survivor, and a deadly power. Most notably, it can possess its human prey out of sheer malevolence. Generations of madness in one family is thought to be the result of having injured a *Fox Fairy* (in one of its transformations) long ago.

Invisible by daylight, the *Fox Fairy* can be seen at night around the home in various forms. It is often sighted prowling the roof of the house, and is offered delicacies and incense. The *Fox Fairy* is always treated with great respect, if not actually worshiped outright. It can transport people through the air and empower its worshipers with the ability to enter houses through walls and closed windows as it is able to do.

LORE

One morning a young man was carrying a load of vegetables across a field with several companions. All of a sudden he seemed struck by some force that froze him in midstep. He dropped his baskets, and at once began to rave like a madman. Soon the whole village was talking about the incident. The young man claimed to be possessed by a *Fox Fairy*. When a person is possessed by a *huli jing* he not only becomes a raving maniac, he gains the power to heal. This young man was suddenly able to cure diseases. People came from all over, begging to be cured. Word of his powers spread and people came from afar. He grew so wealthy that he erected a beautiful shrine to the *Fox Fairy*.

Once there was a wealthy man living in northern China. He had a large, ever-growing pile of straw in his yard that was left untouched by his servants, who only added more fresh straw as it was believed to be the abode of the *Fox Fairy*. One day the spirit, in the shape of an old man, came to the master of the house and invited him into the straw pile for a drink. The man at first refused, but when he finally consented and went through the hole in the straw, he was astonished to find that in the simple straw there were elaborate rooms, furnished luxuriously. The two sat down to drink tea and wine, and later, when the rich man left, he turned to say farewell only to find that all the furnishings had vanished.

The *Fox Fairy*, up to mischief, continued to visit his neighbor in the old man guise and would leave suddenly for "other engagements." Burning with curiosity, the rich man asked him where he went each night and the demon answered that at night he usually visited friends and asked if his neighbor would like to join him. After declining at first, the rich man decided to go. That night they flew through the air like a gust of wind and arrived at an inn. There the "old man" led his victim to the gallery above a large and crowded room, and went himself to fetch food from the banquet table below to eat in the quiet gallery. When the rich man spotted some fruit on a table below, he asked for some. The *Fox Fairy* said, "I cannot get them for I cannot go anywhere near that man who's standing near the fruit, as he is a very good and upright man."

The rich man suddenly realized that he might not be an upright man since he consorted with a *Fox Fairy*, and he determined not to involve himself with such spirits any longer. Just as that thought crossed his mind, he seemed to fall from the gallery and crashed into the party beneath. The guests at the banquet were astonished to see him, especially because there was no gallery above, only a wooden rafter. At first they thought him a malevolent spirit, but when he explained how he had arrived, they all recognized it was *Fox Fairy* mischief. They gave him money to return to his home, which turned out to be more than a thousand *li* away.

DISARMING & DISPELLING TECHNIQUES

Burning paper charms against the *Fox Fairy*, and then putting the ashes into tea and drinking it, may help. It is most important never to harm the creature. When in female form, plying it with wine until it's drunk will make it revert to its true shape, and once discovered it will vanish. If, in its fox form, the tail can be somehow cut off (because the tail is the source of its power), it will leave the premises and never return.

MARE
Norway

The Norwegian *Mare* is a female shape shifter who visits her sleeping victims (usually men) and torments them while they sleep. The *Mare* can fit herself through a keyhole in a door, a crack in a wall, or blow through an open window. She can be beautiful or ugly, a dwarf or a giant. Most often, though, she takes the form of an animal, most commonly a horse. When she has gotten into her victim's bedroom, she mounts their chest, causing pains, tightness, troubled breathing, and horrible dreams. In Germany she is the *Mahr*, in Danish, *Mare*, in America the *nightmare* is her descendent.

By day, the *Mare* appears as a normal human woman. She is overcome by a late-night urge. At night, in prowl mode, she roams around until she finds a victim. But after sunrise she turns into somebody's mother, wife, or a shopkeeper and is indistinguishable from real humans. If she cannot find a human victim, sometimes a *Mare* will ride an animal instead. Horses in their stalls wake up doused in their own sweat and cows are shaky when being milked and will give sour milk.

LORE
Once there was a farmer's son who was tormented nightly by a *Mare*. One evening he asked a friend for help. Together they closed all the holes in his room except one, through which the *Mare* could slip in. As soon as the friend saw anything out of the ordinary he was to plug up that hole as well. He did this, and in the morning the farmer's son found a beautiful girl in his bed. She did not know where she had come from, nor did he, but he was enchanted. The two were married and had many children. One day he showed her the hole through which she had slipped into his room. She slipped out of it and was never seen again.

DISARMING & DISPELLING TECHNIQUES
To protect oneself against the *Mare*, one should never sleep with an open mouth. It is believed that if a *Mare* can

count a person's teeth, he will surely die. When leaving shoes by the bedside, the toes should be pointed away from the bed, lest they be used as a sort of trail to the sleeper. A horseshoe over the bed is a helpful deterrent, as is anything made of iron or steel near the bedside or under the pillow. Lighted candles around the bed also keep the *Mare* away. Prayers often work, as does reciting this ditty:

> *Mare, Mare, Mare hear!*
> *Are you now inside of here?*
> *Do you remember the blow on the nose*
> *that Sigurd Sigmundarson gave you, my dear?*
> *If you're inside then out you'll go,*
> *bearing rocks and stones,*
> *and everything within here!*

To protect livestock from the *Mare*, metal hung around the barn, or spruce and fir twigs, will keep the *Mare* away. A metal bell around the animal's neck may avert the demon.

KITCHEN FAIRIES
China

Kitchen Fairies are a large, industrious, invisible population, and since they cast no shadows they can be accounted for only by the unusual amount of work they accomplish for their owners. They obsessively sweep and dust, so it is very obvious whose house is inhabited and whose is not.

Some people want *Kitchen Fairies.* They can be caught at any crossroads by burying two different kinds of animals, digging them up later, and putting their remains in an incense burner. One won't see the *Fairies,* but the house will be instantly cleaner.

Two problems exist. First, for their very hard work *Kitchen Fairies* expect a year-end bonus: one human to eat. To avert having to provide this fare, one simply explains to the invisible group that they have broken pottery and owe the owner, so they will have to wait a year for their meal. This postponement works for years, because they are not bright.

The second, and far more serious, problem is getting rid of them if one wants to do so. The only way to do it is to marry them off in the following manner: Prepare packets of ash from incense and silver, which embody the spirits themselves, and place them randomly on the road. A person unfamiliar with the custom will eventually pick up the silver and find himself with a new presence in his home.

LORE

Once a poor man saw a packet of silver lying on the road and knew it was a *Kitchen Fairy,* but he couldn't resist the money, so he grabbed it and went to the river (because like many other demons these can't cross water). The *Fairy* had leaped on his hat, so he threw the hat into the water and left with the silver. He grew rich. Meanwhile the hat was found by a passerby and hung to dry on a tree branch. The tree withered. Much later the rich man went to sit near that very tree, and when asked why the tree was so withered, he laughingly told the old story of the *Kitchen Fairy,* the hat, and the silver.

Unfortunately the spirit was still there, invisible, and over-heard the tale. Infuriated, it jumped on the man and ate his soul. The man withered and died.

DISARMING & DISPELLING TECHNIQUES

Because *Kitchen Fairies* are said to live in kitchen pots, it is a custom to leave a small amount of water in each to discourage them from setting up house. The silver packet road dispersion is another last resort but, as in the tale, can lead to trouble.

FAIR LADY
Hungary

The *Fair Lady* is one of the malevolent fairies so powerful as to be seen in many shapes: a beautiful woman, sometimes naked; a horse; a long-haired woman in a white dress looking like a common housewife. She never travels far from home. She is often seen under the eaves of the house — always a dangerous place — and other times she'll show up in the stable. She weaves dangerous spells that can leave a person struck dumb or worse.

The *Fair Lady* is said to have a "platter" of her own, embodied by a common household object, like a spoon, a plate, linens, or the bed. The object is secretly under her spell. The expression "Stepping into the platter of the Fair Lady" means to fall under the spell of the spirit. Sometimes water dripping from the eaves of a house forms a puddle that can become her platter; if a person takes one step into the puddle he becomes hers. The seat under the eaves is especially dangerous at noon. The noon presence of the *Fair Lady* is a highly unusual characteristic as most demons are only out at night (with the rare exception of demons thought to cause sunstroke in places like Polynesia).

Sighting the *Fair Lady* is a portent of grave trouble. She dances in storms, kidnaps children, and has been seen dancing men to their deaths. Her song is her lure. *Fair Ladies* have been spotted flying through the air in groups, singing bewitching songs. If they are heard by a mortal man, he may be inspired to reckless and fatal acts, for instance, plunging into the lake to his death.

LORE

Once there was a young man who one morning put on a new pair of sandals that he had never seen before. He went out walking and found himself singing a new tune. Before long, there appeared three beautiful women beckoning him to join them in a dance. Naturally, he was delighted to do as they asked, and it wasn't until many hours later that a neighbor passed by and saw him twirling around by himself in a field.

"For the love of God," shouted the neighbor, "what are you doing!"

At the word "God," the young man fell down dumbstruck. The neighbor ran over and looked at the poor young man lying there. He saw that the new sandals were worn away and the soles of his feet were already quite bloody. It wasn't until much later that the lad recovered from the incident that he'd brought on himself by donning enchanted sandals and thus stepping into the platter of the *Fair Lady*.

DISARMING & DISPELLING TECHNIQUES

Eaves must be avoided. The place under the eaves has been a notable hangout for malevolent spirits since ancient times. Any household item that seems oddly attractive, new, or in the wrong place should be left untouched. Prayer, crossing oneself, carrying a Bible, wearing mistletoe around the neck, all are said to be effective repellents. Like other fairies, the *Fair Lady* is also repelled by church bells, crowds, and human laughter.

NISSE
Norway

The *Nisse* is a species of fairy so minute that he can hide anywhere, or vanish altogether. He has a gray or white beard, simple gray clothing, and a pointed red hat. His body is covered in thick wooly hair. He has an exceptionally large lower lip and no thumbs. He is considered rather ugly.

The *Nisse*, like many household fairies, can be a very helpful friend or a destructive enemy. He is said to live in the barn, and sleep in the stalls. The *Nisse* is powerfully strong and seems to enjoy hard work. He is solitary and labors long and finishes his tasks quickly. A *Nisse* needs to be fed only every Thursday and on Christmas Eve. But they are nasty if crossed. The *Nisse*, like many fairies, spends his free time on pranks. He trips people, shoves them down the stairs, and releases animals from their pens at night. But if treated with the respect he demands, he can be a good and loyal if occasionally impish worker. He takes one-third of the crop as wages.

The *Nisse* will not tolerate mistreatment of the animals in his charge, and humans who disregard the welfare of their livestock often receive harsh thrashings. The *Nisse* is also known for stealing hay and grain from other farms to feed the animals in his care. During these nightly raids, if the fairy happens to meet another of his species, a kind of "inter-*Nissene*" warfare will break out. Grain has been seen flying around the air wildly on such occasions, by itself.

LORE

There was a *Nisse* who gave all his attention to his favorite black horse. This horse grew fatter and sleeker than the other horses and its coat was better groomed. The farmer grew angry at the stable boy and accused him of neglecting all the horses but one. "That's not me," said the boy. "That's the *Nisse!*"

That evening, after the horses had been fed, the farmer went down to the barn to see for himself. Indeed, the black horse had been fed extra hay, so the farmer angrily took some of it and threw it to the side, whereupon he got a quick, powerful blow to the head that knocked him to the ground. No visible being was around! After that, the horse was allowed to eat all that he received, and the farmer never complained again.

Once a girl was on her way to feed the family *Nisse*, and instead sat down to eat the good sweet porridge herself. When at last she brought his offering, he noticed she'd replaced the good food with plain porridge and sour milk, served up in a pig's trough. The invisible *Nisse* grabbed the girl and began to dance with her. He danced faster and faster throughout the night until she was gasping for air. While dancing, he sang: "If the Nisse's porridge you did steal, the Nisse will dance until you reel!" The girl nearly died by morning.

DISARMING & DISPELLING TECHNIQUES

The only sure way to get rid of a *Nisse* is to give him a new set of clothes. He will leave immediately. Many people have moved their homes or burned down their farms hoping to escape from the family *Nisse*, only to find it perched in the back of their wagons with all of their other possessions, moving with the human family to their next home.

PSYCHE

"The mind is its own place, and in itself
Can make a Heav'n of Hell, a Hell of Heav'n,"
says Satan. He later realizes:
"Which way I flie is Hell; my self am Hell."
— JOHN MILTON, *PARADISE LOST*

The terrain of Psyche is understood differently by various traditions to be Soul, Self, Mind, collective unconscious. For the purposes of the Guide, it is the abode of those species who actually inhabit the human being and use that living person as an instrument of their will. The indwelling demons are never experienced by an outsider as they are by their host or hostess. Although these "hallucinations" or subjective realities remain concealed, what does give them away are the startling outward manifestations of their presence as expressed by their human puppets. They do not leave voluntarily, so it is always necessary to get outside help when inhabited. Much of the lore of the Psyche centers on methods and techniques of transformation, exorcism, and healing.

Some humans seek the state of being possessed for reasons of their own. There is the shaman, witch, or magician who intentionally performs a rite or dons a mask or animal hide to become an Other, and allow his corporeal self to be taken over and imbued by a spirit. In this case the host is a volunteer. However, an average housewife or student who is simply performing routine tasks when subsumed by a dybbuk or a Fox Spirit is a victim. Since most people do not want to become the abode of a demon, the majority of tales involve the plight of the helpless host and the ways the unwanted tenants were evicted.

An important Psyche species is the raging indwelling animal — an ordinary human can move mentally one small step to become his/her "animal" nature, as in the Werewolf or Fox transformations. Other afflicted people were believed to be inhabited by "unclean spirits" long before modern explanations for mental illness, hysteria, epilepsy, and schizophrenia. Treatments to drive out the demons were usually conducted with no concern for the host and addressed only the spirit. The patient (if he survived) later had no recollection of his or her possessed state. Then there are those indwelling demons who cause notice when some proclivity of the human they inhabit becomes grotesquely enlarged: when a person lives only to eat or profit or lust, he may be infected with one of the Seven Deadly Sins.

In all cases, "naming" the demon seems to reduce and disempower it. Modern explanations of the phenomena resulted in new names. The Id and the Shadow, included here with their methods of depossession, are redefined demonic species. The Buddhist Mara represents the demon both as an interior obstacle and potential teacher. A transformative approach to the Tibetan Buddhist Yama (Death) illustrates a radically different approach to the field. This leads to the ultimate Quantum Daimon as a species for the new millennium. It is in Psyche that the reader may find some personal demons. Everybody houses some.

THINGS TO KNOW ABOUT POSSESSION

Before the eighteenth-century Age of Enlightenment in the West, many individuals and groups were routinely considered to be affected by "demonical possession." This was described as a mental state wherein the individual was not responsible for his actions or words. The victim displayed hysterical symptoms and convulsive writhing that resembled epilepsy, as if a violent struggle were raging within. The face would appear contorted, the body out of control, and there would be an accompanying radical change of vocal timbre: the new and demonic voice was usually deep, gruff, and weird. Often, it spoke languages unknown to its human host.

The onset of dramatic symptoms was sudden, although there is a suggestion of preexisting states of melancholy in cases of the afflicted. The definite signs were a new shrinking away in horror from religious relics or icons; an ability to speak foreign languages; lewd behavior presumably unknown to the host body; supernatural strength; cursing, blasphemous, and lewd speech; animalistic movement; barking like a dog or fox or bleating like a sheep; and afterward, if the exorcism was successful, no memory whatsoever of the episode by the individual.

To return the possessed to his or her natural state, official rites of demonic exorcism were held by professionals. Since the possession species is worldwide, they continue to be seen frequently in various traditions, and many of the symptoms seem similar throughout the world. The cures or rites are usually in the hands of professionals, but they vary greatly. In India various mantras are uttered and incense is used, in China certain written charms are pasted on the windows and other incantations are burned. Even Josephus, the Jewish historian, in the first century C.E., wrote about a "magic root" that was commonly used among the various practices employed to return the victim to his former self.

In most rites it was of primary importance to "name" the indwelling spirit and then address it directly by name and ask that it leave. In the Catholic Church an official method includes specific wording: "I adjure thee evil spirit in the name of the Lord." This appeal to the specific demonic spirit to leave in the name of Jesus or of various saints was apparently effective. However, when the demon was addressed in this manner its immediate response was spectacular. All hell would break loose. The inhabited person would writhe, vomit (sometimes spitting out strange objects such as glass, nails, animal hair, insects), and hurl himself/herself around the room, all the while screaming abusively at the exorcist in a gruff, unnatural, hideous voice.

Risks of exorcism were possible contagion — the "unclean spirit" might move into the body of the priest. Also, the inhabited would sometimes die before the demon was finished struggling. To make matters worse, it seemed that over a few centuries in the West, entire convents or communities were infested. There were epidemics of possession all over Europe. Many of these involved witchcraft and the accusation and torture of so-called witches — all of which are outside the Guide's concern. The *Compendium Maleficarum*, compiled in 1608 by Brother Francesco Maria Guazzo, lists fifty ways in which one can tell if the possession is the real thing. Among these notable symptoms are: if the possessed feel as if ants were crawling under their skin; if the body is stirred by palpitations in the afflicted area; if the voice heard inside the head is saying things they don't understand; or if the priest's hand upon their head feels like ice.

Many, but not all, of the indwelling demons who were thought to cause these ravings and crises seem to have disappeared or perhaps shape-shifted and have been identified by other names. In some cases the symptoms are now attributed to various mental illnesses. The following lore is spun from the cosmic battles played out in interior habitats. As with other quellings, the focus is on the end of the story, and what is not always revealed is how or why the demon entered the Psyche.

WHO'S WHO IN THE PSYCHE

GERASENE DEMON	Ancient Palestine (Jordan)
WEREWOLF	Global
LOUP GAROU	North America
LEYAK	Bali
DYBBUK	(Judaism)
KITSUNE-TSUKI	Japan
MARA	(Buddhism)
YEZER HA-RA	(Judaism)
SEVEN DEADLY SINS	(Christian West)
MR. HYDE	(Robert Louis Stevenson)
ID	(Freud)
SHADOW	(Jung)
YAMANTAKA	(Tibetan Buddhism)
QUANTUM DAIMON	(Guide)

See also:

WINDIGO in Mountain

MARE in Domicile

FOX FAIRY in Domicile

MADAME WHITE in Water

GERASENE DEMON
Ancient Palestine — Jordan

The Gerasene Demon possession is described in both Luke 8 and Mark 5, and creates the model for the practice of "casting out unclean spirits" in all later Western Christian cases. The host of the possession was a Gerasene man who for some time had not worn any clothing or lived in a house, and when attacked by the possessing "devils" wandered about, living mostly amid the tombs. In a possessed state, he was often restrained by members of his community and bound by chains and fetters, from which he always broke loose and escaped into the wilderness. Every night he howled and gashed himself with stones, and nobody was strong enough to control him, for he seemed to have superhuman powers.

LORE

When Jesus and his disciples arrived at the shore of the Gerasenes, opposite Galilee, a strange wild man fell at Jesus' feet and simultaneously the spirit within the man shouted imploringly: "What do you want of me, Jesus! Do not torture me!" Luke reports that Jesus had been asking the unclean spirit to leave the man when this outburst occurred. And Mark reports that Jesus had said: "Come out of the man, unclean spirit." The indwelling creature was apparently terrified at the sight of Jesus. Then Jesus addressed it: "What is your name?" he asked firmly.

"Legion," replied the invisible devil(s) via the mouth of the man. "For we are many." The voice then pleaded that the unclean spirits be allowed to enter a herd of pigs nearby rather than be sent to the "abyss." Jesus gave permission for them to exit the man and enter the swine. What followed this command was an immediate dash of two thousand pigs across the field. They charged in a pack off the neighboring cliff into the water and drowned. The swineherds ran off and told everybody what they had just witnessed.

Meanwhile the wild man was entirely cured. He was recovered, dressed normally, and sitting calmly at Jesus' feet when the community arrived, shocked by the whole event. The "powers" by which Jesus was able to effect this cure were suspect. Some believed that such powers had been gained traditionally in the past by conjurers who had made a pact with evil spirits like Satan and Beelzebub. (This issue is discussed at length in surrounding chapters of the Gospels.) In this case, because of the sensational events, the ambivalence toward miracles, and the loss of herds of swine, the Gerasenes were alarmed and asked Jesus to leave, and to take his disciples with him. The cured man asked to go with them, but he was told instead to go back to his home and tell the people what "the Lord in his mercy has done for you."

DISARMING & DISPELLING TECHNIQUES

Prayer is the effective technique utilized. The source of dispelling power is attributed to the Holy Spirit, counter to the "envious" accusations that Jesus' power to "cast out devils" is connected to Satanic sources. In the Book of Mark, shortly after the incident with the Gerasenes, there is a moment when Jesus asks the unclean spirits to depart the body of an epileptic boy. His disciples ask him why they were unable to cast it out. Jesus replies: "This is the kind that can only be driven out by prayer."

There is mortal danger to both the victim and the healer as they stand together in the force field of unimaginable powers. Just as the *Gerasene Demon* was sent into the swine, cases exist where the spirit takes up new lodging in the healer. Therefore the exorcist, shaman, holy man, or healer must be impervious (by means of supernatural aid or powers) to the possession species.

As soon as the *Gerasene Demon* is addressed and forced to reveal its name, it is reduced and bound. It is no longer an anonymous ubiquitous unimaginable supernatural force. Like the Djinn or spirit tricked into a bottle, "naming" is a controlling act that encompasses and contains the force and puts the creature under the command of the namer.

WEREWOLF
Global

The *Werewolf* is the most universal form of animal possession — although the wer(man)-tiger and other fierce prowling animal possession exists — and is a human transformed into a wolf. One common belief is that the person who wants to be a *Werewolf* must climb into a wolfskin. During the night he hunts as a wolf, during the day he rests and hides his skin. While wolves usually travel in packs, the *Werewolf* is a loner. Unlike a normal wolf who avoids humans, the *Werewolf* will attack any human he comes across. Pointed ears, hair on palms, large claws, paws, eyebrows that are connected over the bridge of the nose, or hair between the shoulder blades are common *Werewolf* features. As one can see from the depiction, they are not seen as entirely wolf. Robert Burton, in *The Anatomy of Melancholy*, describes the affliction as

Lycanthropia, wolf-madness, when "men run howling about graves and fields at night and will not be persuaded but that they are wolves." He reports that they usually have hollow eyes and dry, pale, and scabby legs.

The best time for the transformation is said to be during the full moon. Wearing a wolfskin, drinking water from the puddle of a wolf's footprint, or the ingestion of magic potions are the principal means of becoming a *Werewolf*. Some people transform themselves by choice, others are transformed into *Werewolves* because of spells or hides that have been placed on them. Sometimes the transformation happens suddenly, or erratically, with no explanation, much to the dismay of the victim, who finds himself suddenly a *Werewolf* for short periods at a time. Often those who do not wish to become a *Werewolf* have time to warn others of their transformation so as to avoid the inevitable.

LORE

Sinfjotli and his uncle Sigmund came across a house set deep in the Norwegian forest. Inside the house slept two enchanted men. Wolfskins hung on the wall above them. The sleeping men had been cursed so that only on every tenth day could they come out of their wolfskin and resume human form. Sigmund and Sinfjotli put the skins on and were instantly transformed into *Werewolves* themselves; that is, they became wolves in physical appearance and spirit, but retained human minds. Together they agreed that they should risk attacking no more than seven men. If they needed help from each other, they agreed to howl, and each went their separate way looking for flesh. But Sinfjotli, despite the agreement, took on eleven men alone, and though he defeated them all, Sigmund was furious. In an instant he pounced on his nephew and tore his windpipe open with one slash of his claws.

He carried the young *Werewolf* to a hut and kept watch over his hurt body. After seeing two weasels fight outside the hut, and watching the victorious weasel place a leaf over the cut windpipe of his victim, Sigmund decided to do the same.

A raven brought him the medicinal leaf, and after Sigmund placed it across the hurt windpipe, Sinfjotli was healed instantly. The two returned to their lair and waited for the time when they could take off their skins. As soon as the moment arrived they tore off the wolfskins and burned them, thus breaking the curse.

Not all *Werewolves* have the same control that these fortunate Norsemen had. An ancient Greek cult that worshiped on Mount Lykaion in Arcadia had a yearly ceremony in which one worshiper would be transformed into a *Werewolf*. In this animal form he was made to roam about for nine years. If during this time he could refrain from eating human flesh he would be changed back into a man. If, however, as a *Werewolf*, he consumed human flesh, he could never return to his human self. In Germany, the transformation was effected by wearing a wolfskin and a belt with a magic buckle. When the buckle broke, the enchantment ended.

A story from Sweden relates the plight of a man who thought he might be a *Werewolf*. Without sharing his suspicions about himself, he asked his wife — if she happened to catch sight of a *Werewolf* — please not to stab it but to hit it with a pitchfork.

That very night she did encounter a *Werewolf*, and she obeyed her husband's request. The *Werewolf* snagged her dress hem in his mouth as he fell. At breakfast the next morning, she happened to notice dress strands in her husband's teeth, and said to him: "I think you are a werewolf." He replied, "Thank you for telling me, for now I am freed!"

The naming cure has many different applications in the case of the *Werewolf* with an equal variety of results. Often, in European lore, after many years of wandering as a *Werewolf*, one can be called by one's human name and suddenly remember one's human self, and thus change back into a former existence. At the other extreme, in Chinese folklore, is a case of a housewife who went out nightly in wolf shape, and then listened to her family discuss the neighborhood *Werewolf* problem; she promptly left the household and was never seen again.

In France, another housewife had less luck. One day a man saw his friend, a hunter, pass by his château, and, waving to him, called out to wish him a good chase. Later, the hunter was attacked by a wolf and attempted to kill the animal but was able only to swipe at it with his knife and sever a paw. He escaped narrowly and, shaken, stopped by his friend's home to tell him about the attack. When he opened his sack to show his friend the huge paw, he was shocked to find instead a lady's hand with a ring on one finger. The friend recognized the ring as his own wife's and went to find her. She was hiding her hand in a bloody kerchief when he came into her chamber, and she was forced to confess. She was arrested and burned to death.

DISARMING & DISPELLING TECHNIQUES

A silver bullet is the only sure way to kill a *Werewolf*, and after it is shot its head must be cut off and burned, the ashes scattered in the wind. If a *Werewolf* is killed in his human shape, he will revert to animal shape at death. But the task is dangerous, for being bitten by a *Werewolf* will turn any human into a *Werewolf*. The sign of the cross will avert attack by a *Werewolf*, and holy water is also effective. A pitchfork can be used to strike a vulnerable spot between the eyebrows and allow time for escape, and special gray stones are said to keep the species at a distance. Voluntary *Werewolves* are able to become human again when a special formula is uttered. However, if the human who knows the formula dies, the *Werewolf* is doomed to remain one.

LOUP GAROU
North America

The *Loup Garou* is a bayou werewolf species that originated in France (the name may have come from a shortened form of *"Loup, gardez-vous,"* which means "Wolf, watch out!"). It is a person transformed, either by a spell cast by another or by choice (which entails rubbing the body with a special kind of grease), into a creature notable for its fiery red eyes, body hair, large claws, long snout, and mean disposition. The *Loup Garou* is seen frequently at special dances in bayou country, in which cavorting in wolf style and acting wild is the common practice. Each *Loup Garou* is said to own a bat the size of an airplane that serve as its transportation. They fly them to other people's homes and drop down the chimney into the bedroom. There they bite the sleeping human victim, who wakes up the next morning as one of them.

DISARMING & DISPELLING TECHNIQUES
The *Loup Garou* is terrified of frogs and will run away if a frog is hurled at it. Like many other demons, the *Loup Garou* can be easily tricked by a simple household colander or sifter hung outside the door. It will become so involved counting holes, it will forget its original mission. It is said that if one can manage to sprinkle the *Loup Garou* with salt, the demon will catch on fire. It will then immediately discard its blazing animal hide like a snakeskin, and resume its human state.

LEYAK
Bali

The *Leyak* is a demonic species akin to one type of werewolf: a human being who intentionally transforms himself or herself by occult arts. At night the *Leyak* can appear as an eerie light or shape-shift to flying monkey or bird. He or she destroys crops, kills people, and is considered the agent of all aberrant, dire events.

While this malevolent spirit flies about like a bad dream, appearing to ordinary people who are out for a midnight walk, the physical body of the human being from which the demon has originated, remains asleep in bed. One would never suspect that the sleeping friend, neighbor, wife, or husband is a *Leyak*. But once in a while during the nightly capers a *Leyak* is destroyed, and then the sleeping human dies instantly without any prior sign of sickness. It is this sudden death that tips off the community to the real identity of the former *Leyak*.

DISARMING & DISPELLING TECHNIQUES

There are no known preventatives or ways that ordinary people can protect themselves from this species. Professionals with amulets must be called.

DYBBUK
Judaism

The *Dybbuk* is described as the spirit of a dead person who enters and takes utter possession of a living person. Spirit possession is quite common in Christianity — being noncorporeal, the species is always wandering and in search of a body, ranging from swine to people. Gregory the Great wrote of a nun who ate a lettuce leaf upon which a demon happened to be invisibly perched. She had not made the sign of the cross before dining, and after the salad was possessed. In Judaism, the cases are less common and were attributed to impersonal Shedim until the *Dybbuk* made its appearance in the sixteenth century. Underlying the *Dybbuk* in Jewish tradition is the idea of the *gilgul,* or transmigrating soul, which can be found in thirteenth-century mystical Jewish ideas. The *Dybbuk,* in exorcism, is always identified as the soul of a specific and recognizable person who has lived.

LORE

The Mayseh Book (The Book of Tales), a collection of folklore published in 1602, describes the first case:

A young man was possessed by the wandering spirit *(gilgul)* of a dead man who drowned at sea. The man's soul had passed into a cow; the cow had gone wild and the owner sold it to a Jew; the Jew was about to slaughter the cow just as the young man passed by; the soul flew into the young man's body. Once settled in its new home, it took over the young man's will, mind, and body. The young man became its puppet. Wise men came to help. They asked, Who are you?, and the *Dybbuk* spoke. He said he was drowned at sea and, since his body was not recovered, his wife was not permitted to remarry and eventually became a prostitute. These events had made him miserable, but he also bore the guilt of having committed adultery when he was alive. His confessions elicited confessions from some of his listeners into whose hearts he could see, thus acting as an agent to rectify their wrongs. He was finally persuaded to depart.

After this, hundreds of tales of the *Dybbuk* housing itself in ordinary women and men began springing up all over Eastern Europe. The *Dybbuk* entries were not necessarily connected to any earlier harm or relationship, just accidents waiting to happen. At times the possession could be traced to some slight breach of ritual or disregard of warnings about unclean spirits. Going into the water (especially the *mikvah*, a ritual bath) was fraught with danger. One could always come out as somebody else. Several demonic women arose from the waters in these stories. The voice, gesture, and behavior of the person-as-*Dybbuk* is always strange enough to alarm intimates, family, and friends. Paradoxically, although all the action takes place within the human host, his or her mind has been erased in the takeover, so all *Dybbuk* tales are told, not by subjects, but by witnesses to the phenomenon.

The Dybbuk, a wonderful Yiddish play by the folklorist S. Anski, is a mystical love story in which the *Dybbuk* is not a wandering spirit but a living scholar who literally dies for the love of a young woman when her father gives her in marriage to another man. On her wedding night, he enters her body, causing her to behave as one possessed. A rabbi is called in and soon ascertains that this has happened because her father broke a vow to his dead friend: he had promised to give this man's son, the scholar, his daughter in marriage. A trial takes place and the father tries to make amends, and the *Dybbuk* promises to leave his true love's body. But he enters her soul, and she chooses to go to the Other World with him, her destined bridegroom.

The *Dybbuk* is not all "evil," but like many demons has an ambiguous reputation. In one Talmudic story we meet Ben Temalion, a unique and intriguing possession species:

Once a certain rabbi named Rabbi Simeon ben Johai went to Rome to plea for clemency for his people in the wake of a series of stern decrees against them. On the road, the rabbi met a demon named Ben Temalion, a *Dybbuk*. He introduced himself and asked the rabbi where he was going. "To Rome," the rabbi said, and explained why. "I'll help you," said Ben Temalion. He then told the rabbi his plan. The rabbi, with a certain ambivalence about receiving help from an unclean spirit, accepted for the greater good.

As the rabbi traveled toward Rome, news came that the daughter of Caesar had been possessed by a demon and that nobody had been able to exorcise the creature. The rabbi knew that it was Ben Temalion who had taken up residence in the princess, so he volunteered to attempt to cast out the spirit. He called him by name and, addressing him directly, bid him depart. Being identified and addressed, the spirit was forced to obey. The princess was cured. Caesar tore up the decree. And this time the demonic possession species voluntarily did a good deed (although his motives have never been disclosed).

DISARMING & DISPELLING TECHNIQUES

In each case, a *Dybbuk* must be expelled by a rabbi, who always addresses the indweller directly and asks its identity. After the rabbi asks several questions, he is usually able to cast it out of the victim's body. A *Dybbuk* traditionally exits by the toe or little finger of the inhabited person. Also a small hole must be made in a window or other manner of egress established so that the demon will leave the house. (This is always a precaution, as one doesn't want to trap a demon any more than an angry bee.)

KITSUNE-TSUKI
Japan

Kitsune-Tsuki (Fox-Possession), is easily diagnosed: when possessed by the wild Fox Spirit the patient may say "I am Inari god of rice" and have severe cravings for rice with red beans (fox favorites). At times the possessed seem depressed and restless and find it impossible to sleep at night. They prefer eating alone and will not make eye contact.

As for special powers, cases have been recorded of illiterate people who when possessed were able to write fluently and draw pictures of the fox as messenger of Inari on their communications. Unlike werewolf possession the victim retains human shape night and day, and never fully metamorphoses to an animal. The creature is said to reside in the stomach or on the left side. These possessions have been observed and noted as early as the twelfth century and continue to the present day.

Kitsune-Tsuki, the idea that the demonic spirits of terrible wild foxes could possess a human being, originated with the Fox Fairy in China. There, the Fox Fairy is greatly feared and always propitiated. It is believed that cases of madness caused by fox possession are retributions for former offenses against the Fox Fairy by a member of the victim's family; however, the Chinese Fox Fairy has been known to possess a human being for the sheer malevolent mischief of it. When inhabited, the human can fly, go through walls, and has other striking powers (see Domicile).

The *Kitsune-Tsuki* enters the body through the breast or under the fingernails, and once inside lives independently. The possessed human, often a woman, hears and understands all that this "double" in her consciousness is saying or doing. She and it often have violent arguments. The two speak in markedly different voices.

DISARMING & DISPELLING TECHNIQUES

A priest is often called in, berates the Fox Spirit, and tells it to get out. The fox negotiates its terms, arranges for rice and other offerings, and if satisfied will finally agree to leave. Cases continue to be reported in contemporary times.

MARA

(Buddhism)

Mara, the agent of Death, travels from Hinduism (as the embodiment of Death itself and of the powers of Evil) to become the principal Buddhist demon. He is the tempter, the archenemy of the Buddha, the obstacle to potential Enlightenment, the personification of greed, hatred, and delusion. He tries to lure all spiritual travelers onto the path of worldly desires, which lead to rebirth and not to liberation.

Mara functions to delay the "Coming of the Law." He embodies ego pleasure, worldly pleasure, and sensual delight. *Mara* is not so much evil (in the sense of sinful) in Buddhist thought as he is the epitome of all that is at the root of *duhkha* (suffering). It is with that understanding of *Mara* as a mental state, an embodiment of dis-ease, that he appears in Psyche.

From the Buddhist point of view, as long as humans live in ignorance, craving, and fear, they stay stuck in the cycle of life and death and rebirth and are caught in the realm of *Mara*. When the Buddha threatens to overturn this rule and is on the verge of bringing a new Way — a new understanding — to the world, *Mara* becomes fiendishly furious. He has everything of this world and every weapon known to the universe at his disposal; most important, he holds the entire wheel of life and death in his clutches, and every living thing must die, and every mortal fears Death.

LORE

Siddhartha Gautama gave up his princely riches and then spent years in the forest as an ascetic. Finally he gave up asceticism, now determined to sit under the Tree of Wisdom until he reached enlightenment. *Mara* approached on his elephant, wild with anger, accompanied by his legions of demons. He was such a terrifying sight that all the gods who stood by the tree fled.

Before expending the hideous forces at his command, the

archdemon tried to interrupt Siddhartha's concentration by insinuating himself as a messenger bearing false and terrible news about Siddhartha's worldly family. The Buddha remained unsnared. Then an assault began, designed to bring fear into the heart of any mortal. *Mara* sent whirlwinds, tempests, floods, fire, and mud at the seated figure. But all the weapons turned to flowers in midair and formed a canopy above the Buddha.

Mara told him to get up because he had no right to be there. He was usurping *Mara's* seat on his earth. Siddhartha, unmoved, reminded *Mara* that it was he, Siddhartha, who sought knowledge and not the archdemon. Siddhartha's reply was met with a hail of stone-throwing by a huge demon army. *Mara* then sent his invincible javelin through the air. Flowers again appeared. *Mara* again challenged the Buddha but then the earth itself bore witness to the generosity and greatness of the Buddha and all the demons fled. Even *Mara's* elephant bowed down.

All his show of force had not worked, and now his army was gone, his most impressive weapons used, so the tempter tried his last, best trick. He sent out his daughters: Rati (Desire), Raga (Pleasure), and Tanha (Restlessness). They manifested themselves as dancing girls of extraordinary beauty. But, as attractive as these dancing girls appeared to be, Siddhartha (as reported in the Lotus Sutra) saw through all the delights of their transient offerings. He saw them as ancient hags, as sacks of pus, as skeletons on the ground in front of his feet, as decay. Thus he remained without craving and was unsnared by illusion. He was unmoved.

Since no fear entered the heart of Siddhartha Gautama at the hideous storms and swords, and no craving entered at the sight of the dancing girls, he had managed with his mind to recognize the rocks and weapons as illusory things, thus disempowering them and turning them into harmless flowers. The daughters of the tempter bowed to his understanding.

The gods all came back when the archenemy was defeated and his armies melted away, and Prince Siddhartha Gautama became the Buddha.

DISARMING & DISPELLING TECHNIQUES

All the demons of the Buddhist tradition are teachers, employed to arrest attention with their grotesque and startling appearance. They serve to awaken the individual to reflect on all that which is ego-driven desire and fear of death. Considered in this way, and seen for the illusory beings they are, they are dispelled. These methods of viewing the "demon" can become tools of indivual liberation if practiced over a long period of time.

YEZER HA-RA
(Judaism)

The *Yezer Ha-Ra* ("evil inclination") has a recurring role in Jewish rabbinical writings as an embodiment of that within the heart or imagination of humankind that functions as *ha Satan* (the adversary) and tempts a man to do wrong. The *Yezer Ha-Ra* is part of human nature and exists in each human being as an always present potential adversary to Good. In most lore the *Yezer Ha-Ra* seems to be a powerful impulse that can erupt in the heart of a rabbi or scholar as easily as in the heart of an ordinary person. The emphasis is on the struggle within each inhabited psyche.

The *Yezer Ha-Ra* usually manifests as an (almost) irresistible lustful urge. It is considered especially dangerous when a man leaves the synagogue on Friday night and goes home. En route he is accompanied by a good spirit and the *Yezer Ha-Ra*. If he is distracted from his spiritual reflection, he can fall victim to the latter. This is also true just after the marriage ceremony; the groom is considered very vulnerable due to the presence of spirits around the sacred rite and human closeness to the spiritual realm.

LORE

One night a rabbi was passing through the woods when he happened upon a small cottage with a light on. As he neared the dwelling, its occupant, a very attractive woman, came to the door wearing scant attire. She beckoned to him graciously and bid him enter. When he did, she offered him not a cup of tea, but herself. At this invitation he was nearly overcome by the *Yezer Ha-Ra*, but resisted it with all his might and managed to shout, "No!" Just as the magic word was uttered, the woman vanished along with the cottage. The rabbi found himself alone again in the dark woods.

In another well-known tale, we again find a rabbi. He had been resisting the impulse to make love to a nubile maiden who was in his charge, but he was unable to hold out any longer and found himself climbing a ladder to her bedroom window. But as he climbed, he continued to struggle fiercely with his own evil impulse. He addressed it loudly. He passionately bid the demonic urge to leave him. Breathless, he arrived at the top rung and there he finally witnessed the *Yezer Ha-Ra* exit as an actual pillar of fire. He won. He was free of the inclination to do evil, and he was able to descend the ladder with a clear conscience and no regret.

DISARMING & DISPELLING TECHNIQUES

The *Yezer Ha-Ra* cannot be quelled by any external action. It cannot be placated, propitiated, or tolerated. It must be acknowledged, seen, and labeled for what it is. Then a mighty wrestling match within the psyche of the host must take place. If the subject wins, he will not become victim of his own *Yezer Ha-Ra*.

THE SEVEN DEADLY SINS
(The Christian West)

The *Seven Deadly Sins* were grouped together by St. Gregory the Great in the sixth century. The Seven later appear importantly in the *Summa Theologica* of the thirteenth century, where they are defined and described by St. Thomas Aquinas as "appetites." The *Sins* are agents of serious moral offenses, transgressions of the divine law that lead to eternal damnation. They are one of the most virulent and chronic of the possession species that roost within the Psyche. They are seen as tendencies, temptations, passions — all interconnected strands of the fabric of the human condition, the stuff of exaggerated cravings that cause mortal suffering.

LORE

Why seven? It is a powerful number. There are seven days of the week, seven seas, and seven heavens, and seven is a popular number in ancient magical incantations. The most extreme use of seven may occur in the following Talmudic prescription for a fever:

> Take 7 prickles from 7 palm trees, 7 chips from 7 beams, 7 nails from 7 bridges, 7 ashes from 7 ovens, 7 scoops of earth from 7 door sockets, 7 pieces of pitch from 7 ships, 7 handfuls of cumin, and 7 hairs from the beard of an old dog, and then tie them to the neck-hole of the shirt with a white, twisted thread.

Seven of the Babylonian Evil Spirits railed against in incantations are specifically identified in this fragment:

> Of these seven, the first is the South Wind,
> The second is a dragon with mouth agape that none can withstand.
> The third is a grim leopard that carries off the young

The fourth is a terrible serpent
The fifth is a furious beast, after which no restraint
The sixth is a rampant [missing] against god and
    king
The seventh is an evil windstorm.

These seven evil spirits are "workers of woe," "bear gloom from city to city," cause "darkness over the brightest day," and "wreak destruction" and can be said to define the traits of the *Sins*, who are also usually seen riding animals or as animals that represent their specialties. In their medieval heyday, the *Sins* were impersonated by actors in morality plays, standing against the Seven Virtues that neatly opposed them to remind audiences to be ever vigilant.

The *Seven Deadly Sins* were seen as agents of actions that always led to worse and worse sins. From Avarice, for a familiar example, springs fraud, treachery, deceit, violence, perjury, and hardness of heart. Each *Sin* has its own escalating consequences. They also have an ordered sequence that is generally agreed upon. Five of the *Sins* are spiritual in nature, and two, Lust and Gluttony, carnal. All of the *Seven Deadly Sins* are notable in their selfishness. They each isolate person from person and act within to inflame personal ambitions, needs, gratifications, to the neglect of family, community, or spiritual development. Medieval scholars placed seven fallen angels as promoters of the seven specific temptations. The efforts of these fallen angels was tireless because their goal was to hinder humankind from goodness and keep it from the presence of the Divine as they themselves had been when they fell from heaven. Because the *Sins* are each so vividly depicted, and recognizable, these hypostatized passions that reside in the Psyche follow in separate glory:

1. PRIDE — LUCIFER

Pride is considered the root of all evil. It is for Pride that
Lucifer (Satan, Iblis) fell from the celestial to the subterranean realm. The selfish sin is to be "vainglorious" and think
oneself better than others. Arrogance blocks the Divine as well
as other persons from the heart. Pride is invariably seen as a
lion. Its opposing virtue is Humility.

2. AVARICE — MAMMON

"By Mammon is meant the devil who is the Lord of Money," wrote Thomas Aquinas. Avarice is a worldly sin, creating misers, thieves, and even murderers. The wolf is the animal usually depicted in medieval bestiaries, coming up from hell carrying Mammon to inflame the human heart with Greed.

Like the "hungry ghosts" of the Buddhist hell, the greedy always crave more no matter how much they have. Wretched and envious, Avarice escalates to a state of infinite dissatisfaction, and the sin's obsession with worldly goods promotes neglect of spiritual wealth. The opposing virtue is Sufficiency.

3. LUST — ASMODEUS

Lust is carried up from hell by the goat, an animal long considered lascivious, or the ass, who played the same role in ancient Rome. This "sin of the flesh" is said to lead to "uncleanliness" and away from its opposing virtue, Chastity. (See Asmodeus in Domicile.)

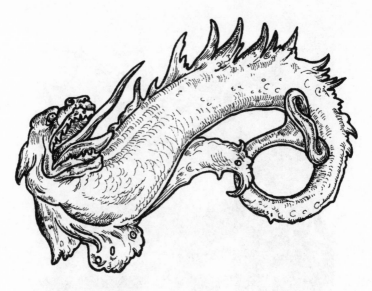

4. ENVY — LEVIATHAN

That the "twisting serpent" from the primordial deep, Leviathan, is Envy incarnate seems appropriate. Dante saw the spirit of evil as a huge serpent, who so entangled himself with his victim that they became utterly intertwined and no longer distinguishable, one from the other.

Envy is a "sin of the Devil," for "Thou shalt not covet" is one of the Ten Commandments. The sin usually is represented by a dog, and often depicted as a heart being eaten away, as in, "Eat your heart out." Overconcern with the possessions of others is seen escalating to hinder sympathetic human relationships. When one is consumed by Envy, the opposing virtue, Charity, is completely erased.

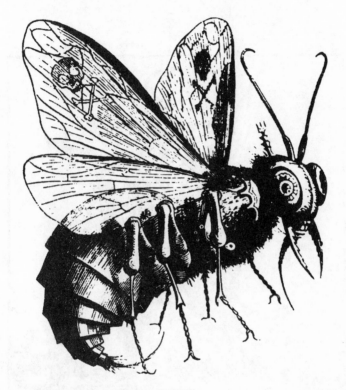

5. GLUTTONY — BEELZEBUB

Beelzebub, seen as Gluttony, started out as a Canaanite deity whose name in Hebrew (Baal Zebub) meant Lord of the Flies and who later came to be equated with Satan. In the Gospels, Beelzebub is called Prince of the Demons. As a sin, he rules over all excessive eating and drinking.

The endless maw of the glutton is never satiated, and he or she is never satisfied. The glutton lives to eat, a state that soon escalates to forgetting gratitude. The pursuit goes on and leads to a specific damnation: the glutton in hell will dine on toads and be forced to drink putrid water. The opposing virtue is Sobriety.

6. ANGER — SATAN

Anger is another sin of the Devil and one of immense importance and fiery power. It is usually embodied by a sharp-toothed animal such as a leopard with bared fangs, or a wild boar, raging, attacking, ready to commit bloodshed. The consequence of this inflaming indwelling passion is to feel vengeance in one's heart. This sin escalates to rage, obliterating all but negativity within, and results in murder and war. Often seen in icons, Anger is a creature stabbing himself in the heart with a knife. The opposing virtue is Patience.

7. SLOTH — BELPHEGOR

Belphegor is depicted as Sloth incarnate. This sin is considered one of the flesh. Usually it is represented by scenes of falling asleep on the job, especially if the job is done by a monk. When in a state of Sloth, negligence and apathy soon set in. The donkey, a slow-moving, lazy creature, is Sloth's representative animal.

Thomas Aquinas wrote that all sins that are due to ignorance are due to Sloth. One needs to be awake and alert to even begin to set out on and maintain a spiritual practice, thus the opposing virtue is Diligence.

DISARMING & DISPELLING TECHNIQUES

The seven penitential psalms were sometimes illustrated by the *Sins* in medieval manuscripts to remind the reader which psalm was effective against which sin, and the recitation of these psalms was considered a way of obtaining forgiveness. The opposing virtue to each sin is mentioned separately as an antidote, and the practice of Patience, Humility, and Diligence were intended to subdue Anger, Pride, and Sloth.

MR. HYDE

(Robert Louis Stevenson)

Mr. Hyde, an unusual, subjectively observed doctor-possession species created in a laboratory, occupies half then slowly takes over all of Dr. Jekyll's mind and body. The case is written up by *Mr. Hyde's* rather stuffy landlord, the respectable, introspective, and somewhat cold Dr. Henry Jekyll, and serves to illustrate some classic possession fieldmarks.

LORE

The doctor observes in his case notes that for years he "concealed" his pleasures and held his head high. It was his "exacting nature" that "severed in me those provinces of good and ill which divide and compound man's dual nature." Henry came to wonder whether it was the curse of humankind that the "polar twins should be continuously struggling. How then, were they dissociated?" Jekyll then experimented in his laboratory with a potion that transformed him to *Hyde,* his polar twin, and allowed *Hyde* to operate autonomously so that he, Jekyll, could observe him from the rational side of the great divide in his psyche.

When he first tried the potion he felt "something indescribably new . . . and incredibly sweet. I felt younger, lighter, happier in body; within I was conscious of a heady recklessness . . . at the first breath of this new life to be more wicked, tenfold more wicked." He also became notably shorter in stature. In the mirror he discovered an ugly countenance, clearly evil, but somehow he was not repulsed by the image but instead felt what he described ominously as "a leap of welcome."

As long as he could control the gleeful pleasure outings with his demonic other self, the doctor maintained his clinical coolness and reflected on his evil twin with a certain *frisson délicieux* couched in philosophical musing. He was always able to return to his laboratory and body and take notes. But soon things escalated and grew all out of hand. *Hyde* hit a woman, ran over a child, and finally murdered a gentleman.

The following morning Henry Jekyll awakened expecting to find himself in his normal respectable day body, but when he glanced at his hand, which was normally a doctor's hand, "white and comely," the hand he saw "in the yellow light of a mid-London morning, lying half shut on the bedclothes, was lean, corded, knuckly, of a dusky pallor and thickly shaded with a swart growth of hair. It was the hand of Edward Hyde."

Finding his physical and spiritual self devoured by the evil demon within and no longer able to transform himself by powders, he wrote his last notes and "died" wondering if this apelike, smallish, hairy, bestial, demonic creature would hang from the scaffold. He, Dr. Jekyll, would never know.

DISARMING & DISPELLING TECHNIQUES

No human can live with a divided nature, either by repressing the demonic creative passionate side that Henry Jekyll describes as his "certain impatient gaiety of disposition" or by allowing it to dissociate by potion or by mental breakdown. Reconciliation to the whole of human nature, poised between animal and angel, might have saved Dr. Jekyll from his Shadow. (See Shadow in Psyche.)

ID
(Freud)

The *Id*, a post-Enlightenment demon, is a powerful species of seething want. The *Id*, coined by Sigmund Freud, is the core portion of his tripartite model of the human psyche: id, ego, and superego. In the ancient model of celestial, terrestrial, and subterranean realms of the spirits, the demonic always resides in the very depths of its habitat — *under* mountain, sea, and domicile. Here, we find the Psyche abode of *Id*, in the unlit, utter darkness of the unconscious. Above it, and in part born from it, is the ego, the partially conscious realm, which we recognize as our own identity; above the ego, also in part unconscious, is the super ego, with its severe moral whip, lashing at the ego from on high with guilt.

LORE

Freud's famous description of the interdependent arrangement goes like this: The ego is like a rider who is attempting to rein in the greater strength of the powerful horse (the *Id*) while using the strength of the horse itself (in part) to do it. The rider cannot be separated from his horse, yet is impelled to lead the horse to where it wants to go. So must the ego "translate the will of the *Id* into action as if that action were its own."

Above the horse and rider flies the attached superego, often demanding an abrupt turn or halt. The ego, sandwiched between, aware of the outside reality, and the only part of the trio to actually respond to experience, has to satisfy both unconscious forces.

The *Id* then is unseen, hidden, indwelling, shapeless, and contains all passions and instinctual energy. It is that which is there pulsating at birth and houses all innate needs and bodily demands. It is from the *Id* that the ego takes its shape and parts of its "horse power" or energy. But the *Id* doesn't know what it wants. It simply *wants*. And it has two primary power drives: libido and aggression.

The *Id* screams from the basement of mind up to the ego,

which attempts to rein it in with rational thought, to hold it steady and gratify its demands with one eye on the outside world. The *Id* knows nothing of the Out There; no light has formed an idea of a "neighbor" or a "parent" or anything external to its incessant bodily demands. It bleats and yells and surges through dreams and whispers to the consciousness of ego via images and obsessive behavior and slips of the tongue and constant internal demands. This is how it makes its presence known.

DISARMING & DISPELLING TECHNIQUES

When the demonic *Id* gets out of control, and the ego cannot bear being in the middle of a raging sandwich, the human will feel overwhelmed. When this happens, the human must seek outside help. The professional leads him slowly to uncover, and discover, all the forces that surge through his unconscious mind by pulling them into the light of consciousness, exposing them to rational discourse, and naming them. By psychoanalytical methods of pulling the "demons" from darkness to light, and calling them by name, their power is reduced, contained, and possibly dispelled.

SHADOW
(Jung)

A personal *Shadow* rests in the depths of the unconscious of every person, ready and waiting to spring. According to Carl Jung's model, the *Shadow* expresses a person's darker dimension, the inner demon, the part of that personality one hides from the eyes of the world (and even from oneself). The *Shadow* includes all those aspects of a person's nature that he believes unacceptable. The *Shadow* lies at the threshold of the unexpressed self, at the border between the known and the unknown.

The unconscious *Shadow* is repressed and hidden away like an unopened trunk somewhere in a corner of a dark and forgotten room. But unlike a closed trunk, it can open by itself. If it does, it may take a form that will make its human host feel that he's fallen prey to a possession species of invisible demon. It leaps out in this form, and projects itself onto another person: maybe a spouse or neighbor whom the host sees as exhibiting the demonic qualities of his/her own *Shadow*.

The stronger the control "Persona" — the mask worn for society — exerts over the individual, the more his true self hides repressed within his *Shadow*, and the less he wants to encounter its existence. Most commonly the *Shadow* remains out of sight of the ego, but not entirely buried. It will spring forth in projections and also in dreams.

In dreams people run down endless hallways, look into twisted mirrors, fight against oppressors (who are often only divided selves or "polar twins" fighting a battle). Often the Psyche will present to dreamers archetypal images of shadow-vampires, devils, goblins, and hybrid animal-human creatures. This is the Psyche's way of saying that each individual *Shadow* partakes of an essence of what humankind has collectively experienced as evil or demonic or destructive throughout history. The dramatic characters in dreams who appear as archetypal images like the Devil often points to the magnitude of a problem as felt by the dreamer. It can feel so impossible, for example, to deal with certain issues that they are imaged as demonic powers — far beyond human control.

In daily life, the *Shadow* manufactures projections onto others. Traits such as vindictiveness, jealousy, rudeness, competitiveness, that are seen in others are often mirror reflections of negative feelings so repressed in oneself that they are hidden from sight. To catch a glimpse of this "power shadow" would be too painful, it would "kill" the viewer, so he represses it, and places his devil "out there," just as Dorian Gray projected his shadow onto his famous, crumbling portrait.

LORE

Long ago, in ancient China, a man lost his ax. He searched everywhere for it but could not find it. When visiting his neighbor, he happened to glance at his neighbor's son, and realized the child looked extremely suspicious. He observed him very carefully, noting the expression on his face, the way he slouched stealthily about, and it was clear to him this guilty-looking boy had in fact stolen his ax. When he went home, with this certainty, he happened to pick up a stone in his garden and there discovered the missing ax, lying precisely where he now remembered leaving it. He looked again at his neighbor's son, and saw that the child had a wonderfully innocent smile, a sweet face, and a childlike walk, and he could not imagine how he had ever suspected the boy of thievery.

DISARMING & DISPELLING TECHNIQUES

If the *Shadow* is admitted into the light of consciousness and faced squarely by the individual, it can be utilized to effect change. In the Jungian model, it is part of the function of depth analysis that the patient listens for the *Shadow*. It is when the deeply planted voice or voices are heard that transformation begins. Uncovering the *Shadow* is like a gardener upturning deeply rooted weeds — it is an essential part of spiritual growth. When the *Shadow* is recognized and respected as a natural part of each Psyche and no longer repressed or projected, the human being can be whole and integrated.

Like all demons, the *Shadow* is always changing its guise, so recognizing it is a lifelong process.

YAMANTAKA
(Tibetan Buddhism)

Yamantaka is usually dark blue, has eight buffalo heads, thirty-four arms, and sixteen legs. He holds a terrible weapon in each of his thirty-four hands. He wears a necklace of severed human heads. He is a Terrifier. However, *Yamantaka* is used by Tibetan Buddhist practitioners as a teacher and an aid on the spiritual path to enlightenment. This tutelary, wrathful deity, the "Terminator of Death," is actually a form of Manjushri, the Boddhisattva of Wisdom, conqueror of the Lord of Death, who appears as the ninth head — nearly hidden on first sighting.

Manjushri, the legendary boddhisattva, traveled to Yama, the Lord of Death, and took on his form. Thus, he became *Yamantaka*, the Terminator of Yama, Lord of Death, in order to overcome Death itself. This complex figure represents a radically different approach to the demonic field and must be understood for what he represents in Tibetan Buddhism.

Tibetan Buddhist texts do not include the Seven Deadly Sins, but they do identify the Five Poisons (or addictions): Lust, Hate, Blindness, Pride, and Envy. And it is these "poisons," they believe, that keep human beings in a state of suffering. It is these transmuted poisons that now, as Five Wisdoms, fill the skull cups worn as a crown by *Yamantaka* (seen just under the head of Manjushri). His necklace of severed human heads represent quelled egos, and the three huge red eyes that glare from his fierce buffalo head challenge the practitioner to gaze upon him and what he represents with clear vision. In one hand he holds the important *vajra* cleaver that is used to cut through ignorance and ego attachment. Each of his thirty-four weapons is poised to attack one's inner demons and destroy all one's own passions, hatreds, and negative emotions (the Five Poisons).

Behind the complex, esoteric practice of Tibetan Buddhism lies a history of shamanic lore, magic, and Tantric art that holds demons in mountains, forests, and water, but in fact the entire landscape lies in the realm of Psyche. It is here, finally, that the "dragons" must be conquered. On an internal battlefield, by visualizing deities of fierce mien and sharp teeth and sword, one harnesses their powers to combat negative emotions and transcend them. Here we find *Yamantaka*, who lends insight to a way of slaying internal dragons of lust, anger, and greed, and emptying the "self" to permit the entrance of Buddha-consciousness.

DISARMING & DISPELLING TECHNIQUES

When the Tibetan Buddhist adept attempts to defeat the poisonous demoness of Envy, he does not do so by reciting the opposing virtue, Charity. He enlists the fierce *Yamantaka*. He imagines himself as a form of Yama the Lord of Death and, completing a ritual learned over many years of arduous practice, calls forth the deity. He has emptied himself and is now only a vessel — a container for the energy of *Yamantaka* —

and as *Yamantaka* he subjugates the powers and conquers the poison of Envy. Suddenly, he sees how deluded a passion Envy really is by gazing from the point of view of death itself. Then, when he is finally able to see Yama — death itself — as illusory, he reaches the opening to Wisdom.

Tibetan Buddhist techniques are intended for use only by those with esoteric knowledge and many dozens of years of daily spiritual practice. They are as extremely dangerous as they are powerful. The approach to this fascinating field is briefly outlined in this Guide because in its model and alchemy, it illuminates a radically different way of viewing and utilizing the demonic population of the Psyche.

QUANTUM DAIMON
(Guide)

The *Quantum Daimon* is an unidentified flying species inspired by the subatomic universe that is neither angel nor demon but simply potential — an energy flowing everywhere that can become a positive force. Robert Burton in his *Anatomy of Melancholy* of 1621 attributed to Melancholy, the sickness of heart, "black anxiety" and sorrow, fearfulness and suspicion, that state of the human psyche from which proceed visions of demons:

> The Devil he is a spirit and hath means and opportunity to mingle himself with our spirits, and sometimes more slyly, sometimes more abruptly and openly, to suggest devilish thoughts into our hearts. He insults and domineers in melancholy, distempered phantasies especially. He is a prince of the air and can transform himself into several shapes, delude our senses for a time; but his power is determined, he may terrify us but not hurt.

Isaac Bashevis Singer, a twentieth-century writer, believed in the reality of demons and also believed that they were a creation of God for mysterious reasons we could never know. Singer thought, however, that before a demon could enter and take possession of a human being, there had to first be a giving up of will, a lack of hope.

LORE

Once a maiden of dazzling beauty named Pandora was created out of clay and water by the god Hephaestus on orders of Zeus. All the gods gave her gifts, put flowers in her hair, adorned her with jewels, and breathed life into her. Zeus then gave her a large vase containing destructive powers along with a warning never to open it, endowed her with curiosity, and sent her to humankind as a punishment. Pandora arrived on earth and once there was seized with curiosity; unable to resist opening the forbidden vase, she unsealed the lid. From the container flew hordes of miseries — the dark spirits of greed, despair, envy, wrath —blotting out all light with a multitude of wings. Pandora slammed the container shut while it still held a creature called Hope.

DISARMING & DISPELLING TECHNIQUES

The Guide attempts a fin-de-siècle Pandora experiment to recapture the *daimon*, that quantum energy imbuing all nature, bringing with it inspiration, uncanny moments of sudden awareness, and acting as intermediary of the Divine and the terrestrial realm. In the experiment we translate the ancient animistic worldview into the point of view of modern physics. Let's call it the *Quantum Daimon*. Imagine it as transparent. The box it rests in is invisible.

Like the brilliant physicist Erwin Schrödinger's Cat (used in his virtual cat-in-the-box experiment to demonstrate the nature of the subatomic world), the *Quantum Daimon* is neither alive or dead, it is neither particle or wave, it is neither fortune or misfortune, neither good nor evil. It is not one thing or another — until we open the box.

It is how the observer opens the box and with what mindset that not only informs but determines the nature of the spirit about to fly. The millennial Psyche species and the viewer participant together may send positive (or negative) energies out into the universe. The Guide hopes that if any reader sights the *Quantum Daimon*, it will be for him or for her a new and shining spirit.

ACKNOWLEDGMENTS

Sunne lai sunko mala
Bhanne lai fulko mala;
Yo katha baikuntha jala
Bhanne belama turunta aula.

For him who listens
a garland of gold,
A wreath of flowers
   for her who tells;
   This tale now to heavens will go
   But at once fly back
   when it's time to tell again.

In the spirit of this Nepalese verse, which is invoked before telling a tale, our first thanks go to the storytellers and to all the wonderful scholars of myth, folklore, and spiritual traditions whose names and treasury of works are listed as an invitation for further study by the reader. We are indebted to you and thank you for all we've learned from you. We wish next to thank the following friends and scholars who provided invaluable contributions to the making of this book. Thanks first to Glenn Young, whose belief in this project led to this publication; to our editor Sean McDonald for blazing a clear path through the jungle with his rigorous mind and brilliant "pencillings," and to Richard Seaver, for his help and editorial input; to Carol Hill and Jim Carse for their careful readings, excellent advice, and inexhaustible support. With gratitude for their original artwork we thank Cathy Hull and Toby Welles, and for help with photography, David Gillison. Many thanks to our learned friends: to Dr. N. R. Srinivasan for extraordinary generosity in sending us original renderings of Hindu stories; to Tej R. Kansakar for sending us myths and advice from Kathmandu and to Kesar Lall, who translated the Nepalese verse and other material; and to John Wolseley, who sent us tales from Australia. Many thanks for leads, loans, and patient answers to questions to Bob Carneiro, Roger Abrahams, Gita Rajan, Gene Murphy, Harvey Goldberg, Celia Candlin, and James Griffith. Our thanks also to Priscilla Rodgers for reading and advice on Jungian material, and to Jerry Wiener for reading and advice on Freudian concepts. Thanks to Joshua Mack for lending his technical assistance to us Luddites, and to Ana DeBoo for the great fairy hunt; particular thanks to The New York Society Library and to A.R.A.S. at the C. G. Jung Center for their generosity; to our community of friends; and to Peter Mack and our family for all their help and loving support.

BIBLIOGRAPHY

Abrahams, Roger D. *African Folktales*. New York: Pantheon Books, 1983.

Algarin, Joanne P. *Japanese Folk Literature: A Core Collection and Reference Guide*. New York: R. R. Bowker Company, 1982.

Ananikian, Mardiros. *Mythology of All Races*, Vol. 1. New York: Cooper Square Publishers, 1964.

Andersen, Johannes C. *Myths and Legends of the Polynesians*. London: George G. Harrap, 1928.

Bamberger, Bernard J. *Fallen Angels*. Philadelphia: The Jewish Publication Society, 1952.

Barrett, Charles. *The Bunyip and Other Mythical Monsters and Legends*. Melbourne, Australia: Reed Harris, 1946.

Bernbaum, Edwin. *The Way to Shambhala*. New York: Doubleday, 1980.

———. *Sacred Mountains of the World*. San Francisco: Sierra Club Books, 1992.

Berndt, Ronald M., and Catherine H. Berman. *The Speaking Land: Myth and Story in Aboriginal Australia*. Victoria, Australia: Penguin Books, 1988.

Bierhorst, John. *The Mythology of North America*. New York: Quill/ William Morrow, 1985.

———. *The Mythology of South America*. New York: Quill/ William Morrow, 1988.

Birrell, Anne. *Chinese Mythology*. Baltimore: Johns Hopkins University Press, 1993.

Boas, Franz. *Kwakiutl Culture as Reflected in Mythology*. New York: American Folklore Society, 1935.

Briggs, K. M. *The Fairies in Tradition and Literature*. London: Routledge and Kegan Paul, 1967.

———. *Abbey Lubbers, Banshees and Bogarts*. Hammondsworth: Kestral Books, 1979.

———. *The Personnel of Fairyland*. Oxford: The Alden Press, 1969.

———. *The Vanishing People: Fairy Lore and Legends*. New York: Pantheon Books, 1978.

———. *A Dictionary of British Folktales in the English Language*. Bloomington: Indiana University Press, 1970.

Bringsvaerd, Tor Age. *Phantoms and Fairies from Norwegian Folklore*, trans. Pat Shaw Iversen. Oslo: Johan Grundt Tanum Forlag, 1970.

Budge, Sir E. A. Wallis. *Gods of the Egyptians*. 2 vols. New York: Dover Publications, 1969.

Burton, Robert. *The Anatomy of Melancholy*. London: J. M. Dent; New York: E. P. Dutton, 1932.

Callaway, Rev. Canon. *Nursery Tales, Traditions and Histories of the Zulus, in Their Own Words*. Westport, Conn.: Negro University Press, 1970.

Campbell, Joseph. *The Masks of God: Oriental Mythology.* New York: Viking Press, 1962.

———. *The Masks of God: Occidental Mythology.* New York: Viking Press, 1964.

———. *The Masks of God: Creative Mythology.* New York: Viking Press, 1970.

———. *The Mythic Image.* Princeton, N.J.: Princeton University Press, 1974.

Carrol, Peter J. "Mimi from Western Arnhem Land," in *Form in Indigenous Art,* ed. Peter J. Ucko. London: Gerald Duckworth and Company, 1977.

Carus, Paul. *The History of the Devil and the Idea of Evil.* Chicago: Open Court Publishing, 1899.

Casal, V. A. "The Kappa." *Transactions of the Asiatic Society of Japan* 8 (December 1961): 157–91.

Christiansen, Reidar Thorwald. *Folktales of Norway,* trans. Pat Shaw Iverson. Chicago: University of Chicago Press, 1964.

Colombo, John Robert. *Windigo: An Anthology of Fact and Fantastic Fiction.* Saskatchewan: Western Producer Prairie Books, 1982.

Coomaraswamy, Ananda K., and Sister Nivedita. *Myths of the Hindus and Buddhists.* New York: Dover, 1967.

Conway, Moncure Daniel. *Demonology and Devil-Lore,* vols. 1, 2. New York: Henry Holt and Co., 1881.

Croker, Thomas Crofton. *Fairy Legends and Traditions of the South of Ireland.* New York: Scholar's Facsimiles and Reprints, 1983.

Curtin, Jeremiah, and J. N. B. Hewitt. "Seneca Fiction." *Bureau of American Ethnology, 32d Annual Report,* 1918, pp. 37–819.

Davidson, Gustav. *A Dictionary of Angels, Including Fallen Angels.* New York: Free Press, 1967.

Davis, F. Hadland. *Myths and Legends of Japan.* New York: Dover Publications, 1992.

Davis, Stanley. *Pre-Columbian American Religions.* New York: Holt, Rinehart and Winston, 1968.

Dawood, N. J., trans. *Tales from the Thousand and One Nights.* London: Penguin Books, 1954.

Dennys, Nicholas B. *The Folklore of China.* Amsterdam: Oriental Press, 1968.

De Plancy, Collin. *Dictionnaire Infernal.* Paris: Plon,1863.

DeVisser, M. W. "The Tengu." *Transactions of the Asiatic Society of Japan* 35 (1908): 25–99.

Donie, J. Frank. *I'll Tell You a Tale.* Austin: University of Texas Press, 1960.

Dodds, E. R. *The Greek and the Irrational.* Berkeley: University of California Press, 1951.

———. *Pagan and Christian in an Age of Anxiety.* New York: W. W. Norton, 1965.

Domotor, Tekla. *Hungarian Folk Beliefs.* Bloomington: Indiana University Press, 1982.

Dore, Henry. *Researches into Chinese Superstition.* 12 vols. Trans. L. F. McGreal. Shanghai: Tusewe Printing Press, 1920–1938.

Dorson, Richard. *Folk Legends of Japan.* Rutland, Vt.: Charles E. Tuttle Company, 1962.

Douglas, George. *Scottish Fairy and Folktales.* London: Walter Scott, 1893.

Erdoes, Richard, and Alfonso Ortiz, eds. *American Indian Myths and Legends.* New York: Pantheon Books, 1984.

Eiseman Jr., Fred B. *Bali, Sekala & Niskala,* vol. 1. Berkeley: Periplus Editions, 1989.

Frazer, Sir James G. *The Golden Bough.* New York: Macmillan, 1922.

Gaster, Theodor. *Myth, Legend and Custom in the Old Testament.* New York: Harper and Row, 1969.

Gay, Peter. *Freud: A Life for Our Time.* New York/London: W. W. Norton, 1988.

Gorion, Micha Bin. *Mimekor Yisrael: Selected Jewish Folktales,* ed. E. B. Gorion, trans. I. M. Lask. Bloomington: University of Indiana Press, 1976.

Graves, Robert. *The Greek Myths.* 2 vols. New York: Penguin Books, 1955.

Graves, Robert, and Raphael Patai. *Hebrew Myths.* New York: Doubleday and Company, 1964.

————. *Hebrew Myths, The Book of Genesis.* New York: Greenwich House, 1983.

Gregg, Robert C. *Athanasius: The Life of Antony and the Letter to Marcellinus.* New York: Paulist Press, 1980.

Grimm, Jacob. *Teutonic Mythology.* 4 vols. Gloucester, Mass.: Peter Smith, 1976.

Griffith, James S. *Beliefs and Holy Places: A Spiritual Geography of the Pimeria Alta.* Tucson: University of Arizona Press, 1992.

Gutch, Mrs. *County Folk-Lore, Vol. II: Concerning the North Riding of Yorkshire, York and the Ainsty.* London: Folklore Society, 1901.

Hamilton, Edith. *Mythology.* Boston: Little, Brown and Company, 1940.

Henderson, William. *Folklore of the Northern Counties.* London: Folklore Society, 1879.

Howey, M. Oldfield. *The Horse in Magic and Myth.* London: William Rider and Son, 1923.

Hudson, Charles. *The Southeastern Indians.* Knoxville: University of Tennessee Press, 1976.

Hultkrantz, Ake. *Religions of the American Indians,* trans. Monica Setterwall. Berkeley: University of California Press, 1979.

Hunt, Robert. *Popular Romances of the West of England.* New York and London: Benjamin Blum, 1916.

Huxley, Francis. *An Anthropologist among the Urubu Indians of Brazil.* New York: Viking Press, 1957.

Ivantis, Linda J. *Russian Folk Belief.* New York: M. E. Sharpe, 1989.

Kaczkurkin, Mini Valenzuela. *Yoeme: Lore of the Arizona Yaqui People.* Tucson: Sun Tracks, 1977.

Kawai, Hayao. *The Japanese Psyche.* Texas: Spring Publications, 1988.

Keightley, Thomas. *The Fairy Mythology.* London: George Bell and Sons, 1900.

Knappert, Jan. *Bantu Myths and Other Tales.* Leiden: E. J. Brill, 1977.

————. *The Aquarian Guide to African Mythology.* Wellingborough, England: The Aquarian Press, 1990.

Kramer, Samuel Noah. *Mythologies of the Ancient World.* New York: Anchor Books/Doubleday, 1961.

Kvideland, Reimund, and Henning K. Sehmsdorf, eds. *Scandinavian Folk Belief and Legend.* Minneapolis: University of Minnesota Press, 1988.

Lall, Kesar. *Folktales from the Himalayan Kingdom of Nepal.* Kathmandu: Ratna Pustak Bhandar, 1993.

————. *Nepalese Customs and Manners.* Kathmandu: Ratna Pustak Bhandar, 1990.

Lambert, Johanna, ed. *Aboriginal Tales of the Ancestral Powers.* Comp. K. Langloh Parker. Rochester, Vt.: Inner Traditions International, 1993.

Langdon, Stephen H. *Mythology of All Races,* vol. 5. New York: Cooper Square Publishers, 1964.

Langton, Edward. *Satan, a Portrait.* London: Skeffington and Son, 1945.

Larousse Encyclopedia of Mythology. London: Hamlyn Publishing Group, 1968.

Larrington, Carolyne, ed. *The Feminist Companion to Mythology.* London: Pandora Press, 1992.

Lawrence, Robert Means. *The Magic of the Horseshoe.* Boston: Houghton Mifflin and Company, 1898.

Martin, Luther H. *Hellenistic Religions.* New York: Oxford University Press, 1987.

Masaharu, Anesaki. *Mythology of All Races,* vol. 8. New York: Cooper Square Publishers, 1964.

Massola, Aldo. *Bunjil's Cave: Myths, Legends and Superstitions of the Aborigines of South East Australia.* Melbourne: Lansdowne Press, 1968.

Matthews, Washington, comp. and trans. *Navaho Legends,* vol. 5. New York: for The American Folklore Society, by Houghton, Mifflin and Company, 1897.

Mehr, Fargang. *The Zoroastrian Tradition.* Rockport, Mass.: Element, 1991.

Mercatante, Anthony S. *Good and Evil: Mythology and Folklore.* New York: Harper & Row, 1978.

Moore, A. W. *The Folklore of the Isle of Man.* Felinfach, U.K.: Llanerch Publishers, 1994.

Mountford, Charles P. *The Dreamtime: Australian Aboriginal Myths in Paintings by Ainslie Roberts.* Sydney: Rigby, 1965.

Narayan, R. K. *Gods, Demons and Others.* New York: Viking Press, 1964.

Neugroschel, Joachim, comp. and trans. *Yenne Velt: The Great Works of Jewish Fantasy and Occult.* New York: Pocket Books, 1978.

Norman, Howard. *Northern Tales: Traditional Stories of Eskimo and Indian People.* New York: Pantheon Books, 1990.

Nozaki, Kiyoshi. *Kitsune: Japan's Fox of Mystery, Romance and Humor.* Kyoto, Japan: The Hokuseido Press, 1961.

O'Flaherty, Wendy Doniger. *The Origins of Evil in Hindu Mythology.* Berkeley and Los Angeles: University of California Press, 1976.

Orbell, Margaret. *Traditional Maori Stories.* Auckland: Reed Publishing, 1992.

————. *The Illustrated Encyclopedia of Maori Myth and Legend.* Canterbury, N.Z.: Canterbury University Press, 1995.

Painter, Muriel Thayer. *With Good Heart: Yaqui Beliefs and Ceremonies in Pascua Village.* Tucson: University of Arizona Press, 1986.

Parker, K. Langloh. *Wise Women of the Dreamtime: Aboriginal Tales of the Ancestral Powers,* ed. Johanna Lambert. Rochester, Vt.: Inner Traditions International, 1993.

Parrinder, Geoffrey. *African Mythology.* New York: Peter Bedrick Books, 1967.

Perrin, Michael. *The Way of the Dead Indians.* Austin: University of Texas Press, 1987.

Piggott, Julie. *Japanese Mythology.* London: Hamlyn, 1969.

Porteous, Alexander. *Forest Folklore, Mythology and Romance.* London: George Allen and Unwin, 1928.

Queffelec, Henri. *Saint Anthony of the Desert*, trans. James Whitall. New York: E. P. Dutton & Co., 1954.

Rappoport, Angelo S. *The Folklore of the Jews.* London: Socino Press, 1937.

———. *The Sea Myths and Legends.* London: Senate, 1995.

Reed, A. W., and Roger Hart. *Maori Myth and Legend.* Auckland: Reed Publishers, 1972.

Reichel-Dolmatoff, Gerardo. *Amazonian Cosmos.* Chicago: Unversity of Chicago Press, 1971.

Robbins, Russell Hope. *Encyclopedia of Witchcraft and Demonology.* New York: Crown, 1959.

Roberts, Moss, ed. *Chinese Fairytales and Fantasies.* New York: Pantheon Books, 1979.

Robinson, Roland. *Aboriginal Myths and Legends.* London: Paul Hamlyn, 1969.

Russell, Jeffrey Burton. *The Devil: Perceptions of Evil from Antiquity to Primitive Christianity.* Ithaca, N.Y.: Cornell University Press, 1977.

Ryan, Judith. *Spirit in Land Bark Painting from Arnhem Land.* Victoria, Aust.: National Gallery of Victoria, 1990.

Saxon, Lyle. *Gumbo Ya-Ya: A Collection of Louisiana Folktales.* Boston: Houghton Mifflin Company, 1945.

Saxton, Dean, and Lucille Saxton. *Legends and Lore of the Papago and Pima Indians.* Tucson: University of Arizona Press, 1973.

Schwartz, Howard. *Lilith's Cave: Jewish Tales of the Supernatural.* San Francisco: Harper and Row, 1988.

———. *Gabriel's Place (Jewish Mystical Tales).* New York: Oxford University Press, 1993.

Scott, Sir Walter. *Letters on Demonology and Witchcraft.* New York: Citadel Press, 1970.

Seki, Keigo. *Folktales of Japan*, trans. Robert J. Adams. Chicago: University of Chicago Press, 1963.

Sikes, Wirt. *British Goblins.* London: Sampson, Low, Marton, Searle and Rivington, 1880.

Singer, Isaac Bashevis. *The Magician of Lublin.* New York: Farrar, Straus and Giroux, 1960.

Singer, June. *Boundaries of the Soul: The Practice of Jung's Psychology.* New York: Anchor Books, 1972.

Speiser, E. A., trans. *The Anchor Bible Genesis.* New York: Doubleday and Company, 1964.

Stevenson, Robert Louis. *The Strange Case of Dr. Jekyll and Mr. Hyde.* Orig. pub. 1886. Lincoln: University of Nebraska Press, 1990.

Theal, Geo. McCall. *Kaffir Folk-Lore.* Westport, Conn.: Negro University Press, 1970.

Thompson, R. Campbell. *The Devils and Evil Spirits of Babylonia.* vols. 1 and 2. London: Luzac & Co., 1904. Reprint AMS Press, 1976.

Thompson, Stith. *Tales of the North American Indians.* Cambridge: Harvard University Press, 1929.

Thurman, Robert A. F., and Marilyn M. Rhie. *Wisdom and Compassion: The Sacred Art of Tibet.* New York: Harry N. Abrams, 1991.

Trachtenberg, Joshua. *Jewish Magic and Superstition.* New York: Behrman's Jewish Book House, 1939.

Tremearne, A. J. N. *Hausa Superstition and Customs: An Introduction to the Folk-Lore and the Folk*. London: John Bale, Sons and Danielsson, 1913.

———. *The Ban of the Bori: Demons and Demon Dancing in West and North Africa*. London: Heath, Cranton and Ouseley, 1914.

Turner, Alice K. *The History of Hell*. California: Harcourt Brace and Co., 1993.

Von Franz, Marie-Louise. *Reflections of the Soul*, trans. William H. Kennedy. La Salle and London: Open Court Publishing, 1980.

Weinreich, Beatrice Silverman, ed. *Yiddish Folktales*, trans. Leonard Wolf. New York: Pantheon Books, 1988.

Werner, Alice. *Myths and Legends of the Bantu*. London: George G. Harrap and Company, 1933.

———. *Mythology of All Races*. Volume 7. New York: Cooper Square Publishers, 1964.

Werner, Edward T. C. *Ancient Tales and Folklore of China*. London: Studio Editions, 1995.

Whitmont, Edward C. *The Symbolic Quest: Basic Concepts of Analytical Psychology*. Princeton, N.J.: Princeton University Press, 1969.

Wilbert, Johannes, and Karin Simoneau. *Folk Literature of the Mataco Indians*. Los Angeles: University of California, 1982.

———. *Folk Literature of the Toba Indians*. Los Angeles: University of California, 1982.

———. *Folk Literature of the Bororo Indians*. Los Angeles: University of California, 1983.

———. *Folk Literature of the Tehuelche Indians*. Los Angeles: University of California, 1984.

———. *Folk Literature of the Guajiro Indians*. Los Angeles: University of California, 1986.

———. *Folk Literature of the Mocovi Indians*. Los Angeles: University of California, 1988.

———. *Folk Literature of the Gunjiro Indians*. Los Angeles: University of Los Angeles Press, 1986.

———. *Folk Literature of the Cuiva Indians*. Los Angeles: University of Los Angeles Press, 1991.

———. *Folk Literature of the Sikuani Indians*. Los Angeles: University of Los Angeles Press, 1992.

Wilde, Lady. *Ancient Legends, Mystic Charms, and Superstitions of Ireland*. 2 vols. London: Ward and Downey, 1887.

Witthoft, John, and Wendell S. Hadlock. "Cherokee-Iroquois Little People." *Journal of American Folklore* 59 (1946): 413 – 22.

Yeats, W. B. *Fairy and Folk Tales of the Irish Peasantry*. London: Walter Scott, 1880.

Yen, Ping-Chiu. *Chinese Demon Tales: Meanings and Parallels in Oral Tradition*. New York & London: Garland Publishing, 1990.

Zimmer, Heinrich. *Myths and Symbols in Indian Art and Civilization*. Princeton, N.J.: Princeton University Press, 1946.

ILLUSTRATION CREDITS

"Basic Demon," after "Satan," from *The History of the Devil and the Idea of Evil*, by Dr. Paul Carus, Open Court Publishing Company, Chicago, 1900. Courtesy of The New York Society Library.

"Common Fairy," after "Ariel," adapted by Cathy Hull from Henry James Townsend's painting circa 1845, New York Public Library Picture Collection.

"Asura," original image by Toby Welles from Indian miniature painting "Gods and Demons Churning the Milk Ocean," anonymous, circa eighteenth century, Victoria and Albert Museum, London.

"Tiamat," *Treasury of Fantastic and Mythological Creatures*, by Richard Huber, Dover Publications, New York, 1981.

"Mermaid," courtesy of The Warburg Institute, London.

"Merman," after the river god Achelous, *Treasury of Fantastic and Mythological Creatures*, by Richard Huber, Dover Publications, New York, 1981.

"Rusalka," ("Mermaid" after woodcut 1550), *Treasury of Fantastic and Mythological Creatures*, by Richard Huber, Dover Publications, New York, 1981.

"Kelpie" ("Seahorse" after a Roman amphora, fourth century B.C.E.), *Treasury of Fantastic and Mythological Creatures*, by Richard Huber, Dover Publications, New York, 1981.

"Nixie," after "Melusina," Puce Church, Gironde, from *Curious Myths of the Middle Ages*, by S. Baring-Gould, M.A., Rivingtons, Oxford, England, 1876. Courtesy of New York University Library.

"Merrow," *Music: A Pictorial Archive of Woodcuts and Drawings*, selected by Jim Harter, Dover Publications, New York, 1980.

"Humwawa," after sculpture of "Mask of Humbaba," circa seventh century B.C.E., British Museum, London. Courtesy of A.R.A.S., C. G. Jung Center, New York.

"Tengu," *Treasury of Fantastic and Mythological Creatures*, by Richard Huber, Dover Publications, New York, 1981.

"Mahisha-Asura," *Treasury of Fantastic and Mythological Creatures*, by Richard Huber, Dover Publications, New York, 1981.

"Akvan," *Treasury of Fantastic and Mythological Creatures*, by Richard Huber, Dover Publications, New York, 1981.

"Pan," courtesy of The Warburg Institute, London.

"Rakshasa (female)," original image by Toby Welles from Indian miniature painting, private collection.

"Ravana," *The Complete Encyclopedia of Illustration*, by J. G. Heck, reprint of original publication by R. Garrigue, New York, 1851. Courtesy Cathy Hull.

"Oni," original image by Toby Welles after "an Old Japanese Painting," *Demonology and Devil-Lore*, volume 11, by Moncure Daniel Conway, Henry Holt & Company, New York, 1879. Courtesy of The New York Society Library.

"Kitsune," New York Public Library Picture Collection.

"Set," after Brugsch, from *The History of the Devil and the Idea of Evil*, by Dr. Paul Carus, Open Court Publishing Company, Chicago, 1900. Courtesy of The New York Society Library

"Djinn," from Turkish manuscript included in *Iconography*, Didron, volume 2, from *The History of the Devil and the Idea of Evil*, by Dr. Paul Carus, Open Court Publishing Company, Chicago, 1900. Courtesy of The New York Society Library.

"St. Anthony Assaulted by Devils," after Schoengauer's engraving 1420–1499, *The History of the Devil and the Idea of Evil*, by Dr. Paul Carus, Open Court Publishing Company, Chicago, 1900. Courtesy of The New York Society Library.

"Ahriman" (after Didron, *Iconography*), *The History of the Devil and the Idea of Evil*, by Dr. Paul Carus, Open Court Publishing Company, Chicago, 1900. Courtesy of The New York Society Library.

"Namarrgon," *Treasury of Fantastic and Mythological Creatures*, by Richard Huber, Dover Publications, New York, 1981.

"Satan," after "Devil," *The History of the Devil and the Idea of Evil*, by Dr. Paul Carus, Open Court Publishing Company, Chicago, 1900. Courtesy of The New York Society Library.

"Croucher," after "Evil Demons" (from Chaldean stele in British Museum after Lenormant), *The History of the Devil and the Idea of Evil*, by Dr. Paul Carus, Open Court Publishing Company, Chicago, 1900. Courtesy of The New York Society Library.

"Asmodeus," *Picture Book of Devils Demons and Witchcraft*, by Ernst and Johanna Lehrner, Dover Publications, New York, 1971.

"Lilith Tempting Eve" (from medieval missal), illustration from Moncure Daniel Conway, *Demonology and Devil-Lore*, volume 11, Henry Holt & Company, New York, 1879. Courtesy of The New York Society Library.

"Pazuzu," from "Demon of the Southwest Wind" (after Lenormant, statue in Louvre), *The History of the Devil and the Idea of Evil*, by Dr. Paul Carus, Open Court Publishing Company, Chicago, 1900. Courtesy of The New York Society Library.

"Fox Fairy," Fox spirit original image Toby Welles after "Japanese Demon," Moncure Daniel Conway, *Demonology and Devil-Lore*, volume 11, Henry Holt & Company, New York, 1879. Courtesy of The New York Society Library.

"Fair Ladies," *The Book of Knowledge*, volume 14, The Grolier Society, New York, 1911.

"Werewolf eating his family," courtesy of The Warburg Institute, London.

"Kitsune-Tsuki," original image by Cathy Hull based on image from A.R.A.S., The C. G. Jung Center, New York.

"Pride," *Picture Book of Devils Demons and Witchcraft*, by Ernst and Johanna Lehrner, Dover Publications, New York, 1971.

"Avarice," *Picture Book of Devils Demons and Witchcraft*, by Ernst and Johanna Lehrner, Dover Publications, New York, 1971.

"Lust," represented by "Asmodeus," *Picture Book of Devils Demons and Witchcraft*, by Ernst and Johanna Lehrner, Dover Publications, New York, 1971.

"Envy," represented by "Leviathan," *Treasury of Fantastic and Mythological Creatures*, by Richard Huber, Dover Publications, New York, 1981.

"Gluttony," represented by "Beelzebub," *Picture Book of Devils Demons and Witchcraft*, by Ernst and Johanna Lehrner, Dover Publications, New York, 1971.

"Anger," represented by "Satan," *The History of the Devil and the Idea of Evil*, by Dr. Paul Carus, Open Court Publishing Company, Chicago, 1900. Courtesy of The New York Society Library.

"Sloth," represented by "Belphegor," *Picture Book of Devils Demons and Witchcraft*, by Ernst and Johanna Lehrner, Dover Publications, New York, 1971.

"Yamantaka," original image by Cathy Hull after statue of Yamantaka Vajarabhairava Ekavira.

INDEX